Islam and Modernity

An unfinished project

Rafik Abdessalem

AFRO-MIDDLE EAST CENTRE

AMEC

AMEC

Published by the Afro-Middle East Centre
PO Box 411494, Craighall 2024, Johannesburg, South Africa
www.amec.org.za

First published 2017
ISBN (print) 978-0-9947048-1-8

© 2017 Afro-Middle East Centre

Copyedited by Mary Ralphs
Cover picture by Madi Alexander
Proofread by Mary Starkey
Designed and typeset by Karengraphics

Contents

Chapter 7
The new Islamic reformists 257

Foreword

Since the late 1990s, much has been written and discussed about a clash of civilisations between 'Islam' and 'the West'. Increasingly, another older discourse has intersected with this, portraying Islam as a 'backward' philosophy, ideology and civilisation that has not kept pace with modernity and is imprisoned in a rigid framework many centuries old. Of course, these views have been contested, and their fallaciousness has been the subject of a great deal of intellectual activity.

For the kind of work that the Afro-Middle East Centre does, these debates are not in themselves a matter of gripping and abiding interest. They are, however, significant and deserving of careful reflection because of the manner in which they affect international relations, and have been used to further various hegemonic agendas. Indeed, attempting to properly understand the rapidly changing geopolitical situation in the Middle East and North Africa (MENA) region without taking this into consideration, or factoring in the real or supposed confrontations between 'Islam' and 'modernity' on the one hand, and 'Islam' and 'secularity' on the other, is a futile endeavour.

This is not to suggest that all politics in the MENA region are about Islam, or that all violence in the region is related to clashes between 'Islam' and 'the West' or 'Islam' and modernity'. However, the manner in which these categories are deployed, correctly or incorrectly, intentionally or unintentionally, is shaping the geopolitics of the region – meandering and unpredictable as this is. A deep understanding of these issues is therefore helpful and necessary for understanding and analysing the region.

In this compelling book, Rafik Abdessalem unpacks two major lines of thought. First, he examines why many Westerners dismiss Islam's vast intellectual, social, theological and cultural heritage as flawed, violent, rigid and fanatical, despite knowing virtually nothing about it. He usefully traces the genesis of this attitude, focusing on how scholars such as Weber, Habermas and others have helped to consolidate the West's view of itself as civilised, superior, developed and progressive, and how the demonisation of Islam acts as a necessary foil for these notions.

Second, he explains that Islam is subject to a variety of interpretive choices and schools of thought ranging from legalistic fundamentalism, through rigid rationalism, to spiritual Sufism. He shows that, since the eighteenth century when the modern West gained the upper hand, Muslim elites have engaged in a process of reinterpreting Islam, investing it with new meanings and contextualising its thought and practice. In response, leading Islamic reformists have considered the reasons for the rise and fall of civilisations, diagnosed great maladies within Muslim culture and consciousness, and made suggestions for dealing with the challenges of modern times.

By treating Islam, secularity and modernity as distinct and separate, rather than as interconnected and overlapping, Abdessalem makes no attempt to reconcile Islam with modernity or secularity, nor does he place one in opposition to the other. Instead, he looks at the interconnections between these broad and complex subjects. Viewing modernity as an 'unfinished project', and revealing Islam's own internal dynamism, Abdessalem throws light on the contingent character of both, rejecting the essentialism of Western discourse that tends to view Islam as fixed, and modernity as linear and fully realised. Here, Abdessalem usefully foregrounds the arguments of classical and contemporary Muslim reformists. Without aligning himself with any single line of thought, he points out that to make use of the tools of technology or democracy, one does not have to decide between being a believer or a democrat; belief in one can encompass commitment to the other.

Abdessalem's analysis is useful in encouraging us to rethink both modernity and Islam, and their relationship with each other. In this rethinking lies the potential for a better understanding of the geopolitics of what is often called 'the Muslim world', including the MENA region.

Na'eem Jeenah
Executive Director, Afro-Middle East Centre, Johannesburg

Introduction

Islam is often at centre of the contemporary international politics. Articles, books, debates and documentaries abound, many of which simplify, distort, and even vilify the Islamic world, while others reflect a real will to understand and reveal its complexity. In the west, Islam is, of course, generally perceived as the antithesis of all that modernity claims to be and to have accomplished. Islam's tendency to resist both secularisation and western-style modernisation means that questions related to secularity and modernity often lie at the heart of the concerns of western commentators.

In this book, I treat Islam, secularity and modernity as distinct and separate, rather than as interconnected and overlapping phenomena. I make no attempt to reconcile Islam with modernity or secularity, as many from both the Muslim and western worlds have done. Nor, indeed, do I oppose one to the other, as many fundamentalists continue to do. To an avowed Muslim fundamentalist, there is no common ground between Islam and modernity – Islam is closed and self-sufficient, with ready-made answers to all situations, requiring nothing from the rest of the world. In this, Muslim fundamentalists are no different from western secularist fundamentalists, who see modernity as pre-eminent and complete. This group sees anyone who does not unreservedly embrace secularism and modernity as entirely rejecting both.

My aim is to look at the interconnections between these broad and complex subjects, and to examine them from new angles and different perspectives. After unearthing the etymology of the word 'secular' in

Chapter One, and examining its syntactical and linguistic definitions within the languages of Islam (including Arabic) in Chapter Two, I question whether secularity and modernity are homogeneous or absolute, and explore the roles of some of the (sometimes forgotten) characters in the 'great narratives' of both modernity and Islam.

I see modernity as a fairly ill-defined phenomenon that has no claim to universal validity, but rather offers a variety of possibilities. In my view, western forms of modernity, which derive from the Enlightenment tradition with its secular inclinations, have not exhausted all the possible forms that modernity can take. To coin a phrase from Habermas, I see modernity as an 'unfinished project', and the convergence between secularism and modernity in the west as little more than a historical accident. If their convergence was neither necessary, nor indeed, the ultimate possibility, a non-secular form of modernity is conceivable, both philosophically and practically.

Running parallel to secularisation is a counter movement of de-secularisation, a phenomenon that has become an undeniable trend in many parts of the globe. Western sociologists and political theorists constantly invoke the triumphant march of secularisation, but rarely refer to the counter process occurring across vast areas of the world. When attention is directed towards de-secularisation, it is often depicted as an irrational reaction, the 'revenge of the sacred', rather than a conscious and mature choice.

At the same time, I question the notion of unity and homogeneity in Islam. Islam is subject to a variety of interpretive choices and schools of thought that range from legalistic fundamentalism, through rigid rationalism, to exotic Sufism. I show that since the eighteenth century, when the modern west gained the upper hand in the balance of power over the rest of the world, Muslim elites have been engaged in a process of reinterpreting Islam and 'modernity' and reinvesting these concepts with new meanings. For the last two centuries, both Islam and modernity have remained strongly present and closely intertwined in the consciousness and the conduct of the Muslim intellectual and political elite. My aim is to throw light on the contingent character of both Islam

2

and modernity, thereby casting doubt on the essentialist approach dominant in western discourse, which tends to view Islam as fixed and fully determined, and modernity as finite and fully realised..

What I mean by Islam is not the theology determined by the Qur'an and the tradition of the Prophet Muhammad that forms the source of Islamic legislation, nor the modes of interpretation adopted by the different Islamic schools, from *al-fuqaha* (the jurists) to *mutakallimun* (theologians) or *falasifah* (philosophers). For me, Islam is a source of cultural norms and values, a form of symbolic capital – in the Bourdieuian sense – evenly distributed throughout society, and acting as the basis for the legitimacy of the rule of the state, and various other political and social forces.

Since the 9/11 catastrophe, increasing numbers of politicians, analysts and journalists comment on Islam. With rare exceptions, few of these people possess any knowledge of Islamic culture, its great languages, or the complexities of its social structures. Since Islam is hardly ever allowed to speak for itself, it has become a legitimate target for examination and appraisal – anyone can claim to be an expert. In many analyses, Islam emerges as a synonym for political terrorism, arranged marriage, women's subordination and political despotism. In short, all that western modernity stands for is portrayed as completely missing from Islamic culture. All the problems that Muslim societies face today are seen as deriving from their loyalty to Islam and its norms that supposedly crush the human will, preach predestination and instil passivity and obedience to despotism. Muslim states are described as economic and political failures, and Islam as a religion of deficiency and redundancy. Muslims, therefore, are portrayed as having no choice but to cling to rigid fundamentalism that shuns reality, or to wholeheartedly and unreservedly endorse the modernity that comes ready-made from the west.

The work of American writer Francis Fukuyama offers telling examples of the kind of literature on Islam that, since the mid 1990s, has been in high demand. Fukuyama entered the fray, having found in recent events an opportunity to rehash his poor Hegelian theory of the end of history. The tale Fukuyama told is far too brief and straightforward to be credible. It may be summed up as follows: 'we' have arrived at the end of history because only one system is capable of continuing to dominate world politics, namely liberal democracy in its American incarnation. Those who have shown resistance to this process Fukuyama labelled as 'retrograde areas', and according to him, Islam, which dominates these dark and shady corners of the globe, will inevitably fall under the massive sway of the mighty American model.[1]

Although in the west, topics related to Islam were, for decades, restricted to the scholarly tradition loosely known as Orientalism (and later as Middle Eastern, or Near Eastern and Islamic studies), Islam is widely, if implicitly, introspected in modern western discourse, through different forms of representation. When the triumphant march of western modernity (with secularity its close ally) is invoked, the world of Islam is implicitly or explicitly referenced as the hallmark of theological and historical deficiency, and as the absolute negation of what the modern western world, as 'the epicentre' of the globe, has achieved in the past two centuries. Islam is depicted as having been isolated from most fields of knowledge – theology and philosophy, as much as from political theory – and survives only at the periphery of academic institutions due to an assumption that it is a deviant sect with nothing to offer. This view of Islam, dominant since the days of medieval Christianity, has been reproduced within European consciousness, and passed from one generation to the next. Such views are prevalent among intellectuals just as much as in the general public, and are shared in religious and secular circles alike.

Over centuries, the west has produced and accumulated a fragmented knowledge of Islam, which, albeit inconsistent and full of contradictions, has enjoyed pre-eminence – its terms binding, its concepts and referents unchallenged. Not only is such knowledge effective, it possesses a capacity for self-reproduction and circulation in a wide range of social arenas. Borrowing a term of Foucault's, it is a coercive species of knowledge that imposes itself upon and 'preconditions' knowledge of the Islamic world.[2]

Although this view of Islam has persisted for centuries, it was in the nineteenth century that a scholarly tradition concerning Islam came to be institutionalised, and was branded as scientific and objective knowledge. As I show in Chapters Three and Four, throughout the nineteenth century, in the general context of western imperialism, the 'non-European' world – including the world of Islam – was prevented from raising its own voice and defining its own self-image, and was instead rendered a mere exhibit, an object of contemplation and categorisation.[3]

Three elements seem to have been principally responsible for shaping this modern western conception of Islam. The first is a memory of Islam recycled from medieval Christianity that has remained active even in this era of secularisation. The medieval Christian view of Islam as a deviant, irrational religion continues to thrive even though Christian theology has lost its vanguard role, and its content has been swallowed by modern essentialist philosophy. The second element is the shift in the global balance of economic and political power in favour of the west, and the fact that the international order has conceded the upper hand to the European powers and the United States of America. The third element is the deep political crisis and disintegration that accompanied the rapid decline of the Ottoman Empire, and which has characterised the Muslim world since the beginning of the nineteenth century. These three interconnected elements allowed the modern west to silence Islam's voice and impose itself as the source of *logos* – understanding, reason and order – in relation to Islam and its societies.

In this process, the so-called 'Orient', 'East' or 'Islam' has been transformed into a silent and passive object, standing powerless before a European gaze that sees it as chaotic, backward and needing to be 'rationalised', 'organised' and 'made sense of'. In the context of European military expansion, the world of Islam turned into a theatrical display, and the western 'spectator' became this 'exhibit's' source of meaning and value. Everything seemed to have stood before the Europeans as an appearance behind which some hidden reality lay. Thus modern Europe transformed the 'Orient' into a great 'external reality' or 'other', and made Islam the most common object of its 'metaphysics of representation'.[4] The modern west's bid to distinguish itself from the Muslim world, or the so-called east, conferred legitimacy on representations of the strangeness of the east, as well as on the west's quest to separate itself from that 'external world', and to transform the east into an (at times picturesque) representation, but one that was always abstracted from reality. This process required a 'fixed *cogito*'; that is, an active and 'rational' subject had to stand apart from and outside the passive object. To represent a geographical and cultural hemisphere as the 'Orient' or 'Islam' is after all to 'orientalise' and 'islamise' it, to impose a set of features upon it. Moreover, the act of representing Islam was never detachable from the act of defining the 'Occident'. As Edward Said explained, Orientalism 'was not just a particular instance of the general historical problem of one culture portraying another', it was primarily an internal cultural strategy that helped the west to shape its own image by being made to represent its opposite, its shadow, and all that it did not want to be.[5] Thus Orientalism and imperialism are not separate fields of endeavour, one referring to 'knowledge power' and the other to 'military power'; the two constitute a united realm of activity, in which power games and military strategies are interconnected and accumulated. Knowledge is not merely a recipient of political power, it is itself a generator and producer of power, and has the ability to consolidate, reshape and redirect political power. If imperialism taught the west how to conquer, Orientalism taught westerners how transform harsh military conquest into the art of rulership.

To avoid simplifications and generalisations, it might be wise to note that Islam has not only been negatively portrayed in modern western literature. In fact, two other intellectual traditions arose that are similar to classical Orientalism in some ways. The first approached the Islamic world through exotic and romantic eyes. Islam here was represented as an emblem of the east, a sphere in which fervent passion, exotic forms of sensuality, poetry and romance reside. Goethe's writings are a case in point. The second tradition invoked Islam as the prototype of 'natural religion', of a moral order that glorifies worldly things, recognises no ecclesiastical authority and serves as the antithesis of the papacy and of western decadence. Diderot and Nietzsche were pioneers of this view. To the latter, Islam was a masculine and combative religion that celebrated the body and 'presence' in this world, thus standing in sharp contrast to the asceticism and puritanism of Christianity.[6]

Amid these diverse narratives and approaches, classical Orientalism has been the dominant school of thought, and because its discourse is consistent with medieval Christian views of Islam (which, as noted earlier, remain vividly present in European consciousness), it was able to claim the status of a scholarly tradition. Where Islam found itself in the balance of power during the nineteenth century did little to undermine the views of classical Orientalists. The prominence enjoyed by the modern west, and the enormous gap that separated it from the rest of the world both economically and militarily, was crucial in shaping discourses on the Muslim 'other'. Moreover, finding itself dependent on a Europe that it had once defeated in its own back yard shook Muslims' views of the world and shattered their sense of self-worth. Although the Muslim elite were aware of the west's superiority in the fields of military and bureaucratic administration, it was when they suffered direct military occupation that Muslims began to question their belief in their own role in the leadership of the planet.

The military expansion that shaped and conditioned Europe's outlook during the nineteenth century devalued the 'non-European' world, stripping vast areas of historical dignity and relegating them to mere subjects of ethnological study and contemplation by the European gaze and imagination.[7] Islam, in all its complexity and diversity, found itself a passive subject redefined by the eyes and imagination of the Orientalists, and, later, by other self-appointed experts and commentators on its systems and societies. For reasons that had much to do with European (un)consciousness, Islam was portrayed as the hallmark of intellectual redundancy and historical deficiency, as a religion that generates fanaticism and intolerance, facilitates political despotism, and preaches violence while allowing no space for human freedom. Muslim societies, with their rich histories and long traditions, were dismissed as no more than a network of scattered sects and tribes. In contrast, the 'rational west' was seen as being able to provide some order and stability to this chaotic world, and it is no coincidence that the notion of exporting of 'civilisation' to 'savage backward' nations flourished alongside the elaboration of the 'Orient's' irrationality, with the latter helping to legitimise the ruthlessness and brutality of western imperialism.

Amidst the unequal distribution of power and resources between the Muslim world and the modern west, Islam became synonymous with epistemological and historical failure. With the balance of power shifting in favour of the west, Islam was made a silent subject of categorisation and reification. In western political discourse, Islam never spoke, it never illustrated its image, presence or history; instead, the Orientalists, and later 'experts' on the Middle East, spoke for and represented it. The processes involved in the objectification of Islam by the west have never been confined to innocent academic endeavour; they are driven by politics and political strategies. As Nietzsche explained, to know something is to master it. Knowledge is, after all, a desire for control and power, and such was the impetus behind western studies of Islam.

Orientalism, like all nineteenth-century science, was haunted by a sharp dualism between 'Orient' and 'Occident'. What Orientalism offered up for study was not only a set of languages, religious beliefs and methods of government, but a series of absolute differences according to which the 'Oriental' could be understood as the opposite of the European. Difference was expelled from the European view of itself, which was asserted to be unified, homogeneous and whole. Difference was perceived to exist only between the self and its opposite. Such an opposite makes possible an imaginary, undivided self. In contrast, the Orient could be viewed as backward, irrational and disordered, and in need of European order and authority. Western domination required the creating of a 'west', as a singular identity.[8] In this, the machinery of modern political discourse aimed not only at the externalisation of the other, but also at the absolute exclusion of the other from the self. To establish this stringent dualism, the west had to overlook differences within, and rule out all possible interaction between the so-called self and its alleged other. Thus, for western modernity to determine itself as the seat of reason, civilisation and order, it had to represent all that it saw as irrational, disorderly and libidinous as being outside itself.[9]

As Armando Salvatore pointed out, the making of 'generic Islam' is strictly dependent on the making of the 'west'.[10] Western political hegemony has been accompanied and consolidated and legitimised by what is referred to as a 'scientific and methodological' approach to 'Oriental' societies. So-called Oriental societies are accordingly treated as a field of knowledge analysable through a set of 'western categories'. The category of the 'irrational despotic Orient' was invented largely in response to a specific historical need to centralise power and to exclude from the distribution of wealth and power those who did not conform to the established codes of rationality.

Does this mean that the west's conception of Islam offers nothing more than lies and fantasies, to be abandoned and overcome?

In Chapters Four and Five, I attempt to show that western literature on Islam is a structural discourse with its own body of theory, narratives and practices. That is to say, the narrative on Islam has its own set of truths, which generation after generation of academics, politicians and thinkers have faithfully adhered to, corroborated and defended. This grants the status of an unchallengeable pre-eminent paradigm to a discourse that is replete with shortcomings and inconsistency, and casts all attempts at offering a more balanced representation of the world of Islam to the periphery of its knowledge system. What gives the Orientalists' 'official' view of Islam supremacy over the diversity of other views and interpretations is the institutionalisation of this discourse and its close affinity with well-entrenched Christian narratives that came to be introspected within western consciousness and memory.

The Orientalist discourse on Islam, written, reproduced, and handed over from one generation to the next, cannot be dismissed entirely as myth and fiction, however. It is a mixture of reality and imagination, of 'truth' and 'falsity'. Thus Orientalism is not a mere illusion to be overcome and abandoned; such is the quest of positivism, which claims to establish 'scientific truth' on the ruins of the epistemological illusion of metaphysics. If we were to equate Orientalism with illusion, the illusion would not be merely a transient epistemological moment, but a condition that is vital for the very existence of the deluded. Orientalism is haunted by the illusion of the uniqueness of the western experience and by the need to implant the latter as its centre of reference. Such illusions are essential to the existence of the 'west' itself. Without this, the notion of the 'west' risks being little more than a myth or an accident of circumstance. For this reason, circumscribing the presence of illusion in Orientalist discourse calls for an enormous and, indeed, incessant intellectual and moral effort.

Even if we accept that hermeneutical activity has succeeded in implementing its will to dissolve the Cartesian yardstick in favour of what it refers to as the interpretive game or the deconstructive project, we still need to ask if hermeneutics has really emancipated itself from oppressive categories, and whether in its deconstructive play, it may be said to be free of power games. To the majority of 'post-modernists', hermeneutics remains 'the magical recipe' for overthrowing the west's claim to the ethnocentrism that has stamped its mark on the entire discourse of modernity. The Cartesian yardstick, they insist, is very narrow, as it deals with the problematic of knowledge, not in terms of an egalitarian hermeneutics but in terms of a 'discriminating cognitive elitism'. Indeed, although Descartes maintained that reason was 'une lumière naturelle', and that all minds were equal in their capacity for intelligence, western philosophy did not then extend such equality to all cultures and systems.[11]

Hermeneutists are not in the least interested in the oppressive character of inequality in the distribution of wealth and power in the socio-political contexts that feed and empower symbolic coercion. As Gellner points out, hermeneutists are enormously sensitive to the manner in which concepts constrain, but less than attentive to the socio-political structure of oppression. The correlation and interaction between symbolic and socio-political constraints (and the reverse) is, however, a strong one. Indeed, conceptual constraints over other cultures and societies are a feature of the machinery of coercion, and manifest in the balance of power. Treating different cultures and symbolic systems as equal does not necessarily mean they are equal in the potential they possess for symbolic universalism.

Islam and secularity

My aim in this book has also been to listen to Islam's 'internal voice' (or voices), not to speak on its behalf, or impose any ready-made categories upon it. However, seeking to escape from the cage of distorted questions and straightforward answers requires a significant intellectual and moral effort, with a view to extending issues and interpretations within Islamic culture to their limits while avoiding imposed questions and answers. It involves searching for new perspectives on the issues of secularity and modernity. I seek to move away from prejudice, and not confine myself to the conventional limits and barriers often forced upon Islam, secularity and modernity. I tried not to succumb to the pervasive influence of simple questions and ready answers, but to apply myself to the arduous task of inventing novel questions and answering them.

Although I use a variety of strategies of interpretation and draw on different schools of thought, ranging from Nietzschean perspectivism to Islamic theology, from the Frankfurt School and critical hermeneutics to Islamic philosophy, I do not align myself with any single line of thought. In this I seek to walk in the footsteps of the great Muslim philosopher Abu Hamid al-Ghazali (d. 1111). In his master work, *Tahafut al-Falasifah* (The incoherence of the philosophers), al-Ghazali relied on myriad schools of thought and a diversity of methods, including those of the philosophers he sought to refute, so as to make plain the internal contradictions and shortcomings of a discourse. However, I attempt to go beyond the 'game of deconstruction', and seek to open new possibilities and advance new answers, so as to fill the gaps and vacuums that are generated. If I must attach a label to this, I would classify it within the new *ijtihadi* school, which presents a new *ijtihad* not in the field of Islam alone but in those of secularity and modernity too, as well as in the possible interconnections between these three fields. I use *ijtihad* not in the limited juristic sense of the term, relating to the interpretation of Islamic texts or to the devising of new solutions to emergent problems, but in its much wider meaning. The term *ijtihad* literally means exertion. In the terminology of Islamic jurisprudence it means to exert, with a view to form an independent judgment on a legal question. In Arabic more generally, the word has two principal meanings: it may refer to the word *juhd*, which means exertion, or *jahd*, which means burden or expense. A synthesis of the two etymological definitions denotes a process of rigorous and arduous intellectual effort aiming at the construction of a particular vision of the subject in hand, and this is the sense in which I use the term.

The controversial relationship between Islam, secularity and modernity provokes a multitude of questions and issues. In this book, I aim to cast doubt on ready-made questions and answers by deconstructing what I call Islam's great narratives, along with those of secularity and modernity. Although I agree that some features of Islam remain irreconcilable with certain aspects of secularism and modernity, I do not accept the view of Islam as self-enclosed and completed. Instead, I argue that the concepts of *ijtihad* and *islah* (reform) stand behind Islam's internal dynamism.

Islam has declared itself the final pillar upon which Abrahamic monotheism rests – its prophet Muhammad being the final seal of all prophets – but it also identified itself as a *shir'ah* and *minhaj*, a general way of life and a set of guidelines for human conduct on earth. In this, Islam makes a distinction between the *muhkam* and *mutashabih*. The *muhkam* denotes that which is indubitably clear and absolutely explicit. Examples of this include the need for prayer, for the observance of Ramadan, for almsgiving, and for the prohibition of theft and murder, to name just a few. The *mutashabih,* on the other hand, refers to the equivocal and ambiguous, which call for the effort involved in interpretation.

In Islam, only the great pillars of the religion are fully determined. These form a circumscribed restricted category *beyond which all is subject to* ijtihad *or interpretation*. In fact, the majority of Islamic juristic, philosophical and theological schools that call for 'rational' interpretation see in this distinction between the *muhkam* and the *mutashabih* a basis for their own legitimacy. Ibn Rushd (Averroes), for example, maintained that only philosophers, with their arsenal of rational arguments, are entitled to legitimately and consistently interpret the *mutashabih*.[12]

Since the early stages of its development, Islam has been subject to numerous strategies of legitimisation. Thus, Islam has always been, and still is, subject to widely diverging readings and lines of interpretation, varying from one school of thought to another, according to different methods and changing historical conditions. In view of Islam's flexible nature and its history of diversity, readers would be wise to beware when extremists from either the Islamic or western traditions try to present Islam as predetermined and self-enclosed.

From a fundamentalist viewpoint, Islam is an absolutely closed system, to be rigorously and harshly implemented. Ironically, western fanatics, on the opposite side, leaning on a set of cherished and deeply rooted stereotypes and prejudices, find themselves largely in agreement with this characterisation of Islam – condemning it as a religion that is closed, rigid, and absolutist to the point of being draconian. But to read the wide universe of Islam through a handful of extremist splinter groups that feed on the deep political crises, and the massive internal and external oppression suffered by Muslim societies, is to commit a grave error of judgement. The Taliban, al-Qaʻida and the Islamic State ought to be seen as the outer expressions of the far-reaching, deep-rooted crises that have haunted Muslim consciousness and political reality for the past two centuries – crises that inevitably colour what they perceive as western attempts at hegemony. These organisations and individuals are symptoms of the problems, not their solution. In devastatingly fragmented communities, staggering under the crushing weight of despotism and imperial interventionism, such extremist tendencies serve only to extend the damage, rather than building crucially needed forms of consensus or conciliation.

Islamic extremism is a superficial answer to a cluster of intensely complex questions and crises confronting Muslim societies. It is also undermining what Islamic reformism has accomplished over the last two centuries. Since the beginning of the nineteenth century, Islamic reformism has been engaged in creating new forms of Muslim consensus and internal unity in the hope overcoming maladies in the *ummah* (the Muslim community) and of bringing forth a 'renaissance'. Faced with the decadence of the political body of the state and its growing 'modern' despotic inclinations, reformists have embraced the notion of the *ummah* and called on its different components to seek consensus. In so doing, they have transformed the traditional view of consensus as a juristic principle into a much wider political concept.

The crucial question for the modern reformist was how to ensure the survival of the Muslim *ummah* and how to reform its internal structures in the absence of a unified state or political body. Essentially, the question has been how to overcome all forms of sectarianism, that is, all religious and political divisions, with the aim of achieving internal unity and facing the 'external' challenges posed by European imperialism. In this context, the reformists' insistence on relying on authentic sources of the Qur'an, the established *hadith* of the Prophet, the principle of *ijtihad*, and their rejection of scholastic *taqlid* (imitation), is easily understood. Considered in this light, however, their invitation was revolutionary in the context of modern Islamic thought. It urged Muslims to break the shackles of sectarianism, unite under the wide auspices of Islamic legitimacy, and apply themselves to the task of creative *ijtihad* and interpretation.

To read the Islamic world as comprising only radical, confrontational and violent movements is a massive oversimplification of a truly intricate phenomenon, but limiting Islam to the narrow spaces occupied by secular Muslim elites would be just as mistaken. Westerners undoubtedly – and understandably – find some ease in conversing with such secularist elites, in whom (consciously or unconsciously) they recognise their own reflection, and with whom they share a common set of aspirations.

For the past two centuries, secularist discourse has been an undeniable fact in the Muslim world, but only as one among several conflicting and overlapping discourses, and not the dominant one at that. Similarly, while one can insist that the process of secularisation is a sociological fact in the greater part of the Muslim world, to evaluate the entire cultural and political scene through secularised and official post-colonial state institutions risks leaving one with nothing but a much-distorted vision. One of the gravest errors committed by many western historians was their bid to reduce the history of the modern Muslim world to that of its political rulers and statesmen.[13] As Edward Said pointed out, to read the Muslim cultural and political scene through small narratives and daily histories offers us a more coherent view of the story of secularisation. It is not in the rulers, strategists, bureaucrats, civil servants and statesmen that the history of a society is to be found, but in the small, silent, un-registered histories of the peasants, of housewives, merchants, students, craftsmen and employers.[14] We therefore need to look at the process of secularisation from both angles: that of the macroscopic histories of the Islamic states and their official institutions, as well as that of ordinary people with their smaller narratives and 'microscopic histories'.

It is obvious that secularity is in crisis in many parts of the Muslim world. However, it is not in the supposedly 'marginalised' or traditional sectors of society that secularity is being defeated but, significantly, in the more 'modernised' ones. It is no secret that Islamic revivalism in Turkey and the Arab world is strongest among students (in predominantly scientific universities) and professionals. Indeed, unlike many writers and academics, who see Islamic dress as a sign of alienation from modernity and of subordination to patriarchy, many women in the Muslim world see Islamic veils as instruments of emancipation that facilitate women's presence in the public sphere and enable them to assert their femininity therein. Many of the mothers and grandmothers of these women remained hidden behind the walls of their homes, and never adopted this form of dress. In western societies too, increasing numbers of Muslim girls at schools and women in universities or professional life are opting to wear Islamic dress, while their mothers or grandmothers remain immersed in their Pakistani, Bengali or Moroccan traditions.

A cursory examination of Muslim societies might try to explain resistance to secularism in relation to an inability to cope with the present and a desire to cling to the past, including to the traditions of religion.

Outsiders frequently see Islamic culture as the main obstacle preventing Muslims from embracing secularism and modernisation. Similarly, a great many academics and politicians trace the far-reaching influence of Islam in Muslim societies to their political leaders' alliances with traditional madrasas. Accordingly, it is argued that any attempt to reshape the cultural map of the Muslim world must start with the reformation, or better still, the abolition of the madrasas, that reputedly entrench so much social backwardness and resistance. It may come as a shock to anyone who thinks this way to learn that, in much of the Muslim world, Islamic revivalism is most active in the modern universities and schools, and is only marginally present in the more traditional sectors of society. In fact, many of the most famous religious schools, including al-Azhar in Egypt and al-Zaytouna in Tunisia, have resisted religious revivalism, and remain impervious to the influence of political Islam in all its forms – from moderate and conciliatory to extreme and confrontational.

In seeking to read Islam on its own terms, I have begun to see the relationship between Islam and secularity as operating on the basis of two principal points. Firstly, if secularism is understood – according to its hermeneutical tradition – not as doctrinal orthodoxy, but as referring to worldly matters and human conduct, then Islam may be deemed a secular religion that establishes no sharp dualism between the worldly and otherworldly, the profane and the ecclesiastical. I argue, therefore, that Islam is a 'natural religion' even though it was founded on a revelation. Thus, the worldly is fully embraced and accepted; this makes Islam a thoroughly 'secular' religion, albeit one with transcendental foundations. I employ the term 'secular' with great reservations because I am convinced that it is almost impossible to escape the early Christian theology inherent in the term, as well as the effects of the later polarisation between Christianity and secularity. Indeed, it is crucial to liberate the term secular from the systematisation of secularism and to distinguish secularity (as a deeply rooted term and concept) from secularism (as a body of doctrine with its own theoretical foundations and prescience).

Secondly, theoretically speaking, Islam's controversial relationship with secularity may be understood on two levels. If we take secularity to refer to a theory of meaning and value based on immanence with no reference to transcendence, as was popular in the nineteenth and twentieth centuries, Islam would have great difficulty in accommodating such a notion. In my view, the worldly and otherworldly are seen as overlapping elements in Islam. That is, the 'worldly' is fully endorsed as having been infused with a spiritual dimension, while transcendence is placed at the heart of Muslim consciousness and the Islamic social order. Thus, if the term secular can be said to characterise a political culture based on religious pluralism, political representation and anti-sectarianism, then the term aptly describes the culture of Islam, in which such elements are already embedded, and could be easily incorporated.

One of my main aims in this book is to examine secularity with a fresh eye.

Secularity, it seems, ought not to be perceived as a unified theory or as a systematic doctrine (as secularism), for that fails to reflect the labyrinthine reality of the modes and processes of secularisation.[15] Secularity, like any 'great historical event', bears the marks of a wide variety of experiences and interpretations. The historical complexity of the phenomenon is larger than any attempt at theorising it; theory can scarcely reflect the uncomfortable and ugly faces that secularity has come to assume in some historical contexts.

As Michel Foucault explained, all 'theories of truth' have to practise some form of exclusion and selection.[16] Living human experience is no doubt greater and wider than any 'narrative', just as human life is more colourful and complex than any abstract theoretical system. In order to break away from what Heidegger described as the 'Cartesian philosophy of representation', we need to be intensely conscious of the enormous gap that separates 'text' from 'reality'. Indeed, even language is not a simple mirror that depicts and reflects what already lies in 'an external reality' out there. All theory is a recreation and reshaping of reality, never a mechanical registration of 'brute facts'. Thus, it would be a simplification, even a distortion, to attempt to read the histories of secularisation through a theory or theories of secularity (through secularism).

The topic of secularity lies at the heart of innumerable discussions and countless questions on the topic of Islam. Many Middle East experts, intellectuals, western diplomats and politicians of the post-colonial era have predicted the 'conquest' of the Muslim world by the process of secularisation, which they see as irreversible. To these thinkers, the westernised Muslim elite, who have dominated the political scene in the Islamic world since the beginning of the twentieth century, have been actively engaged in the project of 'modernisation', and prove the soundness of their predictions.

However, Turkey, to give just one example, offers us an insight into the conflicting and polarising strategies that secularity can be subject to. The military generals, who aimed to control the political scene through a kind of rule by veto, identified 'secularism' with a strong form of étatisme, on the basis of which they thought they could 'legitimately' intervene in every corner of society, intruding even into individuals' most intimate private choices. On the opposite bank, the active forces in civil society, including its 'non-secular' currents, have been compelled to swallow the secular framework, but have done so with the aim of softening the harsh effects of 'military secularism', and in order to transform the draconian Turkish model of secularism, into something more liberal and pluralistic. Thus, before being removed by the military machine, even Necmettin Erbakan, Islamist prime minister from 1996 to 1997, advocated a non-interventionist and neutral form of secularism, in the hope of emancipating the religious sphere from the control of the generals. What seems to complicate the political process of secularisation (and, indeed, that of democratisation) in the Middle East is that secularisation cannot survive here within a democratic environment; that is, without the constant intervention of the state, with its official apparatus of oppression and control. No form of secularism has ever survived in this region unaided by the military or state machine; Algeria is no exception. Part of my aim in writing this book is to try to explain why democracy and secularism are incompatible in the Muslim world, but also that there is no necessary contradiction between Islam and democracy.

Another part of my aim in this book is to explore the shadow side of secularity. Secularism is frequently assumed to promote religious and political tolerance, the rationalisation of politics, democracy and an 'enlightened' worldview. Secularism is, accordingly, held to be a necessary precondition for democracy, and as the sole generator of what John Rawls calls the 'overlapping consensus'. By the same token, religion is implicitly deemed to be the antithesis of the secular and consequently also of the democratic. Religion is thus identified with an enchanted, irrational conception of the world that includes sectarianism, hatred, disarray, political despotism and oppression. Religion is, in short, 'a conversation stopper', as the 'enlightened' American pragmatist Richard Rorty explained.[17] That is, religion imposes taboos and barriers on free and mutual communication, which are taken to be prerequisites for any free liberal society.

In this work, I seek to deconstruct the assumptions that lie at the heart of the allegedly essential categories relating to both secularity and religion. My research is founded on a denial of the existence of a secularism *per se* and of religion in itself, and on the premise that numerous configurations of religion exist, just as there are various types of secularity. In certain historical conditions, secularity may generate tolerance and democracy, while in others it may serve to legitimise political despotism and social disintegration. I argue that it is therefore best not to read secularity through the texts of its philosophers or political thinkers (through secularism), but through the lens of the historian and genealogist.[18] The great narrative of secularism is, after all, a self-created one; it is the image in which secularism likes to see itself and be seen. Any great narrative is an act of exaggeration, creation, undermining and expulsion. Any serious enquiry must seek to distance itself from such narratives and seek out the elements that have been erased, forgotten and repressed. As I note frequently in this book, secularity, as it has been implemented in the Middle East, is seen by the majority of its inhabitants as an ally of political despotism and oppression, and as an obstacle to democratisation. The reasons for this are related to the historical circumstances surrounding the process of secularisation, which, in effect, have nothing to do with the character of secularity itself.

Modernity and secularity

Essentially, I aspire to disarticulate the allegedly necessary interconnectedness between secularity and modernity, and to demonstrate, both philosophically and empirically, that a non-secular form of modernity is possible.

In the dominant philosophical and sociological discourse, secularity is generally conceived as one of the principal pillars of modernity. Modernity – in this view – is achievable only in a highly rationalised context, the latter being predicated on the existence of secular culture. As shown in Chapter Five, the German sociologist Jürgen Habermas provided the most systematic work on the topic of modernity. This is so, even though Habermas never advanced a systematic analysis of secularity; the concept is present throughout his discourse, and particularly in his writings on modernity. Generally speaking, Habermas preserved Weber's approach to secularity and the theory of the disenchantment of the world. For both thinkers, disenchantment was not only a necessary precondition to the process of rationalisation, but a cognitive achievement through which the boundaries of what may be called 'rational' are defined anew. Disenchantment, as Weber and Habermas used it, refers to a moral and cognitive accomplishment realised in the modern west.

Habermas's view of secularity as a foundation stone of modernity was by no means unique or exceptional, but predominant amongst a great many sociologists and philosophers. The works of French sociologist Alain Touraine, Italian philosopher Gianni Vattimo and American philosopher Richard Rorty illustrate this point.

Although championing the thesis that modernity is incompatible with any form of religious fatalism, Alain Touraine – while still firmly rooted in the Weberian tradition – strongly criticised the ideology of modernisation with its commitment to the utopia of reason's triumph in history's progressive march. Moreover, he challenged the Weberian model of modernity, stressing that what it preaches is not modernity *tout court*, but a specific mode of modernisation that is characterised by a great concentration of means at the service of economic rationalisation, and by the violent repression of traditional, social and cultural ties. Touraine argued that the capitalism of Weber's *Protestant Ethic* is neither a general nor a conclusive model of economic modernity, but the outcome of reason's brutal rupture with faith and with traditional forms of social action. If thinkers in the western world largely agree that 'their' modernisation can be equated with modernity in general, Touraine objects, this is largely due to western modernisation taking temporal precedence over other forms of modernisation as well as its hegemony over the west for the past three centuries. Rather than recognising the historicity of the model, these thinkers erroneously declare discontinuity with the past and the creation of an elite 'proprement capitaliste' as the necessary condition for the emergence of a modern society.[19]

Although Touraine exposed the limits of Weber's paradigm of modernity, he remained faithful to its frontiers. What remains of the ideology of modernisation are critique, deconstruction and a sense of disenchantment. Thus, although Touraine pronounced the war that militant atheism waged against Christianity as a peculiarly French phenomenon,[20] he failed to furnish his readers with an answer to the question of the attainability of a non-Weberian, non-secular mode of modernity, and was, in the end, unable to liberate himself from the boundaries of 'the Weberian cage'.

Gianni Vattimo advanced a more sophisticated approach to modernity and secularity, due to his ability to devise new questions and his mastery of the deconstruction game, but he too left the relationship between modernity and secularity intact. In Vattimo's eyes, modernity's later phases may be described as a Nietzschean thematic; that is, as that era in which being modern becomes a self-immanent value. Secularisation for Vattimo described not 'only what happens in a certain era and what nature it assumes, but also the "value" that dominates and guides consciousness in the epoch in question, primarily as faith in progress – which is both a secularised faith and a faith in secularisation'.[21]

For Vattimo, modernity in its mature form denotes a consciousness of a lack of foundation, ending in what Nietzsche describes as full nihilism. Secular modernity has no basis for subordination to a given transcendent power and, in a world devoid of references and moorings, 'everyone is equal and the imposition of any system of meaning on others is violence and oppression, for it can never legitimate itself by referring to an objective order, the only possible foundation for the predominance of an order of meaning is force'.[22] Disenchantment is the full recognition of the lack of foundation, in the sense that there are no objective structures, values or laws; and that human beings create everything posited. Accordingly, nothing remains in the world beyond a mere play of forces.[23]

Modernity can be characterised as an age of the abandonment of the sacred vision of existence in favour of secular values. Intellectually, the cardinal element in the process of secularisation is the faith in progress that is fundamental to Judeo-Christian theology. With modernity's emptying of the notion of progress, all that is left is an affirmation of the new as having fundamental value. As Vattimo maintained, 'secularisation itself, in short contains a tendency toward dissolution accentuated with passage of the pathos of the new toward the field of art'.[24] Modernity dissolves the norm of teleological progress and transforms it into a process of unending progress. Progress is thus both the generator of movement and its product. That is, the only fundamental element preserved within modernity is a providential vision of history.

Radical as Vattimo's non-foundationalism was, with its bid to purge modernity of all substantial essence, it fell short of realising its goal. Rationality, progress, subjectivity, along with the rest of the Enlightenment's idols, may all have come under Vattimo's Nietzschean hammer, but secularity remained the 'non-foundationalist foundation' of his radical modernity. Secularity was left out of the game of radical deconstruction. If Vattimo's endeavour was to live up to the Nietzschean benchmark, nothing should have been exempted from the deconstructive process; not only should the sacred fall to Nietzsche's hammer, but so too should its closest counterpart, the secular.

Rorty's approach to secularity largely remained faithful to the tradition of western liberalism, with its insistence on drawing a sharp line between the private and the public spheres. This dichotomy runs through Rorty's neo-pragmatism. To him, the private is concerned with the meaning of life, which is personal and enjoys a high degree of autonomy from other spheres. The focus of the public sphere is on human solidarity, on that which binds individuals together in a context of shared institutions and practices. The dualism of public/private is, indeed, the backbone of the characterisation of the religious (as distinct from public institutions such as the Church) as that which 'we do in our solitude'. In this, Rorty sought to stretch the Jeffersonian compromise to its farthest boundaries, privatising religion and casting it out of the public sphere, or, in Rorty's words, 'making it bad taste to bring religion into discussions of public policy'.[25] Effectively, this radically restricts the religious, narrowly limiting it to a personal hobby that 'mature, public-spirited adults do not use as a basis for politics'. Religion, Rorty maintained, is a 'conversation stopper', and as such is detrimental to communicability within the public sphere. Religion's incompatibility with public communication is, Rorty added, 'the main reason religion needs to be privatised'.[26]

What appears to be missing from Rorty's argument is the possibility that secularism can play a similar role and be just as much of a conversation stopper in certain contexts. Anyone familiar with secularism as it operates in the Muslim world must surely concede that it does not necessarily trigger open debate, nor foster pluralism and tolerance. In fact, secularism itself can also generate a plurality of taboos and restrictions. The generals in Turkey, who, as custodians of the secular regime, cast their shadows over every corner of Turkish political life, and the French educational establishment, which finds itself in crisis at the sight of a Muslim teenager with a scarf on her head, lay bare the rigid limits of secularity.

For Rorty the accomplishments of the modern west are only understandable in the context of its willingness to go secular, to give up on transcendence. He maintains that secularisation is one of the forces that helped make a social democratic utopia plausible.[27] Against left-wing intellectuals, who insisted that no culture be deemed of lesser validity than any other, Rorty unabashedly preached the pre-eminence of modern western culture. In fact, much of what Rorty said thrives on the ancient Aristotelian symmetrical dualism between 'us' and 'them' that is characteristic of much of Enlightenment literature. The difference between Rorty and his Enlightenment predecessors is that he sought to found his claims of superiority on historical efficiency. In his view, it is now history, not human nature, that justifies ego-centrism, and in the gift of efficiency lies the secret of the west's affluence, prosperity and astounding accomplishments. According to Rorty, 'Most people – especially people relatively untouched by European Enlightenment – simply do not think of themselves as, first and foremost a human being.'[28]

What is striking is Rorty's reverence for that which the 'modern' western imagination deems sacred, its posting of a 'west' vis-à-vis an 'east', along with the silent bid to 'orientalise' the latter, so much so that one often wonders if one is reading a contemporary 'new pragmatist' text or an eighteenth-century manuscript by Montesquieu. In his work, the Orient becomes a synonym for cultural stagnation and resignation, thereby stressing the 'peculiarity of the west'. Rorty tells us that the west has developed 'a hope of a better world as attainable here below by social effort – as opposed to the cultures of resignation characteristic of the East'.[29] Furthermore, underlying Rorty's supposed non-essentialism lies a two-faceted essentialist claim, to the moral prominence of what he refers to as the European–North Atlantic culture of hope, and, consequently, the superiority of the American or North Atlantic liberal model over all other conceivable models, including the European one. While Rorty made no explicit statement to this effect in his political work, in my view, this assumption infuses all his writing.

Many questions remain unthinkable in the Habermasian theory of modernity. At the forefront of these is the bond between secularity and modernity, already discussed. Linked to this is the question of the bond between rationality and secularity. Is the convergence between secularisation and rationalism merely a historical and epistemological phenomenon, or is there a unique and necessary relationship between them that precludes the emergence of one without the other? Is the connection between modernity and secular rationality only one among many possible narratives and not necessarily the 'great narrative' of modernity?

In my view, modernity, rather than secularisation, requires demystification (although demystification is essential to secularisation). By demystification I mean the abandonment of the view of the world as a haven for spirits and metaphysical bodies. I argue that the connection between secularity and modernity is questionable, and I reject the dominant view that rationality inevitably dissolves into secularity. I understand rationality here in functional terms – that is, as the investment of the power of reason in different ways and forms in everyday life. I also seek to cast doubt on the interconnectedness of secularity and modernity by maintaining that modernity does not necessarily require the erasing of religious meaning and presence from worldly affairs. Indeed, there is no empirical evidence that religion has been, or is being, eroded throughout the world. In fact, in many places, the opposite seems to be true.

My methodology is two-faceted: on the one hand, I have attempted to extend the Habermasian view of modernity; on the other hand, I aim to reveal the limits of Habermas's theoretical framework. To play a double game with Habermasian texts is no easy task. One has to engage in the game using its terms and rules, while seeking to deconstruct them at the same time; to attempt to reactivate the potentials embedded in Habermas's theory of modernity and to overcome its limits.

What Weber referred to as the disenchantment of the world, and described as a necessary condition of modernity, is only partially true. Weber, I submit, was right to argue that modernity disenchants the world in the sense that it relieves it of its mythical burdens, but he was mistaken in perceiving this claim as also entailing an elimination of religious meaning and presence from worldly institutions and activities in favour of nihilism. If modernisation is capable of modifying the role of religion, the inverse is conceivable too; religion can alter the function of modernity. Modernised societies tend to allow religion a higher degree of flexibility than traditional societies. This, in turn makes religion more capable of meeting individuals' worldly needs. In other words, religion is potentially just as conditioned by modernisation as modern-isation is conditioned by religion. This is not to say that all religions are apt to 'survive' in a modernised context, but that some can both act within and react to modernity.

In my view, the secular liberal compromise that draws a line be-tween a private religious sphere and a secular public one is only one possibility among many. And this compromise is, it must be noted, not even stable or uniform across the spectrum of western liberalism. The United States provides a clear example of this.[30] Islam needs to be in-voked here too, to demonstrate that certain religious systems have re-acted negatively to modernisation. To the simple minded, Islam is the world's most fundamentalist religion and is incapable of accommodat-ing itself to modernity. A more thorough reading reveals the tensions evident in Islam's relationship with western forms of secular moder-nity, as well as the root causes of those tensions. On the theoretical and practical levels, Islam has neither fully rejected western secular modernity nor passively welcomed it. Reactions have ranged from en-dorsement to recycling and from modification to rejection. There is no doubt that Muslims find great difficulty swallowing the notion of an immanent secular modernity, but, as I attempt to show in this book, far from being linked to any inability to deal with the 'here and now', this is far more related to Islam's own non-secular worldliness.

In effect, I propose a non-Habermasian and non-Weberian approach, and reject the view that secularity is a necessary pillar of modernity. In my view, a non-secular form of modernity is not only theoretically pos-sible, but is already evident in the many manifestations of non-secular modernisation that exist in various parts of the globe. What I hope to do is to deconstruct the alliance between secularisation and modernisa-tion in readers' minds. The modernity we read about in western socio-logical, political and philosophical literature, and observe in western geo-politics, is merely one mode of modernity, and not modernity *per se*. In Habermas's memorable words, modernity itself is a yet unfin-ished project. Indeed, for these words to express their full significance, Habermas's category needs to be broadened to accommodate the possibility of a non-secular species of modernity. In my view, his model of modernity remains too narrow, and relies too heavily on Weber's terms and parameters. What I seek to do is to extend Habermas's claim, and then to bypass the boundaries he retained by drawing on a variety of traditions within both western and Islamic philosophy.

Modernity and Islamic discourse

In Chapters Six and Seven, I explore a number of questions relating to the intricate relationship between Islam and modernity. For instance, how does the intellectual and cultural body of Islam assert itself in the modern era, and particularly since its encounter with western imperialism? How did Islam's intellectual energy reactivate itself in modern reformism, and what was its response to its defeat by the modern west? In what ways has reformist Islam reshaped both Islamic intellectualism and Muslim consensus in an era marked by political disintegration? To what extent has reformism succeeded in adapting and limiting the political discourse of modernity? How far has modern Islamic reformism succeeded in building a consistent alternative, and to what extent has it achieved its goal of rejuvenating Islam, and rendering it compatible with the perceived needs of modern times?

Of course, Islamic reformism is intensely diverse, and crosses vast geographic, linguistic and cultural spaces, but I would argue that common features and similar agendas characterise various components of this international phenomenon. I seek, therefore, to uncover the similarities beneath the differences. I admit that exploring the various configurations of Islamic reformism in detail is a difficult task, but I am convinced that, underlying the fragmented discourse of modern reformism, are common elements that may be designated as the great pillars of modern reformism's philosophical discourse. Theologically, modern reformism revolves around: monotheism; a belief in the free subject; the premise that religion is the moral ground that gives legitimacy to subjectivity; the unity of the rational and the religious; and a strong belief in a progress that has both moral and religious aspects. Politically, modern reformism is firmly opposed to power monopolies, and champions the rule of law. With the rise of Islamic absolutism and the reception given to modern European thought during the Tanzimat era in Istanbul, Cairo, Damascus, Tunis and other Islamic provinces, modern reformism acquired a deep awareness of the dangers of political despotism. It accords priority to the notion of '*adl* (political justice) and the *ummah* (including its independent associations) over the notion of the state.

The project of modern reformism was initiated in the middle of the nineteenth century by Jamal ad-Din al-Afghani (1838–1897), who called for Islamic revivalism. Al-Afghani began his controversial project in Kabul but also travelled extensively, visiting Istanbul, Cairo, India, Iran and Paris, during his lifetime. Muhammad 'Abduh (1849–1905), al-Afghani's most prominent disciple and closest friend, was well travelled too. He worked with his teacher in Egypt, in the aftermath of the 'Urabi Revolution of 1882 against British occupation, until he was exiled to Beirut. He then moved to Paris at al-Afghani's request to join him in establishing the magazine *al-Urwah al-Wuthqa* (The firmest bond), which influenced a great many educated young Muslims all over the Islamic world. Gradually 'Abduh came to moderate the anti-imperialist views he had inherited from al-Afghani, directing his efforts instead to educational and cultural reform.

Since then, modern reformism has extended to all but a few of the Islamic provinces, claiming a vast number of followers from the ranks of the Islamic elites through its call for Islamic renovation and for the abandoning of blind imitation and scholasticism. Islamic reformism has largely transformed Islam's intellectual map and shifted the might of Islam away from traditional imitation and into critical and dynamic renovation. Modern reformism, which is by no means a homogeneous phenomenon, has paved the way for what may be referred to as a 'new phase of Islamic reformism' and a 'new Islamic discourse'. By this I mean a certain mode of discourse that derives its legitimacy from Islam and problematises the issues of modern times using an Islamised language and system of reference, in a bid to revive and adapt Islam to present conditions.

The emergence of this discourse is intimately linked to the birth of the new Muslim intellectual. The decline of traditional learning institutions has reduced the role of Muslim scholars, and a new Muslim intelligentsia have come to the fore. The part played by modern reformism in shifting Islam and its symbolic heritage away from the sphere of the traditional madrasas and into modern schools and universities is truly significant. Indeed, as I show in my final chapter, contrary to the prevailing view that modern schools and universities are the vanguard of secularisation, these establishments have acted as the primary incubators of the new Muslim reformists.

1

Nietzsche, Weber, and the theory of secularity

The greatest recent event – that 'God is dead', that the belief in the Christian god has become unbelievable – is already starting to cast its first shadow over Europe.

– Nietzsche, *The Gay Science*

Although the term 'secular' is deeply entrenched in western theological and intellectual traditions, it was not until the beginning of the nineteenth century that scholars began to construct a body of doctrine on secularism as a theory of meaning and interpretation. Friedrich Nietzsche and Max Weber played crucial roles in laying the foundations and defining the parameters of this theory. No student of secularity can overlook Nietzsche's cry announcing the death of God, nor the fact that his perceptions of the western world's great willingness to embrace secularism have influenced not only philosophers, but wider intellectual circles as well. Similarly, Weber occupies such a central position in the domains of political theory and cultural sociology that no one dealing with the issue of secularity in relation to world religions or modern times can escape the influence of Weberian tradition.

With his nihilistic views and perspectivist philosophy, Nietzsche fundamentally shaped European culture towards the end of nineteenth century, and his distinctive stamp on Weber's thinking is particularly evident in Weber's later writings, where references to Nietzsche are frequent. Nietzsche's mark is particularly evident in Weber's view of the status of religion in modern times, and in Weber's approach to power.

Although Weber ascribed a powerful role to religion in the generation of modern capitalism and formal bureaucracies, he maintained that religion's function was merely transitory. He argued that the death of God, as declared by Nietzsche, was rendered inevitable by the birth of a rational, organised and godless cosmos. In this context, religion gradually retreats to a tiny shadowy corner that owes its existence to what Weber referred to as the 'irrationality of the world'. Weber also distanced himself from the notion of a transcendental and unifying reason in favour of the wider Nietzschean concept of power that penetrates reason and its historical embodiments, namely the economic market and state bureaucracy. The intentional and rational subject gives way to the 'iron cage of modernity', which dominates the tissue of modern life, transforming it into various species of control and discipline.

My main aim in this book is to cast doubt on the basis of the discourse of secularisation initiated by Nietzsche and Weber, illustrating its genealogical roots and internal boundaries, as well as the theoretical and practical difficulties it faces in relation to Islam. In this chapter, I uncover the philosophical parameters of secularity identified by Nietzsche, and explain how Weber's sociology legitimised and consolidated them. In my view, secularism (as institutionalised in the academic sphere, and articulated in the socio-political discourse of modernity) is little more than a corroboration and extension of Nietzsche and Weber's work. These two scholars (and the latter in particular) exercised both hidden and explicit power in their formulation of a doctrinal body of knowledge around secularism, and by their transformation of the long-rooted hermeneutical tradition that is embedded in the term 'secular' (along with its various concomitants – secularity, secularisation, etc.) into a general body of theory. Thus any criticism of secularism ineluctably finds itself in a kind of dispute or polemic with the Nietzschean and Weberian traditions, as well as with the huge arsenal of categorical theories and paradigms that have prevailed since the dawn of the twentieth century. As Foucault justly pointed out, any discourse has its own limits and 'taboos' that it generates and then strives to safeguard.[1] In my view, secularism is one such taboo within the political discourse of modernity.

In most of Weber's work, secularity is conceived of as a by-product of the long and complex development of rationality. In my view, the genealogy of rationality, with its evolution and moments of maturity, is but another face of secularism in human intellectual and institutional history. Rationalisation is a broad concept that can designate a whole process, but also its various forms and components. Simply stated, Weber's claim is that the emergence and 'maturity' of rationalism denotes a process of disenchantment, and is simultaneously an expression of an awareness of this process.

Weber borrowed Friedrich Schiller's phrase 'the disenchantment of the world' and put it to two uses. Used negatively, the expression came to refer to the structure of consciousness and history from which elements of magic are gradually fading away. In its more positive framing, the expression designated the extent to which ideas achieved a high degree of coherence and consistency or, as Weber termed it, 'intellectualisation'.[2] The increasing power of rationalisation, in both its cognitive and practical expressions, culminated in what Weber then described as the 'disenchantment of the world'. In this sense, disenchantment can be seen as part of the overall process of rationalisation. The German sociologist Friedrich Tenbruck investigated whether the processes of rationalisation and disenchantment overlap in Weber's thought, and concluded that 'there has been a tacit acceptance that they are equivalent'.[3]

Disenchantment can be defined as a venture of human intellectual consciousness and, in the main, as a form of historical self-consciousness. A full grasp of disenchantment is unattainable without recollecting the term's dialectical opposite – enchantment. That is, without enchantment, there can be no moral complexity and no understanding of the full meaning of disenchantment. Although the two concepts are distinct, and even opposed to one another, each requires an acknowledgement of the other. If enchantment is a land of mystery and wonder, a magical garden of mythical polytheism, then disenchantment is its antithesis: no garden, but an austere and arid desert, the inhabitants of which are obliged to construct their own meanings.

Weber used various melancholic metaphors to designate the condition of disenchantment, including 'darkness', 'petrifaction', 'mechanisation', 'emptiness', 'inner death', 'a world of shadow', 'no spirit', and an 'iron cage'.[4] One can say that the terms enchantment and disenchantment are socio-historical concepts as well as metaphors: enchantment is rooted in the archaic, magical origins of so-called primitive religions while disenchantment is profoundly entrenched in the history of the monotheistic religions, and is symbolic of modern times. Thus, the term 'disenchantment' should be read not so much as the final state of a world purged of illusion, but as the outcome of a long process of historical and religious change.

Rationality and the theory of action

It is crucial to note that the concept of rationalism in Weber's discourse is fragmented and even controversial and, as such, it is in need of constructive interpretation. Weber did not employ the term in the same way throughout his life, and even altered its field of meaning several times. As Weber put it,

> We have to remind ourselves in advance that 'rationalism' may mean very different things. It means one thing if we think of the kind of rationalization the systematic thinker performs on the image of the world: an increasing theoretical mastery of reality by means of increasingly precise and abstract concepts. Rationalism means another thing if we think of the methodical attainment of a definitely given and practical end by means of an increasingly precise calculation of adequate means.[5]

Weber's clearest and most systematic discussion of rationalism appeared in *The Protestant Ethic and the Spirit of Capitalism*, in which he noted that

> by this term, very different things may be understood as the following discussion will repeatedly show. There is,

for example, the rationalization of mystical contemplation, that is of an attitude which, viewed from other departments of life, is specifically irrational, just as much as there are rationalizations of economic life, of technique, of scientific research, of military training, of law and administration... Hence, rationalizations of the most varied character have existed in various departments of life and in all areas of culture.[6]

In his work, Weber constantly attempted to uncover the historical context of the process of rationalisation, which, as he explained, may take different and even conflicting forms. Thus, rationalisation in one sphere may have irrational concomitants or consequences in another; that is, instabilities and tensions exist in even the most rationalised order.

Broadly speaking, the term 'rationalisation' can be used to describe general trends of historical development. The first of these is the tendency of social and historical processes to become increasingly dependent on calculation and technical knowledge, with the aim of gaining control over nature and the human condition. Rationalism may also refer to the human endeavour to purge ourselves of magical and metaphysical beliefs, relying instead on what is empirically verifiable.

The term 'calculation' is key in this context. Weber used it to designate the point at which 'the spirit of capitalism' – with its claim to rationality – penetrated human consciousness and so many spheres of life. That is, Weber used the notion of calculation to convey the modern condition whereby the logic of monetary and bureaucratic reckoning infiltrates almost all other forms of social interaction. Weber was of the opinion that calculation is evident in the modern world at two levels. The first is in the practical domain, whereby quantitative reasoning and instrumental calculation control the ways in which people conduct their personal and public lives. The second occurs at the level of thought, whereby individuals weigh up alternatives prior to taking action, and link means to goals so as to increase their power over their own condition and the external environment.[7]

By rationality, Weber means a standard of awareness, the substance of which lies in relating means and ends prior to taking action. At an intellectual level, increased rationality signifies increasing theoretical mastery of reality by means of a greater range of concepts. In other words, rationality (the equivalent of secularity) refers to a shift in the comprehension of reality – from metaphysical and mysterious to a utilitarian search for power via mastery over the world. In other words, Weber generally used the term 'rationality' to describe an orientation towards reality that systematically weighs up means and ends for purposes of efficacy, and for the attainment of practical goals. In this sense, an action can be designated rational if it relates means to goals through instrumental calculation. With respect to action, then, rationality can be classified into two types: subjective rationality, which refers to the degree of inner evaluation an actor engages in cognitively before taking action, and objective rationality, which refers to the degree to which an action embodies rational principles by adhering to a means–ends calculation.[8]

Weber also distinguished different types of motivations for action, and his typology for this was based on a sliding scale from rationality to irrationality.[9] Actions that he deemed most rational relate to expediency, with the conduct of *homo economicus* being a prime example. On the other end of the scale Weber placed actions that derive from sentiment and tradition. Weber described conduct that is based on tradition as 'unreflective' or 'irrational' in the sense that it is sanctified and deemed appropriate by having 'always been done'.

Elaborating on Weber's sliding scale of rational to irrational motivations for action, French sociologist Raymond Aron suggested that there are four modes of action, that can all be defined in terms of the knowledge or consciousness of the actor rather than the observer.[10]

- Rational action in relation to a goal that an actor conceives clearly, combining means with a view to attaining a specific end.
- Rational action in relation to a value, whereby an actor acts not for the sake of an effective result, but rather in order to remain faithful to a particular worldview.

- Affective or emotional action, whereby an act is determined with reference to the emotional reaction of an actor in a given set of circumstances.
- Traditional action, whereby action is prescribed by customs or beliefs that may have become habitual or 'natural'. In this case, actors may be unaware of their 'presence' in the world, and simply follow instructions or practices dictated by their social or physical environment.

Science and disenchantment

According to Weber, modern science – along with technological innovation – is the most interesting and revealing expression of the long process of rationalisation, or intellectualisation, through which western culture has evolved. In Weber's view, science by its very nature is anti-religious, which is why he argues that science leads the march of disenchantment. Science transforms the world into a subject amenable to instrumental knowledge, into a flat surface that has no value beyond the human will to mastery and control. With the transformation of the world into an object of science, and something entirely secular, Weber argued that the 'categorical conceptualisation' of science also became contingent – a mere 'ideal–typical' construction. Thus, the substantial object of science vanished – being no longer a 'path to God', to 'true being', or even a way to happiness; and with it disappeared the substantiality of science itself.[11] Weber never accepted the neutrality of science, but always saw it as an essentially atheistic force, arguing that science deprives the modern world of the meaning it had been given by religion as a cosmos full of mysteries, and, as such, opens the gate to secular atheism. For Weber, science was not only a fundamental element in the process of disenchantment, but also its catalyst; not an isolated phenomenon but a cultural one, and inseparable from other epistemological fields, such as philosophy and cosmology. He argued that

> Scientific progress is a fraction, indeed the most important fraction, of the process of intellectualization, which we have

been undergoing for thousands of years and which nowadays
is usually judged in such an extremely negative way.[12]

Weber also maintained that a close affinity exists between science and
rationalism. The latter, in its advanced form, is the child of scientific
specialisation and differentiation, of what Weber referred to as 'intellectualisation'. The process of rationalisation also mirrors the trajectory
of secularisation, which has achieved maturity in the modern west as
the locus of the tangibility of universal history. True, Weber did not
subscribe to a linear reading of progress; he did not celebrate progress
as the French philosopher Nicolas de Condorcet did. Modernity, for
Weber, represented an iron cage, not a haven of rational emancipation.
Weber used the iron cage metaphor to expose the fact that the condition
of modernity is characterised by monetary and bureaucratic calculation,
or what Weber calls the spread of purposive rationality over all other
forms of rationality. In this context, human beings become prisoners
and victims of rationalisation as embodied in capitalism and modern
state bureaucracy. Yet, even when Weber turned his back on the utopias of the Enlightenment, during which rationality began to be seen
as wedded to emancipation, he never abandoned his commitment to
the tangibility of evolution. Nevertheless, Weber did not view scientific
progress with the naive optimism of 'big children in university chairs
or editorial offices',[13] but with pessimism, proclaiming it the destiny of
the modern world.

With the progress of rationalisation in intellectual, social and personal conduct, the world has gradually been demystified. Many modern
societies have abandoned all beliefs in magical powers, spirits and demons. That is, a sense of the divine, and of humanity having any sort of
religious vocation, has been lost. Reality has become cold, pragmatic
and devoid of depth, dissolving in a purposive formal rationality with
no end other than mastery attained for its own sake, and through the calculation of the most efficient means to achieve a given end. In Weber's
words: 'There are no mysterious incalculable forces that come into play,
but rather…one can in principle master all things by calculation.'[14]

Cognitive rationality, in Weber's terms, is a systematic and consistent image of the world, an image that reflects reality as it is – a 'disenchanted garden'. It can be said that rational individuals are, if not in possession of the truth, at least looking for it. They are attempting to understand the world as it is, and not as they want it to be.[15] According to Weber, our aim is to understand life as it is lived, and if science cannot provide a substantial value for action, it can at least reveal the essential meaninglessness of the world. It is the mission of science to penetrate the very depths of existence until it realises that existence has no depth; that it is a mere surface that appeals to no references beyond its own. Thus, for Weber, if individuals continue to bestow religious meanings on the world, it is only because they submit to their fantasies and emotional inclinations. Weber saw religion fundamentally as an illusion, albeit one that has the potential to generate dynamism and change in certain historical conditions. The 'other world' that religion creates is a human world (or an image of ourselves in the world) distorted by religious symbolism.[16] It is worth noting that Marx had some influence on Weber's interpretation of world religions, but this should not conceal the numerous points of divergence and difference between the two scholars. While Marx looked at religion as a mere illusion that reflects 'the heart of a heartless world', and as having no history separate from socio-economic structures, Weber insisted that religion is not necessarily a reactionary force. Weber was adamant that religiously inspired movements have often been catalysts of social change and transformations. Nevertheless, he still saw religion as merely an 'active illusion' that cannot challenge the facts of the world – particularly those of the rationalised, capitalist, modern world – even though religious debate helped to spark the emergence of that world.

The intellectual rationalisation that saw its ripening in modern science and its embodiment in technology does not mean that modern societies are any more aware of the ontological conditions in which we live than our ancient predecessors were. It simply means that most of us gaze into the world without feeling a need to appease or appeal to magic or mysterious powers. To put this in Foucault's terms, what separates modern societies from those of our ancestors is not the 'quantity of knowledge' that we have acquired, but the 'order of knowledge' (the 'episteme'). This has undergone a dramatic change, and our mode of understanding our own ontological condition has shifted dramatically.[17] The modern world radicalised the meaning of conflict that marked the Hellenic worldview, and has driven this to its limits. In other words, the polytheism of the modern world replaced ancient polytheism by transforming the principle of the conflict between various gods into one between different worldviews and interests. In the process, personal gods became impersonal abstract forces. As Weber put it,

> Here too, different gods struggle with each other and will do so for all time. It is just like the old world, which was not yet disenchanted with its gods and demons. But in another sense, just as [the Hellenes] sacrificed on this occasion to Aphrodite on another to Apollo, and above all as everybody sacrificed to the gods of [the] city, things are still the same today, but disenchanted and divested of the mythical but inwardly genuine flexibility of those customs.[18]

The historical achievement peculiar to modern western rationalism is disenchantment. This has, in turn, led to the most acute activation of the conflict between different value systems in cultural history.[19] For rationality carries a value theory in its folds. Secularism both motivates for conflict between different worldviews and, at the same time, offers an awareness of this conflict. Although polarisation is not a new phenomenon, the consciousness of it is truly novel. As Weber said, 'It is the destiny of our culture, however, that we will once more become aware of it, after our eyes have been blinded for a thousand years by the allegedly or presumably exclusive orientation towards the sublime pathos of the Christian ethic.'[20]

Secularisation, or as Weber called it, the 'disenchantment of the world' emancipates the modern world from superstitions and metaphysical illusions, but, as I hope to show in this book, it also has the potential to empty the world and the souls of human beings. Secularisation deprives existence of ethical determination. In the end, substantial rationality dissolves its energy in the vicious circle of instrumental rationality and, under modern conditions, the world shatters into pieces. Monotheism has made way for a new kind of polytheism that places value systems and worldviews in a state of irreconcilable conflict.[21] As Weber himself argued, where the gods of Olympus once competed against one another, today:

> Many old gods ascend from their graves; they are disenchanted and hence take the form of impersonal forces. They strive to gain power over our lives and again they resume their eternal struggle with one another. What is hard for modern [people], and especially for the younger generation, is to measure up to workaday existence.[22]

Disenchantment deprives knowledge of a foundation. It becomes, to use Nietzsche's term, 'perspectivist'. Indeed, science provides no answers for existential problems. As Weber put it: 'What should we do? How should we live? The fact that science does not give us this answer is completely undeniable.'[23] The only choice we have is to create our own meaning and value in a meaningless world. That is, historical existence, according to Weber, is essentially the creation and affirmation of values or, as Aron argues, Weber's value theory is that human existence is about engagement. No choices are directed by science, everyone has to make their own choice between god and the devil. Since purposive rationality is defined as the search for means that suit rationally determined goals, it is clear that Weber was not of the view that individuals and societies could agree on common goals or values. He denied the existence of any grounds for the tangible validity of values, and believed that we are each obliged to make our own choices because, in the last analysis, values are incompatible with one another.[24] Moreover, if existence is meaningless, and even nihilistic, human beings have to shoulder their responsibilities through engaging in the adventure of existence.

In this, Weber's theory of values paves the way for his theory of responsibility. The fundamental antinomy of action for Weber is between the morality of responsibility and of conviction. An ethic of responsibility is, after all, defined by pragmatic effectiveness, by finding suitable means for chosen goals, while an ethic of conviction is a morally motivated action without reference to the consequences. In Weberian sociological theory, one of the main characteristics of disenchantment is the shift of social action from being grounded in tradition to being based on conviction, and from conviction to responsibility.

As German sociologist Wolfgang Schluchter maintained, the main peculiarity of the Protestant ethic in Weber's thought was that it fulfilled the necessary condition for the emergence of purposive rational action in the sphere of social labour. The development of ethics, according to Weber, is a process of advancing towards rational autonomy, and culminates in a sense of responsibility. In its earliest stages, systems of ethics assume a stringently religious character, and are referred to in Weberian terms as 'normative ethics'. The shift from normative ethics (law) to the ethics of principle (as exemplified in inner-worldly Protestantism) sheds light on a dramatic change in relation to the symbolic world. The distinctive role that the ethics of principle played in the development of Protestantism lies in the fact that it paved the way for the emergence of a secular form of ethics – that is, the ethics of responsibility. As Schluchter pointed out, the central question posed by Weberian sociology is: under what institutional conditions do religious ethics shape autonomous, subjectively responsible individuals? In other words, how can the ethics of principle lead to an ethics of responsibility, and how far can this transformation reshape the symbolic and material condition of the world?[25]

The influence of Nietzsche and Kant

When dealing with Weber's thought, it is necessary to locate his work within its theoretical lineage, and to trace its affinities with the work of Kant and Nietzsche. It is not difficult to discern Nietzsche's stamp on the character of Weber's philosophy of meaning. Both theorists believed that the world is devoid of meaning and value, and that it is human beings who endow the 'world' with significance. However, this is only part of the truth; the similarities between the views of the two scholars should not blind us to elements of divergence.

For Nietzsche, the absence of meaning deprived the world of any centre of reference, and he conceived the death of humanity as being a natural result of the death of God. For Weber, the disappearance of God or the gods provided the grounds for establishing an aware, intentional subjectivity at the heart of the world, in the manner of Immanuel Kant. Because the entire world is demystified, and no longer has any independent meaning, only the self-sufficient individual, as manifest in the person of a political leader, is true. While in Nietzschean perspectivism, the subject is merely an imaginary and aesthetic formation, Weber's epistemology retained the subject/object dichotomy, albeit with greater flexibility than the Enlightenment tradition usually allows. For Weber, the subject formed a solid tenet of his theory of responsibility, and, rooted in this subject/object dichotomy, Weber maintained a distinction between fact and value, which drove him closer to Kant and away from Nietzsche.[26]

Weber's affinity with Kant is manifest in two aspects of his work: first, in the distinction he made between fact and value; and second, in his conception of reason as a unifying *logos* – a view that the two thinkers shared intimately. Weber's contention that the human mind bestows order and meaning on a chaotic universe bears a general resemblance to Kantian epistemology. However, what distinguished Weber from Kant (and drove Weber closer to Nietzsche) was his intense awareness of the relationship that binds reason to power. For Kant, the *telos* of reason *per se* was neutral and universal. Indeed, for Kant, while interests that are deeply entrenched in the phenomenal world may distort reason, reason is the expression of the transcendental subject, and is thus independent of and distinct from power. Weber's departure from Kant was probably generated by the influence of the Nietzschean tradition, which sited the notion of power at the very heart of philosophical and intellectual endeavour. Indeed, the correlation between reason and power lies at the core of Weberian sociology. The concept of rational domination governs Weber's critical approach, and abolished any lines of cleavage between reason and power. Rational domination describes a situation in which the rationality of institutions overwhelms and stifles individual autonomy. In the end, the autonomous individual will evaporate in favour of a rational and mechanised cosmos.[27]

From 'brotherly religion' to 'unbrotherly world'

An analytical reading of the long and complex history of disenchantment calls for a reflection on two crucial turning points. The first of these is the internal accumulative line of secularisation that evolved within the internal dynamics of religious viewpoints. This mode of secularisation is predominantly unselfconscious and overwhelmed by religious symbols and practices. One may refer to this phenomenon as an internal form of disenchantment. The second is the shift from a secularised religious view to a positivist form of disenchantment without reference to doctrinal religion. In this instance, religious energy is exhausted and dissipates into the 'disenchanted garden'. This gradual movement may be characterised as an external or emancipated form of disenchantment.

In *Economy and Society*, Weber outlined three stages in the evolution of religious consciousness. The first is pre-animist naturalism, where 'there evolved the concept of the "soul" as a separate entity present in, behind, or near natural objects, even as the human body contains something that leaves it in dream, syncope, ecstasy, or death'.[28] In this stage, religious conscience has no awareness of the distance between the believer and the divine, since the soul is a continuous presence, in terms of which any event or personal action is understood. The second stage is characterised by a higher degree of abstraction, and can be described as natural anthropomorphism. Here, 'spirits may temporarily "incorporate" themselves into things, plants, animals or people'.[29] The third and most critical phase is the shift from naturalism to symbolism. By a process of abstraction, concrete objects come to symbolise spirits. 'Thus magic is transformed from a direct manipulation of forces into a symbolic activity.'[30] These transitions in the history of religious worldviews can be designated (using a term coined by Habermas) as the 'linguistification of the sacred', whereby 'the learning process in which the prejudgment power of the life world over the communicative practice of everyday life progressively diminishes'.[31] Weber argued that, with the emergence of ethical religion in its monotheistic form, the internal process of religious rationalisation reached a crucial phase in which the problem of theodicy is approached in a consistent and 'rational' manner. Given his own location in the west, perhaps it is not surprising that Weber insisted that not only is Christianity the clearest manifestation of this phenomenon and the most eminent of all world religions, but that Protestantism is the apogee of Christianity's internal rationalisation. Hence, for Weber, Protestantism lay at the intersection of two veins of rationalisation.

If we follow Tenbruck's interpretation of *The Protestant Ethic*, we find Weber not merely concerned with the process of rationalisation in European history, but with discovering a general 'rationale' of the development of religious worldviews, and as well as their inherent attitudes towards rationalisation:

> With the disclosure of religious rationalisation, Weber brings back reason into history. He restores the unity of human history by readmitting the authentic history of all those forms, periods, or cultures, which scientism and modernism, in their evolutionary bent, had regarded if not as insane, then as senseless aberrations from the due course of development. Weber saw reason at work everywhere, though it did not automatically result in what is now understood as rationality and progress.[32]

Thus Weber's reading of world religions may be summed up thus: throughout world history, all paths to religious rationalisation have sprung out of the rationalisation of theodicy. They have all come to the same end: the disenchantment of thought and conduct. However, in the Judeo-Christian tradition, the secularity inherent in all worldviews reaches its climax.

Weber delved into the very heart of the notion of disenchantment and raised several pertinent questions in relation to both its historical function and its cultural expression. He asked how the modern structure of consciousness emerged, and how it came to prevail over existing religious views. More explicitly, he questioned how the disenchanted vision stemmed from religious views, only to subsequently forsake these to triumph over the metaphysical principles from which it emerged. While Weber touched on these topics throughout his oeuvre, two of his works are crucial in revealing his responses to these questions. The first is 'Religious Rejections of the World and their Directions' (1946) and the second is 'The Social Psychology of the World Religions' (1929).

For Weber, a scientific understanding of the world was the vantage point from which what he saw as the universal historical process of secularisation must be judged. According to him, the lengthy secularisation process was initiated by what he termed (in the sexist idiom of his time) 'brotherly religions' unfolding in an 'unbrotherly secular world'.[33] Indeed, Weber proclaimed,

> The tension between religion and intellectual knowledge definitely comes to the fore wherever rational, empirical knowledge has consistently worked through to the disenchantment of the world and its transformation into a causal mechanism. For then science encounters the claims of the ethical postulate that the world is a God-ordained, and hence somehow meaningfully and ethically oriented, cosmos.[34]

Metaphysical rationality (or, to rephrase Weber, the process of intellectualisation from which the modern structure of conscience has emanated) comprises three different spheres: the cognitive, the evaluative and the aesthetic – each of which follows its own internal logic.[35] According to Weber, the differentiation of the value systems related to each sphere was the outcome of a long process of ethical rationalisation – the hallmark of disenchantment – and was, in turn, a major catalyst for secularisation. For Weber, modern humans are acutely aware of this differentiation, and of the endless polarisation and tension between these three spheres.[36] Thus it can be argued that Weber's sociology is bi-dimensional. On the one hand, he was concerned with the rationalisation of worldview, with the structural aspects of disenchantment and the conditions from which modern conscience has emerged, and with how this came to develop in accordance with its own internal logic. On the other hand, Weber was interested in the institutional embodiment of the modern worldview; that is, in social rationalisation, or societal secularisation, as implemented via capitalism and modern bureaucracies.[37]

Essentially, Weber measured the rationalisation of a culture's worldview with a multi-dimensional yardstick: that is, by the degree of emancipation from magical thought and conduct, and by its levels of internal intellectualisation, or systematic dogmatism. As he said:

> To judge the level of rationalization a religion represents we may use two primary yardsticks which are in many ways interrelated. One is the degree to which the religion has divested itself of magic; the other is the degree to which it has systematically unified the relation between God and the world and therewith its own ethical relationship to the world.[38]

Weber also observed that different types of 'life orders' are in a state of ongoing tension. Individual value spheres, characterised by internal rationalisation and consistency, may seem unable to withstand the inscrutability of life, which is governed by rival powers. However, 'the individual spheres of value are prepared with a rational consistency which is rarely found in reality'.[39] At the level of the intellect, individual conduct, and social institutions, life orders are on a perpetual quest for empowerment, and share a 'will to power'.

> For rationality, in the sense of theological 'consistency', of intellectual – theoretical or practical – ethical attitude, has and always has had power over [human beings], however limited and unstable this power is and always has been in the face of other forces of historical life.[40]

The tension between different individual value spheres is most evident in the endless rift between inner subjectivity and the external world; that is, in sustaining an ethical–religious vision in the context of a disconnected and uncaring secular world. With the inception of prophetic religion, an abnegation of the world began to emerge, along with the activation of suffering in the unremitting yearning for salvation. Thus for Weber

> The principle that constituted the communal relations among the salvation prophecies was the suffering common to all believers. This was the case whether the suffering actually existed or was a constant threat, whether it was external or internal.[41]

In 'Religious Rejections of the World and their Directions', Weber identifies two tendencies towards world negation in different religious positions, namely: the inner-worldly pursuit of asceticism, and the otherworldly pursuit of mysticism. Although asceticism and mysticism have points of convergence in their common inclination towards abnegating the external world, their strategies in dealing with the world are entirely contradictory. In Weber's words:

> Active asceticism operates within the world; rationally active asceticism, in mastering the world, seeks to tame what is creatural and wicked through work in a worldly 'vocation' (inner-worldly asceticism). Such asceticism contrasts radically with mysticism, if the latter draws the full conclusion of fleeing from the world (contemplative flight from the world).[42]

However, Weber shows that the distinction between asceticism and mysticism can be tempered – while still maintaining the line of cleavage between the two – where asceticism confines itself to overcoming the wickedness of the world 'in the actor's own nature'. In this case, an ascetic may attempt salvation less through action, and more through a passive escape from the reality of life. Weber describes this as an 'ascetic flight from the world'. The gap between the two may also be reduced if a mystic pursues salvation, not by evading the world but by remaining in the mundane. This Weber refers to as 'inner-worldly mysticism'.

Nevertheless, as Weber put it, 'the typical attitude of the mystic is one of a specially broken humility, a minimisation of action, a sort of religious incognito existence in the world. He proves himself against the world, against his action in the world. Inner-worldly asceticism, on the contrary, proves itself through action.'[43] That is, the channel for salvation – even for world-rejecting asceticism – is activity in the world, a yearning to conduct oneself as God's warrior. One is immersed in the never-ending struggle against the temptations embedded in 'this' corrupt world, while for the contemplative mystic, redemption is solely attainable through utter withdrawal from the world. The only activity open to mystics is contemplation, from which they are obliged to try to exclude their daily worries. The *uno mystica* hopes only for 'repose in the divine'.

It is worth noting, however, that a negative attitude towards the world became viable only when the dualism that characterises the prophetic religions, with their longing for salvation, was born. Prophetic religions require a worldview that devalues this world in relation to the fullness of the other. This tendency to negate or devalue this world is tied to the idea of achieving salvation in the next. The notion of suffering, a concomitant of religious consciousness, has been further magnified and, as Weber would have it, rationalised, via the association between suffering and redemption created by the prophetic religions.

Ethical rationalisation ended in secularisation when the modern world became detached from the 'external world', thereby turning the external world into a domain upon which ethical maxims and imperatives are projected. The objectified world thus became posited before the subject: the believer. The separation between moral values and the 'external world' has two consequences. First, it divests external reality of anthropomorphism and any form of magic, since it detaches believers from their external entourage. Second, it transforms the world into a domain that can be mastered through instrumental calculability. Thus, the substantial rationality motivated by ethical religion finally made way for a kind of formal and instrumental rationality.

For Weber, this ethical rationalisation emerged when two conditions were met. The first was when the norm of salvation posited a dualism between God and God's creation. The second was when dualism created a sharp contrast between the perfect, 'imaginative' world and the imperfect 'visible' world, and between subjective moral principles and the external or objective and secular world. According to Habermas, Weber was keen to show that the salvation religions, which go beyond dualism to a tensional contrast, satisfy the condition of moral rationalisation better than religious visions that have less of an orientation to salvation and are more mildly dualistic.[44] In Weber's words:

> The more the religions have been true religions of salvation, the greater has this tension been. This follows from the meaning of salvation and from the substance of the prophetic teachings as soon as these develop into an ethic. The tension has also been the greater the more rational in principle the ethic has been, and the more it has been oriented toward sacred rules as means of salvation. In common language, this means that the tension has been the greater the more religion has been sublimated from ritualism and toward 'religious absolutism'.[45]

In Weber's view, the more rational the religion, the more strained its relation to the world becomes. This culminates in a spirit of tension overwhelming all value systems and social spheres, and in 'things worldly' dominating all otherworldly values. As the ethical religions' conception of the world took on increasingly rationalised forms, and magical notions declined, the theodicy of suffering encountered greater and greater difficulties. Stripped of the beyond, wherein they were grounded, otherworldly values faced mounting challenges. As a result, the value of the 'here and now' began to hold sway over yearnings for the other world; 'the cunning of history' (to use Hegel's expression) came to undermine the logic of the divine. The victory of the values of this world over those of the world beyond occurred in accordance with psychological determinations of human conduct that was, in Weber's view, increasingly motivated by material interests rather than abstract ideas: 'Psychologically considered, [the] quest for salvation has been primarily preoccupied by attitudes of the here and now.'[46]

Intellectually and morally speaking, the norm of otherworldly compensation associated with all ethical religions turns into worldly reward. Sociologically speaking, religion's pledge to establish a new community grounded on an ethic of community over and beyond ties of blood and kinship stands in conflict with the secular world. The more the external world became subject to rationality, the further the gap widened. In Weber's words, religion

> has always clashed with the orders and values of this world, and the more consistently its demands have been carried through, the sharper the clash has been. The split has usually become wider the more the values of the world have been rationalised and sublimated in their own laws.[47]

As the pace of rationalism quickened, and burgeoned in all spheres of life, religion was increasingly cast into the margins as a hallmark of the 'irrational'. Religion, Weber asserted, cannot thwart the advance of rationalism, since even at its most extreme (ascetic Protestantism) it remains based on 'irrational' postulates and presuppositions. As Weber put it:

> The general result of the modern form of thoroughly rationalizing the conception of the world and of the way of life, theoretically and practically, in a purposive manner, has been that religion has been shifted into the realm of the irrational.[48]

With the increasing systematisation and intellectualisation of religion in the west, the inner conflict between metaphysical postulates and the reality of the world escalated. The shift in the potential rationality of ethical religion that infiltrates all western social institutions – including capitalism and modern bureaucracy – opened the gate to an endless altercation between religious consciousness and social structure, leading to the slow disintegration of the latter. Weber observed that it follows that the external world becomes a sort of independent cosmos endowed with its own inner movements, rhythms and validity.

> To the extent that religious ethic organises the world from a religious perspective into a systematic rational cosmos, its ethical tensions with the social institutions of the world are likely to become sharper and more principled, this is the more true the more the secular institutions (*Ordnungen*) are systematised autonomously.[49]

This vision of worldly activity as an arena of struggle was a constant feature of Weber's thought. His close friend George Simmel offered Weber a conception of the inevitable triumph of the 'objective' over the 'subjective', of the victory of the rational cosmos over the personal subject.[50] Since ideas and interests are inseparable for Weber, and since ideas represent cultural values, then, when connected with interests, ideas shape the different orders of life. It is, therefore, possible to read the process of secularisation, from above, so to speak, by focusing on the history of secularisation, and from below, by looking at the process of social rationalisation as the practical embodiment of the process of disenchantment.[51] Weber adopted the 'view from above' in his wide-ranging study of the sociology of religion, and a 'view from below' when he uncovered the imperative applicability of the secularisation of worldviews on the social level. As Schluchter pointed out, Weber was not concerned with abstract notions as such, but with the active dynamics of ideas as associated with interests and embodied in social institutions.[52]

Protestantism and the capitalist cosmos

Weber drew attention to the relationship between the 'spirit' of Protestantism and the 'spirit' of capitalism, and revealing the comprehensive correlation between religious ways of thinking and attitudes towards economic action. Weber, following Goethe, spoke of an 'elective' affinity between the religious and the economic spheres, and Aron pointed out, that while no causal relationship exists between Protestantism and capitalism, there is 'a spiritual affinity between a certain vision of the world and a certain style of economic activity'.[53]

The main novelty of the Protestant ethic was not the ethical legitimisation of rational work in this world, but the pursuit of the highest possible profit, not in order to indulge in life's pleasures, but for the sake of increased productivity itself. As Weber put it, 'The only way of living acceptable to God was not to surpass worldly morality in monastic asceticism but solely through the fulfilment of the obligation imposed upon the individual by his position in the world. That was his calling.'[54] In other words, if God has predestined each human being's role in this world, individuals are impelled to work as vessels of salvation. Moreover, in order to overcome the existential loss resulting from the ambiguity of their final destiny, work – rational, regular and constant – comes to be interpreted as yielding to God's command.

In accordance with divine purpose, then, Calvinism seemed to provide both the moral impulsion that derives from salvation and a focus on economic activity. Protestantism, Weber submitted, reactivated what was immanent in western culture. That is, it revived the rational Greek tradition within Judeo-Christian ethics. One may say that ascetic Protestantism lies at the intersection of two lines of rationality, extending the cosmological rationalism of Greek philosophy and the ethical rationalism latent in the Judeo-Christian tradition to their limits. Thus, two systems with great potential for rationalisation came to be juxtaposed in western culture. Indeed, it can be argued that ascetic Protestantism is where these two lines of rationalisation converge.[55] From this perspective, Protestantism is the natural result of what is peculiar to western worldviews.

> The great historic process in the development of religions, the elimination of magic from the world, which began with the old Hebrew prophets in conjunction with Hellenistic scientific thought, had repudiated all magical means to salvation as superstition, and sin came here to its logical conclusion.[56]

The primary achievement of ascetic Protestantism was its intellectual motivation for the emergence of substantial rationality by establishing a systematic method for achieving a rational mode of life. Socially, it spawned a rational ethics of conviction, which later turned into a secular ethics of responsibility that permeated all spheres of life. Ascetic Protestantism thus played a critical role in reshaping a new structure of conscience and a new order of life. That is, its peculiarity lies not only in its disruption of the ancient world, but also in the great energy that caused the unfolding of the new, demystified world. Protestantism's significance is to be found in the religion-free world that it created. For instance, the profane values Calvinism gave rise to – given its massive potential for rationalisation – engulfed and triumphed over otherworldly values. As such, Protestantism became the prime victim of the world it birthed. Once capitalism was established, individuals lost all metaphysical and moral motivation. The hypothesis put forward by Weber is that Protestantism was favourable to the formation of the capitalist system, but was itself swallowed by the system it created. From a historical point of view, there is a difference between explaining the formation of a regime, and the continued functioning of the same regime.[57]

'Religious Rejections of the World and their Directions' can be read as an elaboration of the view that substantial ethics sharply contradict the 'unbrotherly' values of capitalism. The more thoroughly the latter is rationalised, the greater its conformity to its own autonomous internal laws, and the less accessible it becomes to religious ethics of caring for one's neighbour. On various occasions, Weber showed that the conflict between religious ethics and the external world is most obvious in the economic sphere, noting that 'ultimately, no genuine religion of salvation has overcome the tension between their religiosity and the rational economy'.[58]

In effect, ethics stand in an endless confrontation with a rational world that bears the stamp of capitalism and formal bureaucracy. If ascetic Protestantism provided the motivation for the creation of modern capitalism, then, once established, the latter order began the long process of eroding religious ethics in the west. Capitalism is a rationalised structure that transcends all personal intentions; it is an immense cosmos with a set of abstract rules to which the individual must conform.

As Weber put it:

> The capitalist economy of the present day is an immense cosmos into which the individual is born, and which represents itself to him, at least as an individual, as an unalterable order of things in which he must live. It forces the individual, in so far as he is involved in the system of the market relationship, to conform to capitalistic rules of action.[59]

From Weber's perspective, not only is the instrumental rationality of the market simply indifferent to people, but it is also bound to sow hostility between them: 'Capital accounting in its formally rational shape presupposes the battle of man with man.'[60] Money and material interests are the means and the ends of this blind struggle.

Weber also shows that bureaucratic institutions are close allies of capitalism's instrumental rationality, in that they encourage calculation and predictability to the highest degree. In other words, far from being antagonistic to bureaucratic domination, capitalism, in Weber's account, is seen as the single most important motivation for the bureaucratisation of the contemporary world.[61] Rationalised, bureaucratic discipline removes all personal loyalties, heroic ecstasy, cults of honour, 'love, hatred and all purely personal, irrational and emotional elements that cannot be readily calculated and administered through abstract general rules'.[62] Bureaucratic relations of power are systems of formal, depersonalised rationality. They are guided by general and formal norms that have to be applied continually and consistently to every case. Thus, the modern world has become a calculating, mechanised system in which 'all spheres of daily life tend to become chronically dependent on disciplined hierarchy, rational specialisation, and the continuous deployment of the impersonal system of abstract general rules'.[63] Bureaucracy is primarily about the rationality of consistency; calculability is its principal characteristic. Very often, this kind of consistency produces instrumental, irrational effects.[64] Weber argued that in this icy, mechanised world, people tend to become indifferent to religion:

The people filled with the spirit of capitalism today tend to be indifferent if not hostile to the church. The thought of the pious boredom of paradise has little attraction for their active natures; religion appears to them a means of drawing people away from labour in this world.[65]

The system that was initially animated by Protestantism turned into the graveyard of all religious yearning and vocation. The further the system ventured down the path of secularisation, and evolved in accordance with the autonomous, immanent laws of capitalism, the darker the shadows that were cast on religious views and conduct.

For Weber, the free market is a structural, rational system with no reference to personal relations, and closed to emotion, with money as its most abstract and impersonal feature. What is novel about modern capitalism is not the norm of interest or profit – which has existed in all ancient forms of capitalism – but that interest *for its own sake*, that is, the tireless accumulation of wealth, recognises no limits. In Weber's words, 'The more the world of the modern capitalist economy follows its immanent laws, the less accessible it is to any imaginable relationship with a religious ethic of brotherliness. The more rational and thus impersonal capitalism becomes, the more this is the case.'[66]

What is true of economics, says Weber, is equally so of politics. In politics the rational '*homo politicus*' manages political affairs pragmatically and with no reference to religious spirit or personal emotion; the politician acts just like the economist: 'without regard to the person... without hate and therefore without love'.[67] Under capitalism, the political arena, like the free market, is less accessible to any substantial morality or personal loyalty. This runs contrary to the patriarchal political order of the past, which was based on the attraction of charismatic masculinity.

A central thesis in Weber's sociology is the struggle between individuals and groups in human society, and in all spheres of life. Weber was adamant that the ethics of 'brotherliness' were unequivocally defeated in the political domain. The political arena to him, was a Hobbesian world, in which the individual can choose only between 'fight' and 'flight', where people 'strive to share power or strive to influence the distribution of power, either among states or among groups within a state'.[68]

Politics, for Weber, was 'inescapably bound to worldly conditions', with political and economic actors employing the same pragmatic, instrumental rationality. The obligations of politicians, according to Weber, are not substantial or ethical. The 'must' for a politician is less a moral imperative than a pragmatic one, based on a theory of the conditions that give rise to successful political activity.[69] Weber denied the possibility of any accord or reconciliation between politics and religion, and argued that as these spheres become increasingly rationalised, the tension between them heightens. 'The mutual strangeness of religion and politics, when they are both completely rationalised, is all the more the case because, in contrast to economics, politics may come into direct competition with religious ethics at decisive points.'[70]

For Weber, the only domain in which religion retains some sign of life is the military, where 'war creates pathos and a sentiment of community'.[71] He argued that it was only on the battlefield that death and the spirit of commitment 'unto death' continued to have meaning.

Nietzsche and radical secularism

At this point, I turn to Nietzsche for two reasons. First, for his pervasive influence in shaping Weber's thought, and particularly Weber's later writings, in which he championed a sort of warring-gods morality.[72] The second reason has to do with the theory of secularity itself, and Nietzsche's pioneering of an atheist form of modernity. It is no secret that Nietzsche was the most outspoken, radical, and indeed daring voice of philosophical atheism in his age, and influenced most of the great intellectuals of his time.

In Weber's discussion of secularity, his argument was not so much that 'God is dead' but rather that God is redundant. As Weber observed in much of his work (and particularly in *Science as a Vocation*), modern society has the propensity to generate polytheism, and competing gods that are divested of public or private authority. Disenchantment has shattered the unitary cosmos of Christianity and the Greek tradition, replacing it with a pluralistic world where no set of values is capable of furnishing homogeneous significance. In the Weberian view, secularisation proceeds through three phases: disenchantment; social fragmentation; and conflict between partial worldviews.[73]

For Weber, modern culture is a disenchanted garden, even for people who remain fervently religious. Here, Weber shared the views of nineteenth-century philosophers and thinkers, such as Auguste Compte, who proclaimed the inevitability of secularisation. Weber was, however, at odds with those secular philosophers who welcomed secularism with open arms. As noted, Weber realised that disenchantment leads less to human emancipation and more to the triumph of instrumental rationality and the iron cage of modernity. In this, Weber's theory of secularism shares numerous aspects with Nietzsche's. To both men, the advance of science necessarily widens the process of disenchantment; belief in magic and otherworldly forces is progressively eroded by empiricism.

The differences between Weber and his precursor can be summarised in three points:

- Weber saw science as the frontline of a long process of secularisation that is nullifying all meaning and value, as well as any guarantee of human emancipation. What science has to confine itself to is uncovering the meaninglessness of the world, and elevating human consciousness. Weber contended that, although modern societies are not happier or indeed more knowledgeable about their ontological condition than their Enlightenment predecessors, the structure of modern conscience is undoubtedly more mature. Nietzsche questioned the entire notion of 'progress', arguing that human beings are not necessarily rising to better or higher horizons. As Nietzsche proclaimed in *The Anti-Christ*, 'progress' is merely a modern notion, a false idea. Onward development is by no means an elevation, advance or strength, and science is not an end in itself, but has always been cultivated as a means. Nietzsche did, however, concede that if science is pursued with 'something like passion, love, ardour, or suffering', it thrives on what he refers to as 'the will to truth'. The title he chose for one of his principal works, *The Gay Science*, denotes the solid ties binding science and morality. Science, for Nietzsche, originated in philosophy, thus making 'true philosophy' and 'true science' inseparable in his eyes. For Nietzsche, if science offers methodical certainty about particulars, philosophy infiltrates to what is deep, uncommon, to the astonishing and the divine.[74]

- As a philosopher, Nietzsche saw secularism as an achievement of philosophical conscience, and as the self-reflection of an internal morality. For Nietzsche, the vanity of religious truth becomes nothing more than a proclamation when it achieves awareness of itself as mere fantasy, and as a sick will to power. As a sociologist, Weber envisioned disenchantment as a complex product arising at the crossroads between social-historical and intellectual conscience. For Weber, secularity was not only the outcome of a long and laborious trajectory undergone by worldviews, but also had a socio-political history of its own. He saw this history as traceable in the various worldviews of both east and west, as well as in the world's value spheres (science, music, religion, philosophy) and its socio-historical structures (bureaucracy, politics, economy, religious institutions, etc.).

- Although the modern world, as Weber conceived it, was increasingly disenchanted, religiosity retained a certain legitimacy in what he termed 'the ethical irrationality of the world'. In his works *Science as a Vocation* and *Politics as Vocation*, Weber revealed the 'irrationality' of the human condition, arguing that as rationalisation increases, so too does the hold of the irrational. A threefold line of tensions defeated religion for Weber: the first is cognitive, whereby the power of science acts as the main expression of rationality; the second is social, whereby widening social fragmentation shows religion as incapable of controlling social conflict or the polarisation of views and interests; the third is in the esoteric and aesthetic spheres, where the irrational assumes a central position, thereby shattering the monopoly of religion. In this context, religion is not completely eroded but becomes merely a player among other forces of the 'irrational'. Nietzsche believed that, tremendous though it was, the event of God's death had not yet reached the ears of humanity. That is why he saw himself as the herald and precursor of 'philosophers of the future'. He was not saying that there was no God, but, rather, that God had been killed:

> God is dead. God remains dead. And we have killed him. How shall we comfort ourselves, the murderers of all murderers? What was holiest and mightiest of all that the world has yet owned has bled to death under our knives: who will wipe this blood off us? What water is there for us to clean ourselves? What festivals of atonement, what sacred games shall we have to invent? Is not the greatness of this deed too great for us? Must we ourselves not become gods simply to appear worthy of it?[75]

Nietzsche's proclamation was less about the existence of God, and more about the diminished significance of human beings and the degeneration of morality and the value of life. While for Weber, the Christian God (as depicted in ascetic Protestantism in particular) that had instigated the emergence of the modern world could still reign over an isolated corner in the 'iron cage of modernity', to Nietzsche, the death of God is the most pivotal idea in the history of human conscience; it is the most terrible, wretched and poignant of all events. In *The Anti-Christ* he says, 'The Christian conception of God – God as the God of the sick, God as spider, God as spirit – is one of the most corrupt conceptions of God arrived at on earth: perhaps it even represents the low-water mark in the descending development of the God type.'[76] This idea of God in Nietzsche's view was superfluous, impoverishing the human condition. God was thus not dismissed as theologically inexistent – the question of God's existence or non-existence being irrelevant to Nietzsche – but rather because of the mode of life that religion generated, and which he referred to as 'a sick will to life'.

Nietzsche's pronouncement that 'God is dead' was uttered using the language of religion. The form he used derived from the Gospel.[77] The disappearance of God and all gods was alluded to as early as *The Gay Science*. In his first work entitled *The Birth of Tragedy* (1870), Nietzsche noted, 'I believe in the ancient German saying: all Gods must die.'[78] Later, in a central passage of *The Gay Science*, Nietzsche, in prophetic mode, announced the birth of his 'madman', the symbol of the 'future, anticipated humanity'.

> Have you not heard the story of the madman who lit up a lantern in the radiant hours of morning, ran into the market and cried out: 'I seek God, I seek God.' Since many of the people who did not believe in God were gathered there, he provoked a great deal of laughter. 'Is he lost?' asked one. 'Has he lost his way like a child?' asked another. 'Is he hiding? Is he afraid of us? Has he departed on a long voyage? Or has he emigrated?' Thus they howled and laughed. The madman leapt into their midst, piercing them with his stare. 'Where has God gone?' he cried out; 'I will tell you. We have killed him. We are all his murderers. But how could we have done this? How did we manage to drink away the ocean? Who gave us the sponge with which we wiped away the horizon? To where is it moving now? To where are we going? Running away from all suns? Are we not continually plunging down?'[79]

In another chapter, Nietzsche declared:

> The greatest event that God is dead…that the belief in the Christian God has become unbelievable, is already beginning to cast its first shadow over Europe.[80]

Of course, Nietzsche's declaration of the death of God related primarily to the God of Christianity, but he reached further to use God as a symbol for all the ideas and ideals of traditional metaphysics.[81] He maintained that metaphysics, whether Platonic, Kantian or Christian, is quintessentially a hidden theology that imposes a dualism of 'real' and 'apparent' on the world, thereby dividing it into two estranged entities. In his preface to *Beyond Good and Evil*, Nietzsche noted that Christianity is nothing more than Platonism expressed in lay metaphors and allegories, or, as he put it, 'a Platonism for the people'. He proclaimed that to divide the world into 'real' and 'visible' is 'only a suggestion of decadence – a symptom of declining life'.[82]

Nietzsche conceived of the dualism of truth/falsity, not in an epistemological relationship (as in Hegelian dialectics where truth annihilates all forms of error) but as a mode of existence in which truth is inseparable from error:

> Today, on the contrary, we see ourselves, as it were, entangled in error, necessitated to error, to precisely the extent that our prejudice in favour of reason compels us to posit unity, identity, duration, substance, cause, materiality, being; however sure we may be, on the basis of a strict reckoning, that error is to be found here.[83]

He pointed out that the difference between error and truth is one of degree, not genre, and argued that to abandon one necessarily implies relinquishing the other. As he put it, 'Truth is the kind of error without which a defined species of living being cannot live.'[84]

The overcoming of metaphysics is no easy undertaking. It is a fierce battle against the human existential condition. Nietzsche tried to show that, with the tremendous event of the death of the Christian God, no stable foundation for morality or thought remained. For him, disenchantment not only signalled a world devoid of transcendental moorings, an arid spiritless universe, but also one bereft of objective meaning and significance, an amorphous rubble of contingency.[85]

Just as the Copernican revolt shook human narcissism, nihilism deconstructs all centres of gravity and characterises humanity's condition as we become fully aware that we lack any foundation.[86] As Heidegger later illustrated, nihilism for Nietzsche was a historical process 'whereby the dominance of the "transcendent" becomes null and void, so that all being loses its worth and meaning. Nihilism is the history of being itself, through which the death of the Christian God comes slowly but inexorably to light.'[87]

The dissolution of the idea of God pulverised the whole system of metaphysics, undermining its theological and ontological foundations, and transforming the world into a mere power game. As Nietzsche wrote in *Twilight of the Idols*, 'Christianity is a system, a consistently thought out and complete view of things. If one breaks out of it a fundamental idea, the belief in God, one thereby breaks the whole thing to pieces…It stands or falls with the belief in God'.[88]

Nietzsche believed that to overcome nihilism we must first be able to recognise it.[89] In *The Gay Science* and *Thus Spoke Zarathustra*, he conceived of the death of God as a double-faceted event. On the one hand, as a tragedy that betrays the nothingness of existence, and on the other, as a necessary condition for gaiety and childlike innocence. Relinquishing God inaugurates the reign of the void, forcing people to look to themselves for orientation and guidance.[90] Aware of the full extent of the calamity, Nietzsche tried to replace passive nihilism with a flourishing new life in which gaiety and laughter provide an alternative to Socratic dialectics. He laid down a new perspective on values founded on the exaltation of the earth, observing that, with the death of God, Platonic dualism and alienation from the earth was obliterated.[91] The figure of Zarathustra was thus reclaimed to teach the 'human animal' that with God dead the superhuman (*Übermensch*) will acquire mastery of the earth.[92]

For Nietzsche, nihilism was not a symptom of the decay or 'regression' of western culture so much as the hallmark of the self-consciousness inherent in western values – the natural outcome of the intrinsic movement of western history. That this was to be exultantly received in dances and laughter is an assertion of the need to overcome pessimistic nihilism in favour of an affirmative nihilism. However, with the later publication of *Human, All Too Human* Nietzsche argued that to live is not to overcome suffering but to affirm life as it is.[93]

For Heidegger, Nietzsche's atheism represented the crowning of modern metaphysics. Atheism is an advanced phase in the internal movement aimed at disclosing 'the origin' of values. Indeed, the insignificance of origins heightens when the provenance is discerned. Atheism may be summed up as the offspring of the truth of the void – 'the awe-inspiring catastrophe of two thousand years of training in truthfulness that finally forbids itself the lie of belief in God'.[94] Heidegger showed that what Nietzsche declared so vehemently was already inherent in Descartes' discourse at the dawn of the modern age. The Nietzschean bid to dissolve being into the will to power echoed the Cartesian aspiration to make the *cogito* into the master of the world.

The limits of secularism

This brief foray into Nietzsche's philosophy makes it obvious that Weber's terminological and conceptual baggage was the product of a long history of cultural hermeneutics. Weberian sociology can be described as a secular form of Christianity,[95] or as eschatology without a God. Weber preserved the Protestant worldview but used a vocabulary that had been purged of religious connotations and was articulated within a secular context. Weber's ethical thesis was a sociological articulation of his own Protestant background, combined with secular liberalism. His sociology was governed by a double paradigm: a secularised Christian theology and a Christianised secular liberal tradition that stretched back to the eighteenth century. The Weberian approach to secularity thus requires an 'archaeological effort' to reveal the logic that governs it and the parameters of its validity. An etymological analysis offers a useful starting point for this excavation.[96]

The word 'secular' derives from *saeculum*, which is one of the two Latin words denoting 'world' (the other is *mundus*). *Saeculum* is also frequently used to translate the Greek word *aeon*, meaning age or epoch. Medieval Christianity accomplished a synthesis of the Greek definition of secularity, with its spatial connotations, and the Hebrew conception, which perceived the concept temporally. The synthesis resolved the tension between the Greek and Hebrew terms by dividing the world spatially into a higher, religious realm and a lower, timebased, historical world that was designated as secular.[97]

In the late thirteenth century, the adjective 'secular' was employed in English usage to distinguish the 'worldly' clergy living and working in the wider medieval world from the 'religious' clergy who lived in monastic seclusion.[98] From the time of St Cyprian, Christian writers used the term *saeculum* to characterise the world outside the Church and the spirit of that world.[99] Later, the meaning of the term extended to express worldly institutions concerned with civil, lay and temporal matters, as distinct from purely religious and spiritual activities or organisations. That is, the internal dualism inherent in Christianity related to distinguishing ecclesiastical from lay activities was expressed as an internal/external distinction between the 'world of the Church', and the 'temporal world'. From about the sixteenth century, the word 'secular' tended to lose the negative connotations associated with profanity that it had long carried, and became associated instead with the notion of change. Since then, the verb 'to secularise' has meant to make someone or something secular, or to convert something from ecclesiastical to civil use or possession.[100]

In French, the term frequently used to denote worldly is *laïcité*. According to Jean Bauberot, the word first appeared in the French *Dictionnaire de la pédagogie,* which was published between 1882 and 1887 under the direction of Ferdinand Buisson. The latter considered the term to be a necessary neologism, and used it to designate the reform of primary education staged by 'la république des républicains'. Buisson described 'la laïcité' as having two meanings. On the one hand, it referred to the distinction between different forms of public activity, and on the other, to the autonomy of such activities from the religious sphere. In current usage, only the second definition has been preserved. The term gained currency as French schools were increasingly secularised from around 1880, and reappeared strongly in 1905 when a law was passed to decree the separation of the Church and the state in France.[101]

The term secularity and its offshoots, as well as the French term *laïcité*, have convoluted histories, and to understand these concepts it is useful to acknowledge their historical complexity and the power games reflected in their usage and definitions. Theories of secularisation use the terms 'secular', 'secularity' and 'secularisation' both ambiguously and dogmatically. The historians of the eighteenth century began to speak of secularisation to designate the transfer of ecclesiastical and spiritual authority, as well as property rights, to the state. The word was applied to describe the process by which ideas and modes of behaviour 'detach themselves from the religious context of their original establishment, and are derived from universal reason'.[102]

However, if the concept of secularity is not exclusively the product of an internal, linear process within Christian doctrine, the concept is certainly not independent of this process either. Indeed, the term has its own hermeneutical and socio-historical context. To quote German philosopher Hans Blumenberg, secularity – like any concept – has a 'metaphorical background', meaning 'a process of reference to a model that is operative in the genesis of a concept, but is no longer present in the concept itself, or may even have to be sacrificed in the need for a definition'.[103] Thus, for Karl Löwith, western modern and political thought is a mere subversion of Christian theology, and the philosophy of history and its ideology of progress is little more than a 'secularised eschatology'. Though Blumenberg shares Löwith's analysis in many ways, he sees the trajectory of secularisation as a far more intricate phenomenon. For Blumenberg, the continuity between the modern age and the Christian tradition is one of questions rather than answers, since secularisation for him is a secularisation by eschatology, not merely the secularisation of eschatology, as Löwith proclaimed.[104]

The modern age is unthinkable without Christianity. Indeed, its wide residual concepts and norms, as well as its dualisms, are inconceivable without their Christian roots. This is not to say that the term 'secularity' is a mere extension of the medieval Christian definition, so much as to insist on a line of continuity between the present and the past. However, secularity can be seen as an overlapping movement of transformation and retrogression in the Heideggerian sense. The concept has been subject to metamorphosis, acquiring new functions while retaining 'a substance that endures throughout the process'.[105] To uncover the range of meanings contained in the term 'secular' is to understand continuity in discontinuity, to detect the line of unity that lies hidden beneath a diversity of forms and functions.

The seeds of secularisation in European consciousness arguably date back to the beginning of Christianity's institutionalisation. The restriction of religious activity and symbols within a sacerdotal institution casts the rest of society into the sphere of the profane or *saeculum*. Much later, Lutheran doctrine, with its commitment to two separate kingdoms – one ruled by God and the other by human beings – bestowed a theological legitimacy on the secularisation of politics.[106] In modern times, as the power of the Church has decreased, and the Christian worldview has been vanquished, the Churches have found themselves compelled to defend their authority in the wake of the Enlightenment's radically anti-clerical claims, at first militantly, and then in a spirit of silent defiance. However, when the balance of power shifted from the Church to the secular state, religious rejections of secularism were gradually watered down, making way for another adaptation. In other words, secularisation is not the by-product of an internal 'religious consciousness' so much as a fusion of religious horizons with historical powers.

Secularity in its later configurations signals an awareness of the dualism inherent in Christianity, and extends this dualism to its limits. The sacred gave birth to the secular, and then saw the secular gain awareness of itself as an autonomous sphere in modern western history. This consciousness is not reflective, in the Hegelian manner, so much as a historical event. That is, the concept of secularity and its derivatives can be read – using a word of Blumenberg's again – through a model of 'reoccupation' rather than one of stable continuity or radical rupture.

However, no hermeneutical 'reoccupation' occurs in a vacuum; every such recapturing is conditioned by socio-historical forces, and thrives on an intellectual tradition. Secularism is, after all, the outcome of the socio-political movement generally referred to as 'the emancipation of the bourgeoisie'. This movement, which was driven by the 'utopia' of progress, simultaneously harks back to tradition and the past. As Heidegger succinctly noted, the past is not behind us (as Hegel's linear vision of history stipulated), but is that which comes towards us.

Indeed, any understanding is an act of history and within history. Hans-Georg Gadamer has elaborated on this view, noting that understanding is not reconstruction but mediation, in the sense that every 'act' of understanding is a moment in the life of tradition itself, since our language bears the stamp of the past and is the life of the past in the present. In his words, 'It is not really we ourselves who understand: it is always a past that allows us to say "I have understood".'[107]

What any reader of western political history is sure to find striking is the extent to which religious activities occur within the secular world. Hannah Arendt revealed the dilemma of modern revolutions in their proclivity to found a political authority beyond human power. In undertaking to legitimise the validity of laws made by society, and to place those laws above society at the same time, the French and American revolutions invoked a transcendent source of authority. As Arendt asserted:

> Hence, in theory as in practice, we can hardly avoid the paradoxical fact that it was precisely the revolutions, their crisis and their emergency, which drove the very 'enlightened' men of the eighteenth century to plead for some religious sanction at the very moment when they were about to emancipate the secular realm fully from the influence of the churches, and to separate politics and religion once and for all.[108]

In modern representations, secularity is essentially the result of the historical ascendance of non-clerical and anti-religious inclinations. This historical movement did not operate within a hermeneutic vacuum but reverted (in a brutal attack on, or compromise with, religious forces) to the Christian tradition via the model of reoccupation, either explicitly or in a negatively implicit manner. True, nowadays, when Christian theologians insist on the compatibility of Christian doctrine with secularity, or look upon secularity as the legitimate heir of Christianity, they speak the language of modern times. Nonetheless, whether deliberately or unconsciously, they generally recycle Christian theology in favour of the 'historical fact' of secularisation.

Although many Christian theologians now find themselves compelled to adapt to secularisation by legitimising and incorporating it into their own doctrines, sociologists insist that secularity is getting the upper hand over religiosity. What is beyond question is that the modern world has succeeded in evading religion, or at least confining it to the private sphere.

2

Islam and the limits of secularity

Say: Truly, my prayer, my worship, my life, and my death are
for Allah, the Cherisher of the Worlds

– Qur'an, 6: 162

Nowhere have secularist predictions of religion's demise met with as many difficulties as they have in the lands of Islam. It is intriguing that while secularists continue to insist that the modern world will gradually abandon religion, the Muslim world seems to be moving in the opposite direction. Indeed, the present wave of de-secularisation among modern sectors of Islamic societies appears to be stronger than the process of secularisation that began to infiltrate the region during the Tanzimat era (instituted in Istanbul from 1839 to 1876, and in other Muslim provinces at the beginning of the nineteenth century).

In the mid twentieth century, Hamilton Gibb, a leading British Orientalist, was so struck by the impact of westernisation and modernisation on Egypt and other regions of the Muslim world that he expressed concern that Islamic institutions and symbols might disappear entirely. This, he feared, would create a vacuum in Muslim souls, as well as in social, political and economic structures, that would inevitably be filled by modernisation.[1] Yet, as I write this book nearly a hundred years later, many of Gibb's successors are more preoccupied with the decline of secularisation in the Muslim world. Indeed, Islam's resistance to westernisation and secularisation has driven many of the west's sociologists, political thinkers and journalists to write off Islam and the Muslim world as the epitome of 'cultural failure'.

The question of secularity lies at the heart of countless discussions and questions related to Islam. Many western intellectuals, diplomats and politicians have predicted the 'conquest' of the Muslim world by the apparently irreversible force of secularisation. The westernised Muslim elite, who have dominated the politics of the Middle East since the beginning of the twentieth century, and have actively engaged in a project of 'modernisation', seem to prove the soundness of such predictions. The triumph of Kemalism in Turkey (the project of radical secularisation and modernisation that Mustafa Kemal Atatürk embarked on after the ruin of the Ottoman caliphate) as well as the emergence of the Pahlavi royal family in Iran from 1925 to 1979, with its zeal for western-style modernisation, seemed to herald another triumph for secularisation. The emergence of pan-Arabism at the centre of the Mashriq – with Nasserism in Egypt and Ba'thism in Iraq and Syria – seemed to confirm this trend. Thus, while these pan-Arab regimes showed some hostility towards western powers for supporting Israel's occupation of Palestine, and inclined somewhat towards the Soviet's economic model, most were keen admirers of Bismarck's model of nationalism, and his paradigm of using state power to institute modernisation.

However, the eruption of the Iranian revolution in 1979 cast serious doubts on the validity of secularisation in the Arab world. Since then, most of the discussion about the issue has reflected the enormous difficulties confronting anyone advocating secularism in the Islamic world. The emergence of political Islam as a ruling ideology (as in Iran), and in powerful movements opposing the more 'secular regimes' (in Turkey and Egypt, for example), has drawn the attention of many sociologists, political scientists and other intellectuals to the Middle East, and its future prospects. Much of the literature produced by these 'experts' and by Arab secularists preaches the ineluctability of secularisation. The 'hidden spirit' of history, it is claimed, has a ceaseless drive towards secularisation. In making such assertions, thinkers such as Aziz al-Azma, Abdullah Laroui, and Bassam Tibi, to name just a few, find support in the increasing secularisation of state institutions and the judiciary, but they turn a blind eye to what takes place at the heart of society.[2]

Consumed with a desire to establish the theoretical validity of secularism, they utterly ignore the facts on the ground. Thus, for years, Turkey, Tunisia, Egypt and Algeria were considered mature secular states, regardless of all that was brewing beneath their façades.

For many analysts, the secularisation process that they see as ongoing in the Islamic world involves little more than revisiting the secularisation of the past. The separation between religion and politics that prevails in some contexts is seen as mirroring the chasm that existed between the *'ulama* and the caliphs or sultans of bygone days. John Ruedy, for example, has argued that a tacit process of secularisation haunts Islamic history. He maintains this regardless of the fact that, in the course of its own history, Islam (unlike Christianity) has been unable to provide any theological justification for the distinction between the religious and the secular, or to produce anything like the Augustinian dualism of the 'city of God' and 'city of man'. According to Ruedy:

> It should be realised that even though the terms are dissimilar and the discourse is not as explicit, the struggle to define the proper domains of the temporal and spiritual exists in Islam. That struggle began in the reign of the early Umayyad Caliphs during the seventh century and has continued virtually without interruption in the twentieth century.[3]

This theory of the secularisation of the Muslim world is incomprehensible in isolation from the reports of bureaucrats and state ideologues, or indeed from the huge arsenal of writings by erstwhile Orientalists and other contemporary experts on the Middle East. All these voices echo the same unshakeable belief in the triumph of modernity. They partake of a vision of history as a continuous process of transformation 'through which the new would supersede the old, the modern the traditional, the secular the religious'.[4]

An alternative theory casts Islam as a special case amongst world religions. This is the position taken by French writer Maurice Barbier, who argued that while political modernity has flourished in the Occident since the fifteenth century, it has been utterly lacking in the Muslim world. This Barbier explained by referring to Islamic history, which, he insisted, reveals that the value of individuals is not recognised and that no divide exists between the state and society. Barbier does not hesitate to trace the causes of the crises that have beset Muslim society to the Islamic worldview and theology, which apparently crush the individual in favour of the *ummah*. In his own words,

> On pourrait chercher la cause de cette situation dans L'Islam lui-même. En effet, cette religion insiste fortement sur la dimension communautaire: pour sa profession de foi, le croyant entre dans une communauté (*ummah*) qui le dépasse et détermine toute sa vie. [One can seek the cause of this situation within Islam itself. Indeed this religion strongly insists on a communal dimension: in professing their faith, believers enter into a community that supersedes and determines their lives].[5]

Barbier maintained that political modernity is, therefore, unattainable in the Muslim world. For him, the only glimmer of light that this dim part of the globe can aspire to has to take the form of a radical *laïcité*, along the lines of the Turkish or Tunisian models. For Barbier, writing in 2000, even though the process of *laïcisation* had not been fully achieved in Turkey or Tunisia (since religious belief is still a motivating factor among the political opposition), these remain the most politically modernised of all Muslim states.[6]

Like Barbier, much of the academic establishment has a deep-rooted tendency to explain the Islamic world with reference to culture, and in isolation from historical experience. The roots of the perceived backwardness of the Islamic world are seen to lie in a religion that preaches predestination, stifles individual freedom and aborts all possibility of rationalism. Islam is, in short, seen as the direct opposite, the photographic negative, of the west's idealised Christian self-image,[7] which supposedly represents the epitome of individual freedom, social dynamism and political pluralism. The principal vulnerability of these readings and the ground they occupy is their unwavering commitment to the virtues of secularism.

In fact, to obtain any real understanding of Islam, Weber's narrow model of secularity has to be jettisoned. Islam's inner dynamics have to be understood in relation to its own terms and concepts, rather than to a set of externally prefabricated categories. In my view, the main issue is not whether Islam is incompatible with secularism, but how secularisation can be questioned and deconstructed, and whether resistance to secularisation unveils another perspective on both secularity and Islam. So far, most theories of secularism emanate from a Christian or a secularised Judeo-Christian perspective. We do not seem to know yet how cultures whose religious traditions differ from the Judeo-Christian ones respond to this conversation, or what questions and answers they may propose.

It is no secret that Weber's theory of secularity, as institutionalised by western academic and sociological discourse, is beset by immense theoretical and empirical aporias when it comes to Islam. These difficulties are generated not only by Islam's tendency to sacralise all that is worldly, but by the fact that the nature of Islam shatters the dualist model; Islam bestows a spiritual meaning on all that is worldly. The transcendental in Islam finds expression in the mundane, for the spiritual is seen as but an accumulation of what we, using cognitive knowledge, see as material, and the worldly is seen as just another dimension of the otherworldly. In fact, if we consider Islam from the angle of the worldly, it appears to be a 'secular religion'. However, as explained in my introductory chapter, I use the term 'secular' here with great reservation; it would be better not to use the term in relation to Islam at all. Islam challenges secularity, not because of its supposedly inexorably rigid nature, but primarily by virtue of its flexibility. In fact, the absence of a cleavage between the 'religious' and the 'secular' is evident not only in terms of Islam's sacralisation of the whole of existence, but also in the fact that Islam has no clerical institution that represents religious truth. This makes the religion as current as the soil of this earth.

Weber's theory of secularisation can be summed up in the claim that the more religion is rationalised, the more tension inheres in its relationship with the world. For Weber, what applies to religion can also be said of the whole structure of knowledge, so that the more rationalised worldviews become, the more they gain a kind of autonomy, and when this happens, rationalism begins operating according to its own frame of reference and stands aloof from religious principles.[8] The limits of Weber's paradigm are crystal clear when it is applied to Islam. In its place, I shall venture to construct a non-Weberian model that I hope expresses Islam's worldview and historical experience more accurately. The model I propose is a complete reversal of Weber's model, and I would argue that in an Islamic context, increased rationalism consolidates the bond between Islamic religious norms and ordinary Muslims' experience of the order of life.

As a rule, I suggest that religion can affect the world only if it becomes 'worldly', and incorporates the so-called 'secular', thus showing an interest in the politics of the world in its broadest sense. This certainly applies to Islam, where 'natural religion', which is argued to be consistent with human nature, is no more than another way of understanding revelation. The great reformist and jurist Shaykh Muhammad al-Tahir Bin Ashur conceived of *fitra* (human disposition at its most pure and natural) and its protection as the main objective of the *shari'ah*. Islamic law, he maintained, emanated from religious texts, but also from the material context and social environment. In Islam, *shari'ah* and *fitra* overlap, and contradictions between them are inconceivable.[9]

Bosnian politician and writer Ali Izetbegovic analysed the differences in the terminology used in the Gospels and in the Qur'an. He showed that the Gospels are dominated by words such as blessed, holy, angel, eternal life, heaven, sin, love, repentance, forgiveness, mystery, body (as the bearer of sin), soul, salvation and so on. Qur'anic terms tend to be more 'related to the practicalities of this world', and terms that recur frequently include reason, health, cleanliness, strength, buying, contract, pledge, writing, weapons, battle position, force, struggle, trade, fruit, decisiveness, caution, punishment, justice, profit, medicine, interest and so on.[10] Based on this analysis, Izetbegovic argues that the Qur'an affirms natural life and discourages all forms of asceticism; it is 'for richness and against poverty, for...power over nature not only on this planet but if possible also in the universe'.[11] While not necessarily agreeing with the views of the Romanian anthropologist Mircea Eliade on human history as a drive towards secularisation, I must concede that his perspective on Islam seems to have some validity. For him, the Prophet Muhammad stands on the threshold between the old religious age and the new secular one. Eliade maintains that the Prophet forms a bridge between these two periods of human spiritual development.[12] Muslim philosopher Muhammad Iqbal shares this view of the Prophet, but without bowing to secular determinism. Iqbal argues that, culturally speaking, Islam is a worldly religion with a 'secular' attitude, yet because it is based on the idea of a transcendent God and revealed text, it is incompatible with the notion of immanence.[13] Immanence, as used in this text, refers to the belief that the Divine presence is manifested in the material world. Transcendence is the belief that God (or the Divine) is above and beyond the material world.

Religion, secularity, and politics: defining some terms

Before proceeding, I am compelled to offer some further definitions lest we stumble into misunderstanding. Co-signs do not necessarily co-refer, and even the term religion has long been fraught with controversy. The root cause of this is, to my mind, linguistic in nature. Within Islamic and western thought, the same terms have different meanings. In this section, I try to clarify some of the grey areas.

Religion

The first point to be aware of is that terms vary in accordance with their cultural contexts. That is, Islamic concepts and semantics have a peculiarity that is tightly linked to the Islamic context as a whole. Thus, while we can translate *din* as religion, and *iman* as faith, the translations do not precisely match the concepts.

The term *din* has no synonym in the European languages. The Arabic word *din* refers to the lexical verb *dana dayn* (debt), denoting the intimate relationship whereby humans are indebted to divine creation and care. *Din* also refers to the primal relationship forged since the creation through *al-mithaq al-ghaliz* (the great pact) between God and the Adamic race.

The word *islam* is a noun derived from the verb *aslama*, which means to give oneself in total commitment, to submit voluntarily, and with true submission rather than as a result of oppression or weakness. Every act of obedience through which individuals submit to God and abide by God's order is *islam*. This is why the word Islam is also used to designate all the monotheistic religions emanating from the Abrahamic tradition, including Judaism and Christianity. In reference to the free will bestowed by God, individuals may choose to follow the path of *iman* (belief) or *kufr* (denial).

Most Muslim champions of the principle of free will and the notion of conscience refer to the contractual relation between God and humanity as the necessary condition for liberty. According to contemporary philosopher Mohammed 'Aziz Lahbabi, it is through the *shahadah* (the declaration of faith bearing witness to the unity of God and the prophethood of Muhammad) that Muslims have personal value and express themselves as human.[14] The *shahadah* is the Islamic equivalent of *Cogito ergo sum* (I think therefore I am), as it signals an awareness of both subjectivity and free will (in the freedom to choose a religion). For Muslims, freely chosen submission to God requires the practice of religious commandments and ethics, and loyalty to the Muslim *ummah*.[15]

The concept of *din* is closely associated with that of *ibadah* or worship, which the Qur'an deems the primary object of creation: 'Verily I have created jinn and human beings only that they may worship me.'[16] In Islam, worship is not confined to prayer or spiritual purification; instead, all human activities are seen as forms of religious expression and worship. Islam, as Muslims perceive it, is not merely a system of belief and worship because religion is not a part of life that can be said to be distinct from any other. This worldview is evident in the layout of traditional Islamic cities, where the placement of the mosques enables them to play a central role in all aspects of city life. Indeed, the location of mosques at the heart of a city is much more than a reflection of an architectural centralism; the mosques open onto the schoolyards and marketplaces.[17] This reinforces the tight associations between society's principal components, and clarifies the connections and interrelationships between the realms of ethics, economy and knowledge. To a Muslim, it is absurd to confine religious activity or truth to particular compartments of life. It is inconceivable that anyone can be religious within the boundaries of the mosque and unreligious in the marketplace. Thus, the marketplace is seen as an extension of the mosque, and the mosque as a link to the marketplace.

In my view, Islam is not a religion in the strict sense of the term. The meanings inherent in the term religion in the European languages seem to denote a line of separation between what pertains to religion and what abides outside this sphere. When Christianity turned into Christendom, the sphere of the religious came to be seen as synonymous with the Church, and the priests and monks soon claimed to be the sole legitimate repository of religious knowledge and power. The world outside the Church was thereby characterised as non-religious or secular.

Islam rejects the dualism inherent in the term *religio*, along with its implicit commitment to an official religious institution. Instead, every aspect of human life is considered 'religious', and what Christians might designate as 'secular' is seen as merely a different expression of the religious. One may conclude that Islam is a very secular religion but its secularity bypasses both the concept of secularity and the definition of religion. As noted in the introduction, for me, Islam is a source of cultural norms and a form of symbolic capital – in the Bourdieuian sense – evenly distributed throughout society, that act as the basis for the legitimacy of the rule of the state, and various other political and social forces.

Prominent in Qur'anic discourse is the absence of a dualism separating the religious and the profane, or the temporal and the spiritual. Instead, a noteworthy feature of the Qur'an is the fact that the word *dunya* (this world) is repeatedly mentioned simultaneously with the word *akhirah* (the other world). This has left a marked imprint upon Islamic semantics, so that, in general, the two terms are closely associated.

Secularity

Examination of the term 'secularity' within the syntactical and linguistic definitions of the languages of Islam – including Arabic – provides a more accurate picture of the problem of secularity. It is, indeed, interesting that no trace of the term is to be found in Arabic dictionaries before the end of the nineteenth century.[18] Modern Arabic dictionaries, too, lack an accurate definition of the term, or reveal tensions between different definitions. The dominant definitions are: science; a separation between state and religion; the world; and non-religious. The Turkish term for secularity is the neologism *ladini*, which literally means non-religious. As used by the famous sociologist and theoretician Ziya Gökalp, this term was often taken to mean irreligious, or anti-religious.[19] Such interpretations reveal the hostility with which the notion was understood in the Islamic world. Later on, the term was abandoned in favour of *la'ik*, a loan-word from the French (*laïcité*).[20] The great reformist Jamal ad-Din al-Afghani translated secularism using the Qur'anic word *dahriyyah*, meaning belief in the material world as an end in itself; that is, belief in a fully existing present with no reference to the transcendental.[21]

In Arabic, Christian Arabs felt the urge to express the notion of secularity well before their fellow Muslims. The word they invented was *'almani*, from *'alam* (world), referring to the worldly as opposed to the otherworldly. In modern times, the word has been devocalised, and is now pronounced *'ilmani*. It is taken to mean scientific, from the word *'ilm* (knowledge or science),[22] but this is an entirely mistaken analysis of the word's etymology. Before the twentieth century, the word most frequently used in Arabic was *ladini* (non-religious), and the definition most prevalent in contemporary Arabic dictionaries is *al-'almaniyyah*, with reference to the world and worldly things.

What is also interesting is the ambiguity with which the terms secularity and *laïcité* are fraught, and the lack of a clear distinction between the two, although secularity is predominantly defined as a separation between state and religion. This, I assume, is because the separation between religion and state is the most prominent feature of secularisation, and because the Arab world's earliest acquaintance with western culture was through French terminology – *laïcité*. It is noteworthy that many contemporary intellectuals and writers in the Arab Maghreb who are familiar with French make no distinction between the two words, and it is almost always the French model of *laïcité* that is used when the notion of secularity is invoked in the western parts of the Arab world.

The politics of language

Setting aside the linguistic features of specific terms, the confusion over the concept of secularity reveals the ongoing controversy surrounding this issue among the Arab elite. Language itself – as Wittgenstein aptly argued – is overwhelmed by power struggles and strategies.[23] For example, those who define *'ilmaniyyah* as science and reason often see it as bringing enlightenment and a source of guidance to Arabs and Muslims. Meanwhile, those who associate *'ilmaniyyah* with the non-religious are often committed to an unmitigated rejection of secularisation. If we go beyond the elite to consider the broader society, the concept tends to be met with ignorance, rejection, or both.

In my opinion, two factors account for the negative connotations that Arab Muslims attach to the notion of *'ilmaniyyah*. The first is to do with inadequate translations of the notion, which associate it with being anti-religious. The second is historical, stemming from the specific conditions within which secularism emerged and continues to operate. Essentially western imperialism imposed secularised bureaucratic and legislative institutions on Muslim societies that it came to dominate, thereby undermining the role that *shari'ah* had played for centuries. Later, secularity became the face of despotic, post-colonial rule.

Moroccan thinker Mohammed 'Abed al-Jabri has suggested banishing the term *'ilmaniyyah* from Arab–Islamic discourse. Proposing that the terms rationality and democracy be used instead, he argued that these are more neutral and expressive of the needs of Arab-Islamic societies.[24] However, the inscrutability of these terms, and the wide difference between them, makes it difficult to agree to this suggestion. Nevertheless, al-Jabri laid bare the fact that secularity is highly unpopular in the Arab world, and that this presents Arab political discourse – including that of the secular elites – with the challenge of overcoming the alienation and the hostility with which the concept is often received.[25]

Islam as a worldly religion

Although there is no such thing as a standard or static form of Islam, a system of values and symbols that is impervious to certain aspects of secularisation is deeply ingrained in Islam. This value system rests on three pillars: the first defines the relationship between the spiritual and the mundane, that is, between worldly and otherworldly values; the second is the absence of a clerical institution; and the third defines the relationship between politics and religious values, that is, between power and religious meaning.

Islam has always presented itself as having incorporated and surpassed the earlier monotheistic religions, particularly Judaism and Christianity. For Muslims, Christianity is seen as having mended the worldly orientation that infected Judaism. The Christian emphasis on spiritual purification and transcendental salvation is perceived as lessening the worldliness that characterises Judaism, and as excising the 'nationalisation of religion' that the Jewish myth of being the 'chosen people' promoted.[26] Islam aims to re-establish the balance between the worldliness of Judaism and the untainted spirituality of Christianity, offering a synthesis that simultaneously surpasses the two earlier religions.

For Muslim historian and historiographer Ibn Khaldun (1332–1406), politics was an integral part of Islam, the object of which is the management of worldly affairs. According to Ibn Khaldun, this stands in clear contrast to the beliefs of earlier monotheistic religions that intervene in the world of politics by default rather than for any implicitly theological reasons.[27]

From a Muslim perspective, the 'worldly' does not contradict the 'religious'; indeed, it is considered to be a substantial component of religious truth. Thus Islam does not see life as an impediment that human beings must avoid for religious values to achieve significance. The equation may be formulated thus: religious truth is valid only once it has been transformed into a historical concrete value; and all that is worldly, even in its extreme worldliness, is in essence religious and spiritual. Thus, all human activities, even the satisfying of our sexual needs (within marriage), are understood to be acts of worship. It is possible that this positive view of the body, and all that is material, is what associated 'Muhammadism' in western consciousness with savage sexual instincts – even in its Prophet, who led a normal human life.[28]

However, if we compare Islam to the medieval Christianity that was being practised when Islam emerged, it is evident that the mechanism governing medieval Christianity and the stance it took vis-à-vis life was one of reduction and impoverishment – or to use Nietzschean terminology, a *décomposition de la vie* – whereby religious meaning acquired its value through the degradation of life. In Nietzsche's words, 'All the concepts of the church are recognised for what they are: the most malicious false-coinage there is for the purpose of disvaluing nature and natural values.'[29]

Medieval Christianity saw the 'religious' as being opposed to the 'worldly', and vice versa, whereas the impulse driving Islam is the enrichment and fulfilment of life through imbuing it with the notion of the afterlife. Islam shatters Christian dualism in the sense that it overcomes the division of reality into 'material' and 'spiritual' spheres. As the Muslim philosopher Allama Muhammad Iqbal maintained, Islam faces this opposition with a view to overcoming it, and this process of synthesis puts an end to the opposition between the 'real' and the 'ideal'. In Iqbal's words:

> The life of the ideal consists not in total breach with the real,
> which would tend to shatter the organic wholeness of life into
> painful oppositions, but in the perpetual endeavour of the
> ideal to appropriate the real, with a view eventually to absorb
> it, to convert it into itself, and to illuminate its whole being.[30]

For Iqbal, the 'material' or the 'profane' is simply in the process of becoming the spiritual. Thus, he maintained that there is no chasm separating the 'religious' from the 'material', and everything is essentially spiritual. Reality, as Iqbal perceived it, is spiritual, and its life consists in a dynamic, temporal activity:

> The spirit, finding its opportunities in the natural, the material, the secular, is therefore sacred in the roots of its being…The merely material has no substance until we discover it rooted in the spiritual. There is no such thing as a profane world. All this immensity of matter constitutes a scope for the self-realisation of spirit. All is holy ground.[31]

What fuels Islam's denial of the separation of the secular and the religious is the absence of a clerical organisation. The openness of the Qur'an to interpretation repudiates the need for religious institutions and authorities. Furthermore, the consensus of the *ummah* forms the basis of legislation and religious regulation.

By contrast, the Weberian paradigm sees rationalism as being conditional on a rigid separation between the 'profane' and the 'sacred', and the institutionalisation of the latter. If this were truly the case, the Shia tradition would represent the apogee of Islam's internal rationalisation by establishing a hierarchical, religious body akin to that of the papacy. Reality, however, testifies to the ludicrousness of this claim, for in contemporary Iran the principal impediment to political reform is the presence of a formal religious institution that proclaims itself the guardian of the faith. The Iranian experience seems to allow for only two choices: 'Islamise' or 'secularise'. In other words, Iran has two possible options: to forsake Shiism, and be consistent with the general spirit of mainstream Sunni Islam, thereby accepting politics as an open field of *ijtihad,* that is impervious to monopolistic tendencies, or to dissolve the religious establishment and desacralise politics in favour of secularism.[32]

Religion and politics

For long periods of its history, the Christian Church has been active in politics, with all the complexities, calculations, and conflicts of interest that this involves. However, for the most part, this involvement did not occur in response to any intrinsic, religious requirement. It can be argued that Christianity's heavy involvement in politics was not ground-ed in theology because its vision of the world is firmly rooted in the Augustinian dualism of the 'city of God' and the 'city of man'.[33]

Islam's political history reflects the exact opposite. Indeed, the gap that separated the rulers from the religious authorities in the early stag-es of Islamic history was not founded on any theological justification. Even the early *fuqaha* who advocated this separation for pragmatic purposes remained faithful to a vision of religious politics. Abdullah Laroui was, I think, right to point out the error of seeking to read the political history of Muslim states through the political theories of the Muslim *fuqaha* because, even though the *fuqaha* came to accept the Muslim state as de facto reality, the Islamic state of Madinah and the Rightly Guided Caliphate was still their ideal.[34]

The connection between the 'temporal' and the 'transcendental' has always been strong in Islam. This is strongly reflected in the circum-stances surrounding the emergence of the faith. Its birth was associ-ated with the establishment of the state of Madinah, and the Prophet was both a religious leader and the ruler of a civil state. Conversely, early Christianity was established less via political or state authority and more via monastic orders that initially acceded to Roman authority. Indeed, from the beginning, Jesus announced that his kingdom was 'not of this world', and that transcendental salvation was the substance of his mission. Thus, during the first centuries of its existence, Christianity existed separately from, and was antagonistic to, the political commu-nity. While the conversion of Constantine (in the fourth century) sig-nalled the start of state protection and patronage for the Church, it was only when the Calvinist and Lutheran reformist movements offered a new interpretation of the idea of salvation that Christianity established a socially aware and interactive relationship with the world.[35]

From the inception of Islam, the Prophet insisted that his kingdom was of this world. His mission, and that of his followers, was to assert and affirm God's presence in the world. Islam is as intimately entan-gled with the state as it is in all personal and social activity for two main reasons. The first is that for Muslims, Islam has an authority and a legitimacy that far exceeds that of the state. Religious values are seen as transcendental and all-encompassing, while all states have only a historical and relative value. The second reason is that the authority of (and therefore allegiance to) the ideal of the *ummah* supersedes that of the state. The state is seen as an intermediary between religious values and norms (which cannot be incorporated in the person of a ruler or in any state structure) and the concept of the *ummah*, which provides a source of legitimacy and oversight superior to the authority that any state can claim. Perhaps this is why so much Islamic political thought revolves around the idea of the *ummah* rather than the state.[36] The general mechanism governing Islam, it must be noted, tends to adapt and assimilate worldly goods and activities within a spiritual framework.

The political culture of Islam presents countless challenges for modern political norms. However, this is not the result of Islam's rigorous monotheism, which provides no space for consensus between the sovereignty of God and humans, but simply because no political body of any state can adequately express God's sovereignty. It is believed that only the general will of the *ummah* – its collective consciousness – has the potential to embody such sovereignty. Throughout the history of Islam, no state (including the most despotic) has ever succeeded in establishing its own legitimacy; the *shari'ah* and the *ummah* have always been the true loci of such legitimacy.[37]

Ibn Khaldun's distinction between ethics and morality is useful in throwing more light on the Islamic conception of the state.[38] According to Khaldun, ethics transcend the state. For example, the values of unity and religious fellowship are transformed into morality when immanent within the state; that is, these values form the basis for state ideology, and call on Muslims to work tirelessly to preserve harmony and homogeneity between the morality of the state and the ethics of Islam. This is completely at odds with Machiavellian political theory, for example, according to which nothing exists outside or above the state, and where moral law, as such, becomes incarnate within the state.[39] In fact, the differences between Ibn Khaldun and Machiavelli are radical: while the former looks with disdain upon the state, seeing it as subservient to natural law, the latter regards the state as embodying the rule that must be adhered to.

Nevertheless, realist that he was, Ibn Khaldun recognised the existence of force within states and their tendency to manipulate religious norms to legitimise their rule. However, in his quest for the submission of the natural to the religious Ibn Khaldun refused to acknowledge the state as an immanent value, citing the extensive body of judicial literature that stretches back as far as the first centuries of Islamic history. Jurists have long been accustomed to distinguishing between the laws of nature, which Ibn Khaldun refers to as the rule of *'asabiyyah* (blood kinship), and that of the *shari'ah*, or caliphate, whereby blood ties are put to the service of religious ethics and ideals. To these two types of rule Ibn Khaldun added the rule of reason, which he argued was inherent in the rule of nature, and inferior to that of *shari'ah*. That is, Ibn Khaldun considered the *shari'ah* to be more capable of refining politics, and subduing propensities to violence, than the rule of reason. *Shari'ah* in the Khaldunian system seems to fulfil a similar function to that of reason in Rousseau's social contract; that is, it forms the basis for the civilising of politics and for shifting humanity from a state of nature to a state of citizenship.[40]

Throughout Islamic history, religion has been crucial in reducing state violence and regulating rulers' inclinations to absolutism. Islam's transcendental nature surpasses state authority, and the person of the ruler, and insists on the values of *'adl* (justice and equality). From its inception, Islam led a spiritual revolt, aspiring to replace tribal ties with ties of belief, and to replace the coercive loyalty and violence often imposed by blood ties with ties based on voluntary allegiance.[41] From this perspective, it is when politics functions in a completely profane manner, free of any transcendental authority, that it quickly tends to lose its political character and turn into mere oppression and violence. That is, because politics should be about neither blind power nor savage aggression, it always requires a transcendent political morality.

It has been in the reframing of values and symbols, as well as sources of legitimacy and allegiances, that Islam has realised its most significant accomplishments. By instilling the value of allegiance to the *ummah* over and above that of the tribe, sect or family, Islam gave dominion to the spirit of truth over force. Islam has endeavoured to undermine natural bonds in the interests of enhancing religious belief. In fact, it can be argued that it was only because of Islam that the anarchically inclined Arabs came to accept the notion of a state. Islam proved capable of removing elements of violence and savagery from Arab cultures that were founded on tribalism and blood ties.

As Laroui indicated, Islam arose as an ethical revolt against tribal morality and later grew into a political revolution, while preserving its religious premises.[42] Yet, although Islam has always challenged the absolutes of kingship and the notion of divine right, it has been unable to utterly do away with them, and the contrast between Islam and the value system against which it stood has never been resolved. Nevertheless, the real contribution Islam has tried to make is to add moral values particularly to state formations, but also to political life in general. Thus the Islamisation of the Middle East did not involve the overthrow of the basic structures.[43] Rather, Islam seems to have attempted to infuse existing institutional forms with a new vocabulary, concepts and values, and new definitions of personal, social and political identity. Islam did not seek to innovate, elaborate or introduce new political structures or institutions. Its prime contribution occurred at the level of socio-political morality. That is, the aim was to transform the root values that form the basis of power, its axes of reference and its sources of legitimacy.

As Islam spread, it incorporated various different political apparatuses. Roman, Indian, Greek and Persian practices were key in determining the processes and principles of Islamic forms of governance. Indeed, it was from these empires that Islamic rulers procured many of their administrative staff. This meant that Islamic discourse was considerably enriched by translations into Arabic of Greek treatises on political philosophy as well as Persian manuals on statecraft and court etiquette. Arabic's political lexicon was also significantly enhanced by loan words and, more significantly, by translations of Persian, Greek and Latin terms.

However, as Islam made the transition from some of the world's most arid zones to its more central cities and capitals, the moral and political values it aspired to effect took some grave and damaging blows. The political systems that now entered the Islamic fold were the product of eidetic cultures, which drew no line between rulers and God (or gods), as was the case with the Persians and, to a certain extent, the ancient Greeks. Laroui has argued that the cumulative effect of this was that form became an end in itself; that in the long run, form imposed itself as spirit.[44] Laroui then went on to describe the political history of Islam as having gone from being purely 'religious' to 'irreligious' and mundane, but I find it difficult to agree with this. Undoubtedly, some of the changes that have occurred in Islamic history can be described as a transition from caliphate to kingship, and as the triumph of instrumental reason over ethical reason. However, in my view, this victory has been only partial, and the transition from what jurists refer to as the rule of the caliphate is by no means final or complete.

Religious political values remained influential and active, and when the Umayyad dynasty held power (*c.* 660–750), the Islamic state was held together by a combination of kinship ties and religious values symbolised by *shari'ah*. The Umayyad caliphate attempted to subdue the religious element, but Islam's political values were already deeply entrenched, and many Muslims remained immune to instrumental manipulation. The early Islamic jurists' awareness of the perils of this transition, their attachment to the Prophet, and to the model of the 'Rightly-Guided Caliphate', led them to direct their energy away from the state and into the *ummah*, and away from ruling institutions to those run by *ahli* (society/the people). This was particularly true of the running of institutions such as mosques, religious schools and religious endowments. From the early stages of Muslim history, Muslim rulers attempted to claim guardianship over both the religious and political interests of the *ummah*. This was strongly rejected by the *'ulama*, and resulted in a conflict between the two, creating a chasm between what Lapidus has referred to as the 'court milieu' and 'city milieu'. The court milieu, represented by the palace and the king, was dominated by pre-Islamic

Persian heritage. The city milieu consisted of a wide network of civil organisations and institutions that were profoundly influenced by the *shari'ah* and the *'ulama*. As Lapidus noted, the 'new urban centers, economic growth, and the formation of cosmopolitan communities... created an independent urban population, led by religious chiefs'.[45]

Islam's combining of politics with 'religion' does not involve the sacralisation of politics, since the political is an *ijtihadi* and a consensual domain. That is, politics – including economics or indeed any worldly activity – cannot function according to its own logic or independently of the moral restrictions of Islam and the *maslahat* (interests) of the community. Politics is a civic and a rational matter, but it is also a moral one, and (despite the Hobbesian view) does not necessarily function autonomously. In this context, the principal tension is not between theocratic Islam and rational western secularism. Nor is the divide between Islam and modernity, as western discourse would have it. The conflict is essentially between the theory of immanence – a faith in a transcendental reference for being – and an order of values. The peculiarity of the Islamic view lies in the novel vision it advances of the concepts of immanence and transcendence.

To sum up my position on the topic of secularity and Islam, it is enough to say that many expressions designated as 'secular' or 'mundane' are actually vividly present in Islam. The problem is that the term *saeculum* has a strong historical and hermeneutical tradition that is dominated by Judeo-Christian theology. This has exacerbated the modern polarisation between religion and secularisation. The fact that the institutionalised discourse of secularism is the product of the last two centuries of sociological discourse makes attempts to liberate the concept from this polarisation almost untenable. David Martin's call to release the term from sociological language resounds even more loudly in the Islamic sphere, where such a release is even more acutely needed.[46]

So, is Islam a secular religion? Yes and no. If secularity is taken to refer to the values of this world, Islam must undoubtedly be cast as a secular religion, but if by 'secular' one includes the immanent connotations historically inherent in the notion, the term must be excluded from the Islamic sphere altogether. In my view, there is a real need to divest the term 'secularity' of its unitary claims. That is, clear lines of distinction must be drawn between the following three different meanings of the word: i) the profane and temporal; ii) a doctrine based on the notion of immanence; and iii) the rationalisation of the *polis*. Each of these three meanings is discussed in a little more detail below.

Secularity as the profane and the temporal

Secularity was used by early Christians to denote worldly things and affairs, the profane, and the temporal. Islam, it must be noted, has no problem with these connotations, being a thoroughly 'worldly religion'. Islam advocates an interaction with reality, in all its complexity and 'impurity', not a flight from it. The Sufi tradition, which emerged relatively recently in the history of Islam, with its mystical tendencies and quest for salvation in the 'spiritual world', has been unable to reshape Islam's general spirit, which remains dominated by the worldly interpretations of its *fuqaha*. Indeed, in more recent times, even the Sufis have assumed the form of revivalist *jihadi* movements when confronted with the reality of European imperialism. This is true of the Mahdi Sufism of the Sudan and the Senussi movement in Libya. Lexically, *jihad* is defined as exertion and application with a view to achieving a specific end. In this sense, Islam may be seen as a fully *jihadi* religion, as it stipulates that values without power are meaningless and that power without values amounts to blind violence.

Secularism as a doctrine based on immanence

Secularism is silently present in all of the west's social and political orders. It co-exists and overlaps with non-secular life, which has been incorporated in an order founded on immanence. The discourse of philosophers and sociologists tends to bestow a kind of unity on fragmented configurations, which is often not evident in day-to-day reality. In so doing, some scholars have transformed secularity into secularism – a systematic body of theory that has solid foundations and makes firm predictions. As described by its advocates, secularism does not mean giving up on all notions of transcendence, but rather reshaping these in favour of an immanent system of reference.[47] Indeed, secularity does not necessarily mean the erosion of religion; it can mean the transforming of religion's functions and claims to validity within an immanent framework that is no longer determined by religion. Thus, Spinoza's 'theology', and Hegel's philosophy, decisively shifted Judeo-Christian theology towards immanence, and the pantheistic Judeo-Christian tradition towards secularisation. The immanent tendencies inherent in secularism face tremendous difficulties in an Islamic context. Islam's rigorous monotheism, which serves as the ground for all scriptural interpretation and all human conduct, places transcendence at the centre of all forms of activity. From early in its evolution, Islamic theology has stood firmly against Eastern Gnosticism, a view championed by a great many Judeo-Christian sects. Even the Muslim philosophers had difficulty swallowing the 'materialist' features embedded in Greek philosophy, and so chose to reformulate Aristotelian philosophy within a Platonic and neo-Platonic framework.[48] Although some notions of immanence found their way into Gnostic Sufi traditions (via the late 'philosophical pantheism' of Mansur al-Hallaj, Ibn Sab'in and Ibn 'Arabi) in Andalusia and the Mashriq, many scholars have seen this as a deviation from the teachings and spirit of Islam. The modern heirs of the Muslim *'ulama* (Jamal ad-Din al-Afghani and his disciples) condemned Gnostic Sufism as an aberration, and as a source of the stagnation and decline of Muslim society. Al-Afghani and his followers firmly rejected pantheism as legitimating both determinism and the annihilation of the human subject in favour of otherworldly eschatology. They regarded immanent naturalism with similar suspicion, and al-Afghani devoted much time to refuting 'naturalist philosophy', tracing the origins of this movement to the philosophy of Epicurus and that of the Persian Gnostics, and showing that this was incorporated into French naturalism, and then advocated by many of the Ottoman elite.[49] The Islamic order of value and knowledge is, I submit, one of transcendental worldliness or spiritual materialism. The worldly is infused with a transcendental perspective, and materialism with a spiritual significance. In this sense, Islam overcomes the identification of religion with the sacred, thereby trouncing the dialectical synthesis between the 'sacred' and the 'profane', or the 'religious' and the 'secular'. If there is no symmetrical dualism, there can be no dialectical synthesis. Instead, we have an amalgam of 'religious' and 'secular', each infusing every aspect of the other, down to the smallest detail, divesting the notions of the 'secular' and 'sacred' of all content, and rendering them utterly redundant. What we are left with defies differentiation; the spiritual and the material come to be known and understood as essentially one and the same.

Only in Islam is religious consciousness aware of itself as worldly spirituality, and transcendence is transformed into historical immanence. Contrary to the assumption underlying the Hegelian myth that Christianity should be crowned as the heart of world religions, or as the religion of religions, it is only in Islam that religious consciousness finds refuge from the enigma of theodicy. Not only is the world to be tolerated and accepted, it is to be glorified and exalted as a primary component of religious truth. Indeed, what Weber dismissed as indicators of the decrepitude and decadence of Islam are in fact the sources of its vibrancy, strength and uniqueness among world religions and systems of thought.

Secularity as the rational management of the polis

If political secularity is taken to refer to the 'rational' management of the *polis*, based on the art of compromise and political representation, and a rejection of sectarian divisions and religious disarray, then it seems to me that Islam has no problem accommodating this form of pragmatic secularity. In mainstream Sunni Islam, politics is seen as the domain of public interest based on rational *ijtihad* and the will of the *ummah*. Two issues need to be considered here:
* By insisting on the humanness of rulers, as well as their fallibility and equality with other believers in the eyes of God, Islam's spiritual revolution freed the political sphere from the bondage of

theocratic governance in the name of God. From an early phase in its history, Islam leaned firmly towards the *ummah* and the *shari'ah*, and away from rulers. If anything has been called sacred, it is the *shari'ah* as embodied in the will of the *ummah* and the interpretations of its scholars.

- Even when the majority of the traditional *fuqaha* have seemed to accept even the most despotic of rulers, for fear of political disarray and anarchy, they have remained faithful to the notion of governance as a pact between the rulers and the ruled, and the primacy of the norm of political justice has always been emphasised. Although one may have reservations about the traditional political theories of the *fuqaha*, the spiritual and moral revolution that they fostered and the numerous political perspectives they stimulated have served as a basis for a transition towards a more civil and 'rational' management of politics. Indeed, the importance of a text is seen as lying not only in the text itself, but in the range of expectations it makes possible.

One of the difficulties that has faced many Muslim jurists who have insisted on governance as a covenant between rulers and the *ummah* is how to make it possible for every member of the *ummah* to participate in choosing a ruler. The main solution proposed so far is that the *ummah* should seek representation via a circle of enlightened and morally just scholars who act as intermediaries between the rulers and the ruled. In my view, however, political representation through free, democratic elections resolves this traditional political dilemma far more easily.

This leads us to the relationship between religion and state in Islam. The fact that there are no ecclesiastical institutions in Islam makes Islam the property of believers and of the Muslim community as a whole. Any interpretation of the Qur'an found acceptable by the majority of believers is considered legitimate. Although some insist on a consensus of a majority of scholars, most of the *madhahib* (classical schools of jurisprudence) regard the *ummah*'s consensus as being equal to revelation itself when it comes to the source of a ruling.

The separation of state and religion was entrenched early in Islamic history, and was called for by Muslim scholars to prevent rulers from interfering in religious matters. The problems facing Muslim societies today are less about the subservience of states to religious leaders, and more about religion's enslavement to the state and to the will of despotic rulers. What Muslim societies seek is the liberation of religion from state authority. If by political secularity we understand the inter-independence of state and religion, then this is easily accommodated by Islamic political theory, as it frees religion from the tyranny of the state. If, on the other hand, political secularity refers to the freeing of religious morality from politics, it will undoubtedly meet much resistance in any Islamic context. As Ibn Khaldun advised, politics, like any other worldly affair, should be 'civilised' by religious morality, and not allowed to function exclusively in accordance with its own frame of reference.

Modernisation and secularisation

One of Weber's major premises was the inevitable conquest of religion by secularism. Thus, for Weber, while religion may reconcile itself to secular interests in a variety of ways, these arrangements are necessarily transitory and frail in nature. Religious aspirations are rendered helpless in challenging the realities of a world that is led by the logic of capitalism and bureaucracy. The silent but implicit claim here is that all religions are vulnerable to reality and incapable of withstanding the uncaring world. However, in this section of the chapter, I will show that when we apply this claim to the Islamic world, it appears tenuous and unpersuasive.

Weber conceived of an objective history regulated by economic rationality, formal bureaucracy and Hobbesian politics, and saw any phenomena beyond these three as reactive and subjective or symbolic and illusory.[50] In this respect, Weber clearly allied himself with the Marxist approach to religion. Where Weber and Marx parted company, however, was in the former's assertion that, while religion may be irrational and illusory, it can be an active force in certain contexts, principally in the pre-modern world. However, he argued that religion is always eventually overwhelmed by economic and political rationalism. For Marx, religion was a mere phantasm, which, beyond the socio-economic structure, was utterly devoid of significance. In his *Contribution to a Critique of Hegel's Philosophy of Right*, he wrote: 'Religious distress is at the same time the expression of a real distress and the protest against real distress. Religion is the sigh of the oppressed creature, the heart of the heartless world, just as it is the spirit of spiritless conditions. It is the opium of the people.' As a sigh or an opiate, religion cannot be read *per se* through its internal representations, but is merely indicative of the contorted socio-economic structure that lies beyond it. Even if we accept Althusser's reading, which endeavoured to avail Marx of his humanist and enlightenment tendencies by drawing a distinction between the young Hegelian Marx and the mature author of *The German Ideology*,[51] no real change is evident in Marx's conception of religion. According to Althusser, the Marxist view of ideology and utopia gained complexity by being categorised as components of the socio-economic structure, rather than mere reflections of the superstructure, but this had no bearing on Marx's characterisation of religion as illusion and phantasm.

Freud's theories generally affirmed this view. Freud saw religion as a sublimation of inner fears and anxieties, and their projection onto the external world; in short, as an infantile delusion. In general, therefore, modern sociology sees religion as an illusionary escape for the poverty-stricken, marginalised, social wreckage of capitalist society, while modern psychology depicts religion as a remedy for the psychologically unstable. Thus, in depicting religion in modern literature, secularists are by no means neutral. Emblematic of such propensities is the following statement by Émile Durkheim:

> Religion is a unified system of beliefs and practices related to sacred things, that is to say, things set apart and forbidden – beliefs and practices which unite into one single moral community called a Church, all those who adhere to them.[52]

Note that Durkheim's association of religion with the experience of the sacred conceals the fact that he has reduced religion to an attachment to sacred objects, and all religious practice to a religious institution, which he refers to as the Church, offering no qualification of the term, as if the presence of the religious depends on the existence of that formal and hierarchical body. Durkheim thus casts all forms of religious expression that do not comply with this prerequisite outside the sphere of 'religion'. Weber, too, explicitly proclaimed that the only religion 'worthy of the name' was Christianity. And, when judging Oriental cultures and societies, even Marx, who was notorious for his almost unequivocally negative view of religion, turned into a veritable theologian when discussing Christianity.

It seems the anthropologists are correct when they insist on the complex and controversial nature of religion, and rebuke sociologists for their overly narrow determinations. Of course, the definition of religion is itself the historical product of discursive forces. As Parvez Manzoor wrote:

> Whatever the cogency and validity of the secularist argument, it is contingent upon a conception and understanding of 'religion' that is idiosyncratically western. The modern definition of religion as 'the exclusive zone of human reality' bears the distinctive insight of the secular man and applies only to his world.[53]

Modern sociological discourse tends to associate modernisation with secularisation, endorsing the notion that religion loses most of its power over people and their social conditions in industrialised societies. Modernisation, with its drive towards industrialisation and urbanisation, certainly challenges most religious inclinations. Modern cities are deemed to be secular cities perforce. As Harvey Cox declared, if secularisation designates the context of our 'coming of age, urbanisation describes the context in which it is occurring. It is the "shape" of the new society which supports its peculiar cultural style.'[54]

It is generally thought that the way we live determines the meaning we attach to our lives, and vice versa. Much of the literature published by western philosophers, historians and social scientists in the last two centuries postulates the disappearance of God (or gods) in the modern world. Modernisation uproots communities from their blood ties and rituals in favour of an individualist world. To use Durkheim's vocabulary, modern societies are held together by an 'organic cohesion' with no reference to the sacred, while traditional societies are based on a mechanical segmentary solidarity, and share strongly ritualistic forms of religion. In his early work, the American sociologist Peter Berger not only assumed the inevitability of secularisation in the west but also its universality, noting that 'it appears that the same secularising forces have now become worldwide in the course of Westernization and modernization'.[55]

There is no question that secularisation is a fact of life in most western societies, but the assumption that we live in a 'secularised world' is questionable, not only in non-western societies but even within the Euro-Atlantic sphere. The relation between secularisation and modernisation is far more convoluted and complex than its apologists seem to think. The persistence of religion in the heart of 'secularised' industrial societies, or 'the revenge of the sacred', as Leszek Kolakowski described it, appears to cast doubt on the theory of secularisation as a whole.[56] Even in the political sphere, what Michael Sandel referred to as 'the Jeffersonian wall of separation between church and state'[57] seems less than solid given the influence of certain Christian Churches and religious sects on American politics.

In my view, the power of history – rather than theory – casts the most serious doubts on the secularist claim to the evanescence of the 'sacred'. As Manzoor argued, 'the death of the sacred remains more a vain secular hope than a probable historical scenario'.[58] The assertion that secularisation goes hand in hand with industrialisation seems too simplistic – even for western societies.[59] However, I am more concerned with secularisation in the Muslim world, where claims of the necessary correlations between modernisation and secularisation are even more contentious.

While most western sociologists are committed to defending the theory of secularisation, modernisation, industrialisation, urbanisation and the spread of education, they often fail to testify to the advance of secularisation in the Muslim world. The contemporary Islamic upsurge is particularly interesting, since it appears to be more dynamic and powerful in the cities than in the rural areas, and more prevalent among the highly educated and modernised than in the more rural and traditional sectors of Muslim society.

A map of contemporary Islam seems to reveal that the Islamic revival is advancing more rapidly in modernised contexts than in traditional ones. Thus, the Islamist project is more active in Turkey, Algeria, Tunisia, Malaysia, and Egypt than it is in Saudi Arabia, Morocco, and Mauritania. Islamic movements seem to experience greater difficulty in advancing among the more traditional social groups, including tribes and rural farmers. For the most part, these social segments, along with the ruling elite, seem to form the social bases of the more 'modernised secular' states.[60]

In my view, Ernest Gellner's characterisation of the separation between secularisation and modernisation in the Islamic world is largely accurate. According to Gellner, secularisation may assume several different forms, but is a fact of life in most cultures other than Islamic culture. As he observed, 'To say that secularisation prevails in Islam is not contentious. It is simply false; Islam is as strong now as it was a century ago. In some ways, it is probably much stronger.'[61] However, Gellner's analysis of the reasons for this is controversial. He accounts for the absence of reciprocity between modernisation and secularisation in Islam with reference to the absence of a formal clerical institution, which gives Muslims the freedom to adjust to modernisation. The lack of responsiveness to secularity is explained with reference to Islam's supposedly rigid fundamentalism. This contrast probably says more about Gellner than about Islam, and reflects the tension in his work, particularly in his *Conditions of Liberty: Civil Society and its Rivals*, in which he seemed torn between being a researcher so engrossed in his subject that he could not help expressing his admiration for it, and the traditional Orientalist gazing at his subject through a massive arsenal of a priori categories and an active historical imagination.

The truth is that, while the shock of modernity that accompanied western imperialist expansion may have shattered the structure of Islamic conscience and its social fabric, Islam has largely been able, not only to contain modernity within its own hermeneutics and language, but also to benefit from its achievements. The discourse of Islamic reformism, dating back to the beginning of the nineteenth century, has played a crucial part in adapting modernity to the Islamic context, and in monitoring its key notions and terms. This has enabled Muslims to communicate with the modern world using their own language and mechanisms, and has paved the way for the formation of what can be referred to as an Islamic discourse on modernity. Given all the crises in the Islamic world, as well as the sensationalism and exaggeration of its realities and problems, it is not easy to discern the profound shifts taking place in the Islamic cultural sphere. Nevertheless, I attempt to examine these changes in the chapters that follow.

3

Secularity and despotism

Quand les sauvages de la Louisane veulent avoir du fruit,
ils coupent l'arbre au pied, et cueillent le fruit, voilà le
gouvernement despotique. [When the primitives of Louisiana
wish to eat some fruit, they cut down the whole tree to gather
it. Such is despotic government.]
— Montesquieu, *De l'esprit des lois*, Vol. I Ch. XIII

Political secularism is often represented by its champions as the basis of
democracy and as essential for the flowering of values such as pluralism and tolerance. Indeed, many insist that only secularism is capable
of teaching people tolerance and how to co-exist or communicate rationally with others in public fora. Secularists argue that democratisation arises inevitably when religion retreats to the realm of the private.
Within this particular political discourse, the Middle East is generally
invoked as the epitome of resistance to democratisation, and Islam's
iron hold over all aspects of life is said to compel Muslims to reject
secularisation entirely.

   In this chapter, I tell a different story, and attempt to reveal the contingency and historicity of political secularisation. Like any pervasive
phenomenon, secularism occurs in multiple forms and colours, and, in
certain contexts, it is more closely allied to political coercion and despotism than to democracy. My aim in the chapter is to move away from
abstract discourse to concrete reality. Thus, rather than viewing secularism through the eyes of its advocates, I describe its actual performance
in the Middle East.

After briefly outlining the etymology and use of the term 'despotism' in the west from ancient Greece through to the modern era, I focus on the lines of convergence between secularism and despotism in the Middle East. I suggest that secularisation has been an ally of both despotism and democracy, and question whether secularity is necessary for the promotion of values such as tolerance and open-mindedness.

Starting in ancient Greece

In Hellenic discourse, the term 'despotism' referred to the relationship between a master and his slaves. The term *despotès* was closely associated with *oikonomos* (household management), and applied primarily to patriarchs who controlled household life. The despot, in Greek usage of that time, referred to the father of a family, but his power was understood to encompass the lives of his slaves, not his wife or children. In ancient Greece, slavery was considered integral to the human condition. Aristotle, for example, argued that slaves lacked full human capacities, and that, as barely more than animals, they could be exploited as living tools, objects for household use. Classical Greek also allowed for 'despotic rule' to mean 'arbitrary rule'. However, since it was believed that slaves had little capacity for judgement, they were expected to accept their own domination.[1]

For Aristotle, slavery was natural, and a matter of necessity: 'It is thus clear that some are by nature free, so others are by nature slaves, and for these latter the condition of slavery is both beneficial and just.'[2] In his *Politics*, Aristotle distinguished between four forms of power: the power of a king, the power of a magistrate, the power of a father, and the power of a master. He argued that only the first three can be classified as political relationships, since they are exercised between free people. Despotic power, he noted, is the power of a free person over those who have been 'naturally' deprived of freedom.

Thus Aristotle accepted commonly held Hellenic opinions, but he also extended their application to contexts where political power was analogous to that of a master over his slaves.[3] Aristotle saw all monarchies as despotic, even where the power of a monarch – although indistinguishable from that exercised by masters over their slaves – was seen by his or her subjects as sanctified by custom and hence legitimate. He also believed that this type of rule was characteristic of non-Hellenic people or barbarians (whom the Greeks regarded as slaves by nature). Despotism was profoundly repulsive to the Greeks, who perceived themselves as rational agents, and entitled to political self-determination.[4] Just government, according to the ancient Greeks, seeks to further the common interests of the governed. Conversely, despotic authority exercises itself in the interests of the master, and is only unintentionally advantageous to a slave.

Aristotle distinguished the realm of the household, or *oikonomos*, from the sphere of politics, or *praxis*, where public debate took place and citizens asserted their essential identities as 'political animals'. For Aristotle, it was improper to speak of a despotic political power. He employed the term 'despotic government' to designate governments that no longer conformed to the principle of 'absolute justice'. Thus, he saw tyranny as a deviation from kingship, oligarchy from aristocracy, and democracy as a drift from a republic. He saw tyranny, oligarchy and democracy as despotic because, under all these forms of government, leaders – like the master of a household – pursue their personal interests even though they may, in the process, accidentally benefit their subjects.[5]

Aristotle further contended that different forms of government waver between the best and worst forms of themselves. Thus, kingship is never pure; tyranny is never complete, and political regimes continually slide between purity and tyranny, perfection and degradation. In consequence, Aristotle deemed aristocracy to be a middle path between tyranny and kingship, and designated it as the best possible form of government.[6]

During the Greco-Persian wars (499–449 BC), the Greeks described the politics of Persia and 'other Asian peoples' as 'despotic' and 'barbaric'.[7] For the ancient Greeks, barbarians (in this case, Asians) had no capacity for reasoned public debate, and could therefore legitimately be used as slaves.[8] Furthermore, since Asians were deemed incapable of acting reasonably in a public sphere, it was assumed, as Aristotle put it, that the 'barbarous should be governed by the Greeks'.[9]

The medieval tradition

The line of continuity between Greek thought – particularly that of Aristotle – and that of modern Europe is evident in the fact that Aristotle's works were still being read and were translated in the fifteenth century.[10]

From the start of the Crusades in 1095, and for centuries thereafter, the Turks were portrayed in Europe as a source of terror. The fall of the Byzantine Empire in 1453 sent a wave of psychological shock through Europe. The Turks stood on Europe's threshold, presenting a daunting threat on almost every level – military, political, cultural and religious.

Machiavelli, in early sixteenth-century Italy, was probably the first to describe the Ottoman state as the antithesis of European monarchy. In two central passages of *The Prince*, he depicted the autocratic bureaucracy of the Ottoman Porte as an institutional order that was different in every respect from the states of Europe:[11]

> The entire Turkish Empire is ruled by one master and all other men are his servants, he divides his kingdom into *sandjaks* and dispatches various administrators to govern them, whom he transfers and changes at his pleasure…They are all slaves bounden to him.[12]

Ever since, western political thinkers and philosophers have tended to define the character of their own political and cultural world by contrasting it with that of the Ottoman Empire that was so close yet infinitely remote.

Amid the religious conflict in France during the Reformation, French jurist and philosopher Jean Bodin expanded on the contrast between monarchies bound by respect for their subjects and those that ruled by unrestricted domination. The first represented the 'royal sovereignty' of the European state, the second was the 'lordly' power of despotism that was allegedly alien to Europe and encountered only in states such as the Ottoman Empire.

In the eighteenth century, with the publication of the works of Montesquieu, the concept of despotism became even more significant in western political discourse. Replacing the concept of tyranny (which refers to the exceptional abuse of power by an individual ruler), despotism denotes a *system* of total domination.[13] Montesquieu distinguished between three main types of government: republican, which are driven by virtue; monarchies, which are driven by honour; and despotic, which are driven by fear.[14]

It is worth noting that Montesquieu was less interested in the origins of political institutions than in the way they function. He insisted that there is an essential difference between the nature of a government and its principles, with the former revealing its substance, and the latter its form. The difference between a monarch and a despot, he argued, is partly a moral one, but he noted that the differences between monarchies and republics are not moral in nature.

By classifying both democracies and aristocracies as types of republic, Montesquieu sought to nullify the difference between the two. He defined monarchy as a form of government in which supreme authority belongs to the person of the monarch, and where there is a clear distinction between the monarch as a person and as a ruler. Monarchies, he argued, tend to function in regulated and orderly ways, and monarchs are public figures who are politically accountable, and whose commands are executed in accordance with rules and regulations that are sanctified by custom. Monarchies are often based on constitutions, and have well-defined rules that regulate the exercise of power. In this sense, monarchies are a well-organised and coherent form of government with defined rules that prescribe their functioning; no monarchy is arbitrary.[15]

In contrast, Montesquieu described despotism as an arbitrary and personified mode of government, in which no lines can be drawn between rulers and their public roles because the notions of private and public are destroyed. Despots tolerate no regulating laws or independent bodies whose duty it is to compare their decisions with legislative regulations. If despotic power is more restricted than a monarch's, so too are the freedoms of its subjects.[16]

Freedom for Montesquieu depended less on the limitation of power than on its mode of distribution and the rules governing its use. The new idea that Montesquieu introduced was that if power is to be effectively exercised to secure freedom, it must not merely be constrained, but appropriately restricted. Under despotic rule, power is unevenly distributed, and herein lies its vulnerability. Where power is not rationally organised according to precise rules, the parameters of what is lawful and unlawful are ambiguous, and subjects do not know what is expected of them. In theory, citizens are a despot's obedient servants. In practice, however, they can do as they please within undefined limits.

Under the power of a great despot – as was supposedly the case in the Orient – innumerable petty despots take advantage of the uncertainty of the law and the irregularity of power to further their interests and oppress their subordinates. Thus, corruption and tyranny flourish at all levels, security is scarce and revolts are frequent. Not only do the common people obey a despot mostly out of fear, but so too do the despot's subordinates. They too are mere servants who can be stripped of their offices and privileges at any moment. Liberty, Montesquieu insisted, can be guaranteed only by the rule of law, and the rule of law can exist under any form of rule except despotism.[17]

Montesquieu developed the concept of despotism through analysing the problems of his time. Montesquieu's Europe was one in which monarchies inclined towards absolutism and the centralisation of power. Asian regimes were described as despotic as a way of establishing analogies with the political conditions of eighteenth-century Europe, and to help his European readers to draw conclusions regarding the destiny of their own monarchies.

Despotism or 'despotic government' became a watchword of political thought relatively late in western history. Voltaire seems to have been correct in regarding it as an innovation, for it gained currency during his lifetime.[18] However, Voltaire disapproved of the distinction Montesquieu made between 'despotic (again, read Asian) government' and 'monarchy', under which royal power was checked by an 'intermediary body', and which claimed a privileged position in European states.[19] To Voltaire, Montesquieu's concept of despotism was absurd, and he argued instead that despotism cannot be a distinct mode of power but rather denotes a *degeneration of governance*. This is not to say that Voltaire did not employ the term despotism in a political sense, or that he defended the 'Oriental regimes' that were seen as epitomising despotism. However, when Voltaire used the word, he did not do so with reference to a *form of government*, and did assert that despotism is not in a separate category of its own.

A case can be made for reading Montesquieu's definition of despotism as an attempt to articulate the aspects of absolutist power that threatened to reduce public life to the domain of private power. Furthermore, for Montesquieu, despotism indicated a discursive order of power, which corresponded exactly to the ethnic, geographical and conceptual conditions of Aristotle's 'other', and seemed highly relevant to European perceptions of Asian society.

By the eighteenth century, the application of ideas initially conceived in relation to Turkey had spread steadily further east in the wake of colonial exploration and expansion to Persia, then India and finally China. The revival of the term despotism in western discourse occurred in parallel with the construction of the geographical fiction of a 'despotic Orient', and particularly 'despotic Islam'. Over centuries of military conflict with the Ottoman Empire, Islam was perceived in the west as being synonymous with Turkish and Arab culture, and as the epitome of despotism. The secret chain of communication between Paris and Isfahan in Montesquieu's *Lettres Persanes* revived the old fiction – traceable to Aristotle – of 'despotic Asia' vis-à-vis 'monarchic Europe'. The Persians in the *Lettres* are closer to fiction than to reality, and more European than Persian. Through them, Montesquieu presented his fantastic Oriental 'other', and propagated the old western fiction of a despotic Orient. Indeed, his definition of despotism was modelled on his perception of 'Asian societies'. For example, as already noted, Montesquieu considered despotism to be a political system based on fear and the personal caprice of the ruler, and he took this to be opposed to human nature. Paradoxically, however, he noted that 'in spite of men's love of freedom and hatred of violence, the majority of people are submitted to it'.[20] Montesquieu overcame this contradiction by contending that in certain parts of the world – Asia in particular – nature generates human beings with a potential for subjugation who are inclined to opt for this strange form of government:

> As all men are born equal, slavery must be contrary to nature, though in certain countries, it is founded on a natural reason, and we must distinguish these countries from those where even natural reasons reject it, such as European countries where it has fortunately been abolished.[21]

In this analysis, Asia appears to have always been a natural storehouse of despotism, and it is clear that Montesquieu subscribed to Aristotle's views on Asians' political nature. The only difference between the two is that while Aristotle deemed slavery to be a natural phenomenon, Montesquieu condemned all forms of slavery in the name of nature. Nevertheless, when it came to Asian society he invoked 'nature' to justify the very phenomenon that he dismissed as unnatural and excessively unjust for Europeans.[22]

The modern era

In more recent political thought, the notion of despotism has been associated with an active dualism: the opposition between a utopia of flourishing liberal democracies and regions that are subject to despotic rule. One side epitomises absolute good, rationality and liberty, and the other stands for evil, irrationality and oppression. Not content with this, western liberals also sought an imaginary 'other', which they found in the Orient, and deemed it a concrete model of despotism.

Standing outside this tradition, Alexis de Tocqueville's concept of despotism, and its relation to modern democracy, undermined this notion. Tocqueville (1805–1859) foresaw the possibility of modern democracy turning into a new system of oppression, which he struggled to name. 'I seek in vain an expression that will accurately convey the whole of the idea I have formed of it. The old words despotism and tyranny are inappropriate. The thing itself is new, and since I cannot name it, I must attempt to describe it.'[23] For Tocqueville, the 'new despotism' was without historical precedent, and was difficult to clearly conceptualise because modern democracies base their legitimacy on having banished the despotism of the aristocracy, and feel less threatened by despotism since breaking down that form of government.[24] But Tocqueville argued that the new despotism has a different quality. Unlike the *anciens régimes*, it is soft and invisible – it 'degrades its subjects without tormenting them'.[25] The hands and eyes of the state are increasingly active in daily life, and 'in the name of democratic equality, government becomes regulator, inspector, advisor, educator and punisher of social life'.[26] Thus, a nation becomes nothing but '*un troupeau d'animaux timide et industrieux dont le gouvernement est le berger* [a herd of timid and industrious animals with the government as their shepherd]'.

Tocqueville observed that the emergence of democracy had a paradoxical effect. On the one hand, it provided full affirmation for the rights of individuals (which is bound up to 'the wish to remain free'). On the other hand, it subjugated people to 'social power' (which is associated with the need to be led).[27] Thus modern democracies create individuals who feel a psychological need to be led while simultaneously desiring to be free, and the paradox is encapsulated by the combination of state centralisation with the sovereignty of the citizenry.

Tocqueville maintained that, far from being synonymous with the ideals of equality and social justice, liberty can stand in opposition to them, and added that, in modern democracies, people tend to replace the ideal of freedom with the goal of state-secured equality.[28] He explained that, in an egalitarian society, every individual is naturally isolated, and enjoys no real protection from ties of kinship or social class. In these circumstances, individuals can be 'easily cast aside, and mercilessly trodden on'.[29] It is indeed ironic that the democrats who first introduced the value (or utopia) of freedom into political discourse simultaneously opened the door to this new form of despotism. Thus, despotism in Tocquevellian discourse is not a vulgar political system that dominates and deprives its subjects of their rights and individuality, but a microphysical and invisible phenomenon that is generated by democracy itself. Tocqueville attempted to advance new terms to describe this form of despotism, arguing that as 'the political world changes, we must necessarily seek new remedies in new words'.[30]

Imperialism and despotism

Tocqueville's approach lays bare the relationship between secularisation in the Middle East and its imperialist roots. By imperialism, I do not mean military expansionism alone, but all the forms of political, economic and cultural hegemony that it entails. Hannah Arendt, the German political philosopher, advanced an understanding of the affinities between despotism and imperialist expansion, but her analysis may prove valid for the purposes of this chapter only if its context is reversed. I am not concerned with imperialism itself – with its internal impulses and strategies or its effects on its producers and exporters – but with the impact it has on its victims and subjects in foreign lands. To be specific, I am more concerned with the effects of the great imperialist project than with the project itself.

Imperialism's principal characteristic, as noted by Arendt, is its drive towards expansion, which is its permanent and supreme goal. She explained that this is a natural outcome of the marriage between the bourgeoisie and nation states, which meant that economic goals were incorporated into the political arena. For Arendt, imperialist expansionism is a matter of 'flag following trade', with imperial power being extended to protect ever-wider economic interests. In this process, imperialism emancipated the bourgeoisie, who had long been excluded from the political establishment by their lack of a stake in public affairs. Expansionism as an end in itself, and as the ultimate aim of politics, was an entirely new concept in the history of political thought. The novelty of this concept is that it is not political at all, but has its origins in the realm of business speculation, 'where expansion meant the permanent broadening of industrial production and economic transactions characteristic of the nineteenth century'.[31]

Since the imperialist conception of power views expansion as an end in itself, the imperialist powers initially made little attempt to establish new political bodies in their overseas 'possessions'. What the imperialists wanted, Arendt argued, was to 'assimilate rather than integrate, to enforce consent rather than justice, that is, to degenerate into tyranny'.[32] She summed up imperialist expansion as involving i) the export of the means of power without political institutions or regulations and ii) the separation of political means and institutions. The former means that the instruments of state violence (the police and the army in particular) were the main priority on the imperialists' list of items to export. Violence has always been seen as the *ultimo ratio* in political action, and military power as the visible expression of rule and government. The latter means that, in the process of expansion, imperialism transformed the means of governance in occupied lands into machines of violence and coercion. Furthermore, in Europe, the instruments of state violence are controlled by the national civil institutions that exist alongside but separate from them. In the occupied territories, the police and the army were liberated from any limiting institutions. Thus, imperialist violence was 'given more latitude' overseas than civil society in any western country would have permitted.[33]

Arendt also identified two further devices the imperialists use to impose foreign domination. One is race, the other bureaucracy.

According to Arendt, race-thinking emerged in the eighteenth century and gradually spread through Europe. As the deep basis of imperialist policies, racism certainly absorbed and revitalised the western tradition of race-thinking.[34] To Arendt, race-thinking denotes a lack of a foundation for human community beyond blood alliances. She argued that European colonisers ceased to belong to European society, which was founded on concessions and regulations, following the impulse of their own natures instead of imposing a humane order on themselves and the territories they conquered.[35]

Bureaucracy was the other key tool Arendt identified in the imperialists' great project in which 'every area was considered a stepping-stone to further conquest'.[36] Bureaucracy in this context refers to the lawless and arbitrary rules imposed by anonymous agents of expansion who become unbound from any sense of obligation to the rule of law. Arendt's view of bureaucracy contrasts markedly with Weber's. Weber looked at bureaucracy from within Europe, and from the point of view of an official, and defined it as a highly rationalised and responsible form of government that works according to rules, whereas Arendt saw it from the perspective of a subject observing its direct effects.[37]

To sum up: two aspects of Arendt's work on the subject of imperialism are particularly useful. Firstly, she noted that the separation between the political body at home and its institutions of violence overseas meant that the colonial states became little more than machines of violence and punishment. Secondly, for the colonised, the state came to be identified with the institutions of official force, especially the military and police. It follows that the object of politics in these nations was merely to adjust and distribute the means of coercion and manipulation over the social fabric. The roots of this phenomenon are traceable to the mode of governance established by imperialists; since state-employed administrators 'were actually nothing but functionaries of violence, they could only think in terms of power politics'.[38]

Essentially, the alienation of imperialist political structures from the social base within the colonised states was a natural consequence of the absence of a common language and vehicle for communication between the political elite and the wider population. Bureaucracy, as Arendt demonstrated, played a key role in this. As Arendt put it, 'bureaucracy was the organisation of the great game of expansion in which every area was considered a stepping-stone to further involvement and every people an instrument of further conquest'.[39] In the imperialist project, aloofness became the primary attitude of governance, as subjects were looked upon as little more than recipients of politics rather than as its producers.[40]

In the post-colonial era, the relationships between the political elites and their social bases have remained virtually unchanged. The only difference is that native administrators have replaced foreign administrators. In many such states, the 'modernisation' and 'secularisation' supposedly ushered in by the colonial powers meant little more than the stifling of society beneath a mass of bureaucratic regulations that were enforced by the military and the police. Secularisation came to signify little more than the imperialists' bid to destroy local structures and mechanisms of social cohesion in favour of the hegemony of an over-centralised state.

The problem with Arendt's work is that, like many Orientalists, she remained committed to differentiating between civilised Europe and uncivilised indigenous peoples who supposedly live like animals at the mercy of nature. Implicit in her work is the view that, even when the civilised 'degenerate', they remain distinct from the 'natives'. Although Arendt herself described the Afrikaners, the partial bearers of the imperialist project in South Africa, as becoming, like the native population, a rootless herd of wanderers bound together by blood as a tribe and not by location as a nation, she held on to the typology of an 'original civilised nation' versus 'uncivilised natives'. Ultimately, For Arendt, imperialism's moral deviance seems to have lain not in its destruction of people's lives through military force, but in its failure to impose 'order' and 'reason', and to emancipate indigenous populations from their primitive and 'animal-like' lives.[41]

Arendt remained oblivious to the crucial fact that the imperialist project did not conquer populations that were bereft of history, but extended to great centres of civilisation, which possessed cultural resources richer and deeper than those of the imperialists themselves. The Middle East, for example, had a vast array of cultural and intellectual traditions, political institutions and mechanisms of self-regulation. Indeed, the transfer of power from the southern Mediterranean – and the cities of Cairo, Baghdad, Damascus and Istanbul – to the western cities of London, Paris and Vienna does not mean that the former degenerated into incivility. It simply means that the northern centres became more powerful and more capable of controlling the geo-politics of both regions. The tipping points in this power balance were the defeat of the Ottoman army at the gates of Vienna, the discovery of the New World and the ever-increasing control of western powers over international trade.

Secularisation and global politics

In the Islamic world, secularism has always been associated with imperialism, and with the strengthening of a small elite that is alienated
from its social base. In the post-colonial era, this elite has been sus-
tained and supported by the international economic order, as well as by
westernised educational and cultural institutions that have divided the
world into a centre and a periphery. The asymmetrical and 'vertical'
relationship between the periphery and the centre is based on access
to power; the centre constantly consolidates its position through the
ongoing accumulation of the means of power, and thus relegates the
periphery to the margins in terms of political power, access to wealth,
and even participation in global discourse.

Johan Galtung used the terms 'comprador' and 'bridgehead elite' to
explain the ways in which the centre now maintains the periphery in a
state of structural dependence without necessarily requiring a military
presence. These elites are cultivated in the periphery and encouraged to
adopt the norms and values of the centre, and to defend the dominant
culture and interests of foreign powers rather than those of their own
people.[42] Galtung maintained that the

> center in the Center nation has a bridgehead in the Periphery
> nation, and a well-chosen one: the center in the Periphery
> nation. This is established such that the Periphery center is
> tied to the Center center with the best possible tie: the tie
> of harmony of interest.[43]

Westernisation can be considered a key means of producing bridgehead
elites. The political foundations that French political thinker Bertrand
Badie identified as forming the basis of a 'client state's dependence on a
patron state' can be detected from: i) the central role played by political
actors in constructing relations of dependence; and ii) the effective and
deterministic nature of the state in establishing its logic.[44] The links that
tie the patron state to its cliental counterpart are founded on the intersection of interests and the reciprocal exchange of favours between the
two. The 'patron state' provides the 'client state' with the goods neces-

sary for its survival. The 'client state', in turn, offers diverse favours, either relating to the use of its territory or to the symbolic power it holds in the international arena.[45]

To extend this analysis, it can be argued that, on a cultural level, secularisation (westernisation's close ally) is about the generation of a hermeneutic discourse – a communicative vehicle – with foreign powers who remain incapable of relating to the native population. If any sufficiently precise definition of culture is possible, it is that culture is a symbolically mediated communicative system that is dependent on mechanisms of correspondence, and has an inherently performative dimension. That is, culture is fundamentally a symbolic system that provides a medium for the communication of inter-subjectivity in a social domain. The most basic function of a symbol is to allow a sender to communicate with a receiver. However, as Armando Salvatore pointed out, to convey meaning is to perform an act that modifies the consciousness of the receiver, thus expanding or limiting the abilities of both receiver and sender.[46] The westernisation of the global political sphere has been intimately associated with the emergence of narrow political and cultural elites, uprooted from their social entourage and vertically linked to an external patron state. Westernisation has evolved as western states have systematically set about transforming the international scene in their own image. For all its successes, westernisation is seldom based on free choice, and is often linked to forms of pressure and constraint.

Secularism in the Middle East

Islam can certainly be understood as a 'symbolic communicative system', and as a medium of collective identity that revolves around its own internal hermeneutics. Secularism in the Middle East, on the other hand, is the child of colonialism; it remains connected to western hermeneutics, and has always been restricted to a small elite, never succeeding in expanding to wider social circles. Nevertheless, conflicting 'symbolic communicative systems' are clearly evident if we contemplate the general cultural scene in the lands of modern Islam. One communicative system is very limited, and confined to the narrow elite that has emerged from the imperialism and pseudo-modernisation of the last two centuries. This system is especially active in state institutions, but it remains peripheral to the wider and deeper reaches of society. The other communicative system is deeply rooted in society, and can truly be seen as a bridge to the masses. In my view, these two communicative systems reflect two wholly distinct societies on a collision course. I see them as a 'surface society' and a 'deep society', and as symmetrical in their development, rhythms and strategies.

French Islamologist Jacques Berques, who was intensely aware of this dualism and its shattering effect on modern Islamic societies, described it as a rift between 'two interlocking rhythms of change'.[47] The political elite, allied with external forces, attempt to impose their own strategies on a stable society that has a 'long and continuous tradition of thought and of life in common, produced from within itself, partly by its own internal movement, and partly in reaction to forces coming from outside'.[48] Culturally speaking, secularity in the Middle East has been unable to build a consensus between the intellectual and political elites or between these elites and the masses.

Two issues are important to understand here. The first relates to the political disintegration and cultural polarisation within the elite. What complicates things is the fact that the academic institutions, which were expected to act as the vanguard of secularisation, are undergoing a significant process of de-secularisation. In the contemporary era, many universities – and particularly those that focus on science and technology – are becoming the primary base of the new Islamist elite. Thus the institutions that were being relied on to produce new generations of the secular elite are instead turning into hives of de-secularisation. What seems to draw Muslim elites away from secularism may be linked to the étatisation (or nationalisation) of the social and political sphere, and the imposition of secularism by the army and the police. Lacking a social base, supporters of secularisation quickly resort to the state to preserve their status.

The second issue is that although traditional Muslim societies, and the discourse of the *shari'ah*, were undermined by western imperialism, secularism failed to establish a new basis of legitimacy. That is, secularisation in the Muslim world has always been associated with ideological and political disarray, as well as a strong division between the elite and the masses. The major dilemma facing most Muslim countries is how to restore cultural unity and establish a basis for political compromise between these various conflicting forces.

If we briefly compare the secularisation of the west with the same process in the Islamic world, it is clear that, even though secularisation in the west was not innocent of force and violence, it did succeed in establishing a new basis for consensus and vehicles for communication between conflicting social forces.[49] By contrast, in most Islamic countries, secularisation has been associated with political oppression and violence that has made the building of a new consensus impossible. In the west, secularists succeeded in separating the political sphere from the constraints of the Church, either by radically defeating the old system or by converting the religious establishment into a secular framework. In the Muslim world, secularism – with all its radicalism and promise of utopia – succeeded in undermining the legitimacy of the old social system without establishing its own authority or the necessary foundations for new forms of social consensus to emerge. In this regard, secularism continues to face real challenges and would probably not survive without the support of oppressive state apparatuses. This also means that any space created for political freedom in the Islamic countries tends to put the entire secular system and its elites under serious threat.

While the Middle East's secular elites have attempted to create a radical rupture with the socio-cultural tissue of Islamic society (using Turkish radical secularism as their model), the deep loyalty that ordinary citizens feel towards traditional Islam has hardly shifted. It is, therefore, completely misleading to attempt to read modern Islamic societies with reference to the development of their elites, without also contemplating the wider rhythm and discourse of these societies as a whole. Admittedly, there are many expressions of fragmentation and discontinuity in modern Islamic history, but these cannot conceal the chains of continuity and growth that remain within Islamic social culture, despite all the efforts of western media to convince us of the opposite. We would be gravely mistaken were we to accept the simplistic views that dominate traditional Orientalism: that an enlightened and active elite are battling to win over a 'stagnant' and 'backward' citizenry who are overwhelmed by religious values and symbols.

As indicated, two social and intellectual forces prevail. One consists of the secular elite, the other of the rest of society with its rhythms and intellectual forces. Both of these forces are in a state of renovation and dynamism that stems from their own references, efforts and strategies. This is not to say that modern Islam is completely indigenous. Its own hermeneutics have been engaged in a process of 'acculturation' and interaction with those of the modern west for centuries. The writings of Jamal ad-Din al-Afghani and Muhammad 'Abduh, and the movement of Islamic reformism they founded, are a good example of Islam's internal vitality and the reality of its interaction with the west. Nevertheless, the ideas and cultural forces active in the Muslim world, and the norms to which they appeal, still originate primarily from Islam's internal intellectual and historical legacy.[50]

Of course, modes of reaction to external challenges vary from one culture to another, and are related to their own internal capacities and energies. In the case of Islam, the western challenge was associated with military invasion, and led not to the dissolution of Islamic culture but rather to its activation and renovation. As strong as the impact of the western invasion on Islamic thought and society has been, this cannot obscure the fact that Muslims retain a rich order of symbols that are still active and intensely vibrant in their hearts and minds, both conscious and subconscious. In addition, modern Islamic culture retains its own capacities and criteria for selecting, internalising and reinterpreting aspects of foreign culture.

Secularist political discourse has not evolved internally within Arab–Islamic history, nor has secularisation been a process of peaceful acculturation between Islam and the west. Secularism is the child of imperialist expansion, and it ushered in a new balance of power that has favoured the interests of the imperialist forces and their 'bridgehead elites'. As such, secularisation was adopted by a tiny handful of people and remained alien to society as a whole, quickly leading to the marginalisation of the majority. Not only are the secular elite alienated from their social base, they are also in permanent confrontation with it. In this context, the state and its official institutions have become tools for the manipulation and coercion of the masses, and it is therefore difficult to conceive of secularisation persisting were state repression and organised violence to cease. This contention is substantiated by the cases of Turkey under Kemalism and Tunisia before the 2011 revolution: when they venture towards democracy, secularists finds themselves infinitely marginal, besieged by the population and forced to rely entirely on the support of the military and the police.

Secularisation and militarisation

The emergence of secularism in the Muslim world epitomised the shifts in political culture, related to the meaning of governance and the state's relation to its citizenry, away from the concept of organic power to that of mechanical power. Prior to this, the lens through which Islamic political thought viewed political power was that of a living body with members that complement one another. However, from the beginning of the nineteenth century, a material and mechanical model of power began to gain currency among the Islamic elite. Lord Cromer, Egypt's consul general from 1883 to 1907, was one of the earliest advocates of this conception of politics.[51] Cromer saw politics as a machine working on a world in which citizens are the 'raw materials'. The machine's external motivating force, in the Egyptian case, was synonymous with the role of the consul general.[52]

This affinity between secularism and the military derives from this historical context, in which 'the project of modernisation' emerged. It was by using military force that Europe first impinged upon the Middle East, first in the form of Napoleon's expedition, and then via the continued encroachment of Russia into the Ottoman territories throughout the eighteenth and nineteenth centuries.[53] The defeat of Islamic power in the modern age first occurred on the battleground. The elites in the sultans' courts and armies had little choice but to acknowledge the superiority of European weaponry, military science, and even of their discipline and administrative skills. It was no accident, therefore, that modernisation in the Middle East region generally began within the military, who were in the frontline of resistance to European aggression, and were seen as the principal tool in the preservation of the Muslim community's physical integrity.

From the early nineteenth century onwards, Muslim elites in Turkey, Egypt and Tunisia tended to identify with modern Europe and its military powers, and to ascribe the 'backwardness' of the Islamic world to a lack of military and administrative skills. As Albert Hourani noted, their heavy reliance on hierarchy, discipline and rationality makes armies more capable of adjusting the demands of modernisation than any other social institution.[54] It was, therefore, no accident that the first institution to be modernised and secularised in Turkey and other Muslim countries was the army, or that the army came to form the solid nucleus of the drive towards modernisation.

It was in this general context that secularism first emerged in Turkey and the Middle East. The main priorities of the Tanzimat were to create a modern new army that would be capable of defeating or at least fending off the European attack, as well as consolidating the power of central government over the provinces via a centralised administration framework.[55] Perhaps it was because the leaders of this project were soldiers, bureaucrats and state officials, rather than intellectuals, that they were primarily concerned with state efficiency. However, when the military establishment became the target of the political elite, modernisation was transformed into an end in itself.

It is important to keep in mind that the reform movement that began in Cairo, Istanbul and other Islamic capitals had aimed to reconstruct the Islamic order by borrowing aspects of western technology and administrative systems. Two tendencies developed within this project that still exist today. The first remained Islamic in its thought and aspirations, and saw the process of borrowing from Europe as a means of self-renewal. The second, represented today by the secularist, westernised elite, found its ultimate ideals and aspirations met in the west.

Although the latter was initially confined to a tiny minority, ongoing western imperialism, with its concomitant cultural, religious and racial oppression, saw it gradually come to dominate among the elite. From 1908, with the rise of the Young Turks, the balance of power shifted away from the courts of the sultans and into the hands of a political elite who derived their legitimacy from their control of the military and administrative establishments. It is true that the 'sultanate' political order was patrimonial par excellence but it was, nonetheless, capable of managing a complex and heterogeneous society.

In Kemalist Turkey, power resided in the hands of a narrow military and bureaucratic elite, while civil society was censured and oppressed in the name of progress and state security. This huge change in the balance of power reflects a shift in the recruiting grounds of the elite away from the traditional madrasas and to the military schools. If the principal goal of military restructuring in the Tanzimat era was to defeat western military aggression, in the era of the Young Turks the goal was to reconstruct the whole fabric of society. Atatürk inherited a massive military and bureaucratic machine that had been developed during the nineteenth century. The major change Atatürk effected was to transform the foundations on which these institutions rested from Islamic into westernised secular ones. He then established his rule on this base, and recruited the majority of his political staff from its ranks.

Politically, the military became one of the regime's most important agents of secularisation. It was designated as 'the people's school' and the 'republic's ultimate guardian'. A speech delivered by Atatürk at the army club in Konya in 1931 summarised the close alliance between secular nationalism and the army in modern Turkey:

> In our history, in Turkish history, an outstanding exception appears. You know that whenever the Turkish nation has wanted to stride towards the heights, it has always seen

its army, which is composed of its own heroic sons, as the permanent leader in the forefront of this march, as the permanent vanguard in campaigns to bring lofty national ideal to reality…in times to come also, its heroic soldier sons will march in the vanguard for the attainment of the sublime ideals of the Turkish nation.[56]

Legally, the role of the armed forces was defined by the Army International Service Law, which was enacted in 1935. Article 34 of the law stipulates that 'the duty of the armed forces is to protect and defend the Turkish homeland and the Turkish Republic, as determined in the constitution'. Later, the generals interpreted this clause as meaning that they had the right to intervene in the political sphere should the state otherwise 'be left in grave jeopardy'. After their second intervention in 1971 (the first military coup was in 1960), the military established what William Hale called a 'veto regime', under which the civilian government remained formally in place but its actions were directed, or at any rate restricted, by the military.[57] The role of the military as the 'bearer of the revolution' originally derived from Kemalist ideology, and historical experience. Atatürk himself frequently urged young army officers to think of themselves as the 'vanguard of the revolution',[58] and Turkey's military institution has imposed itself as the custodian of democracy and secularism ever since.

With state institutions forming the solid nucleus of the 'modernisation' and secularisation of society, these movements have been closely associated with étatisme and the destruction of civil society. Secularisation was imposed by the state elite, with the social masses passive recipients of the project, not its activators. Serge Latouche referred to this as 'modernisation without modernity', explaining that while the elites adopted some of modernity's formal aspects, its political and moral content never diffused into society as a whole.[59] To use Habermasian terminology, the process can be described as an instrumental modernity, the sole concern of which was the centralisation and accumulation of the means of power in the hands of the state, and, more precisely, in the hands of the military and bureaucratic elite.[60]

What further complicated the process in the Middle East is that the vertical imposition of secularism was (and still is) defeated by a horizontal wave of Islamisation that spread across modern institutions via civil society. Among the mass of the population, this movement manifests itself through a strong religious revivalism, and in elite circles it is expressed via the growth of a new modern Islamic elite. In 1989, the American author Louis Cantori described this process, declaring that 'Egypt has been Islamised up to its neck' – meaning that the wave of Islamisation has overwhelmed that country's entire social and political texture with the exception of the state apparatus.[61] The Egyptian case is by no means unique in the Arab and Muslim world. Every nook of political openness and cranny of civil activity in that part of the globe is accompanied by a great surge of Islamisation that encircles both the state and its elite.

It can be argued that the Jacobin model (with its violent radicalism) combined with various fascist and communist experiments (with their attempts to reshape the fabric of society by deploying state superstructures in the name of industrialisation and progress) exert a strong influence on the secularist elite of the Middle East. In fact, Hannah Arendt's definition of totalitarianism as 'ideology and terror'[62] seems accurate when applied to secularist regimes in the Middle East that have sought to effect radical changes in individual and social consciousness through the marriage of what Gramsci termed 'the ideological state institutions': the schools, the military and police, and state bureaucracy. Where educational institutions fail to spread the message of secularism, the state's instruments of violence are summoned to enforce it. This has been evident in Turkey (the subject of the most radical secularist project in the Islamic world), and in Tunisia (its counterpart in the Arab countries). Here, secularist elites regard society as a mere object for reconstruction and reshaping, or as a subject for punishment and discipline where their project is met with resistance or opposition.

One might well ask, why, of all the possible modes of secularisation, secularists in the Middle East chose to follow the Jacobin as well as the fascist and communist models? In my view, four main factors help to explain this:

- First, the secular elites' preference for the Jacobin model was by no means innocent or spontaneous, but based on clear interests and strategies. The secular elites deliberately sought a political and ideological model that would be compatible with their despotic tendencies. The British, American and Scandinavian states were judged unsuitable by virtue of their compromising, non-military character and neutrality vis-à-vis religion. The French model, with its militant antagonism towards religion, found favour with Middle Eastern secularists, who were deeply anti-religious and desired to alienate themselves from a society they deemed backward.

- The elites' military backgrounds were the second decisive factor in determining their strategies. Napoleon's expedition to Egypt in 1798 was the first wave of western invasion into Central and North Africa. The French mode of occupation was notorious for its endeavours to create pocket-sized elites steeped in the culture of the French Revolution. Missionary schools, which were well attended by the secular elite, acted as bridges to French political and cultural symbols. Thus, the notion of secularity first entered the Arabic lexicon via the word *laïcité* – a French term that bears the marks of the French Revolution's hostility towards both religion and the Church.

- Third, the elite in the Middle East essentially discovered the modern world through the gates of French culture. Atatürk went to Toulouse to pursue his military career, and Habib Bourguiba studied at the Sorbonne in Paris. In fact, even the Islamic reformist elite, such as Rifa'a al-Tahtawi (1801–1873), Khayr al-Din al-Tunsi (1822–1898) and Muhammad 'Abduh, became acquainted with the west via France. In addition, the majority of students from Muslim countries who went to study in Europe during the nineteenth century were sent to France, and a substantial number of French literary works were translated into Arabic and Turkish.

- Finally, the economic backwardness and political disintegration in which the Muslim world found itself in stood in stark contrast to the achievements of the modern west. From the early twentieth century, the communist and fascist models significantly influenced political and bureaucratic actors in the Middle East, due to the ability of the vanguard role of such states to overcome political disarray and to achieve both a degree of unity and quick progress.

French secularism holds great potential for state despotism, or étatisme, which can be briefly summarised in three points. First, the rapid destruction of the '*ancien régime*' generated a firm belief in the possibility of building a new political identity that begins in the here and now – 'an zéro et jour zéro', as Paul Ricœur put it. Ricœur described this 'phantasm of origin'[63] as a desire for irreversible rupture with the past and a resolve to wage brutal war against what Hobbes called the 'kingdom of darkness' for the sake of the 'kingdom of light'. Political freedom, as understood by post-revolutionary political culture in France, was an attempt to eradicate the evil of the past, and break with its institutional and symbolic authority, in the hope of launching a new age that would be governed exclusively by reason, and with reference to no other authority.

Second, Rousseau's notion of undefined raw nature stimulated the illusion of re-fashioning human nature, and the will to abolish all distinctions between the possible and the impossible, the real and the illusionary. What delineates the boundaries of the possible and the impossible is imagination, and French secularists enthusiastically embraced the prospect of destroying what already existed in the hope of producing a new kind of human. Consequently, politics was transformed into an experimental field for the imagination, with an eye to radically changing the human condition. However, when the radical spirit within the French *laïcité* descended from the realm of ideas and ideals to the world of concrete experience, the results were catastrophic. The French Revolution quickly collapsed into 'legitimate terror' ('la terreur légitime') when Robespierre and Saint-Just preached what they called 'la terreur de la liberté'. Revolutionary government, they insisted, must combine the virtue of freedom with the force of terror.[64] Some might argue that this was a necessary price for France to pay for entry into the modern age, but even if that were the case, history bears witness to several other nations (including America and Britain) that took the road to modernity yet were spared the terror of post-revolutionary France.

Third, French *laïcité* lacks a spirit of consensus and generates radicalism. Post-revolutionary France, although it did much to enrich political discourse, stands as a clear example of this. The horrors of the Napoleonic era were no accident, and when this political culture was adopted by the political elites of the Middle East, its effects were truly devastating.

In comparing the French and American Revolutions, Hannah Arendt observed that one of the main reasons why the American Revolution succeeded in setting up a stable political body was the Americans' willingness to learn from the failures and dangerous deviations of the French Revolution:

> It was not the fact of revolution but its disastrous course, and the collapse of the French Republic, which eventually led to the severance of the strong spiritual and political ties between America and Europe that had prevailed all through the seventeenth and eighteenth centuries.[65]

As Arendt noted, one of the lessons the founding fathers of American Republicanism learnt from the French Revolution was that the use of *la terreur* as a means to *le bonheur* could send revolutions to their doom. The other lesson was that establishing a new body politic is impossible if the masses are loaded down with misery and/or marginalised within the political sphere.[66]

This is not to suggest that the pseudo-secular experiences of the Middle East were merely mechanical reproductions of the model of the French Revolution, or indeed, of its fascist or communist counterparts. Secularisation in the Middle East reproduced only certain despotic aspects of those models. Thus, while the French Revolution paved the path for despotism, it also eventually led to a strengthening of civil society and democracy. Turkish Kemalism, Iraqi and Syrian Ba'thism, Egyptian Nasserism and Tunisian Bourguibism are all instances of Middle Eastern secularism, which not only turned to French Jacobinism for inspiration, but extended its despotic tendencies under the influence of more recent forms of totalitarianism, including fascism and Stalinism.

Just as the American Revolution learned from the bitter failure of its French predecessor, Middle Eastern secularists would do well to learn from the breakdown and collapse of their own experiments in the nineteenth century. They should also study the failure of French *laïcité*, as well as the successes of the American and the Anglo-Saxon experiences. In my view, Arab and Muslim secularists need to absorb three key lessons.

First, politics is in essence the art of consensus-building and civil reconciliation, and should not generate political or cultural disintegration. The use of state machinery against the masses with the aim of destroying civil society – as has been done in the Middle East – deprives politics of its meaning and function. In addition, when politics lacks the ability to bind and govern people in a 'rational civil' manner, ruling becomes impossible. Politics can be an expression of the ingenuity of human beings, but it can also expose the worst in us and bring out in us the most savage of beasts.

Second, politics is not a laboratory where the recipes of radical elites may be tested, or where the impossible can be made possible. Politics is the rational administration of the possible, and what delineates the boundaries of the possible and impossible are the economic resources at the disposal of a given society, combined with its culture and its citizens' capacity for activity and creativity. Arab and Muslim 'secularists' (or *laïques*) have to understand that no society is a *tabula rasa*, bereft of history. Every society holds in its fabric a culture and a set of institutions, and any process of change must be congruent with these symbolic and institutional channels.

Third, politics, as Arendt pointed out, is the rational governance of the community and the binding of its members. Any political order that isolates its citizens from one another and becomes alienated from them degenerates into despotism, and destroys the communicative structure that helps to sustain power. This is the root of the crisis facing secularists in the Middle East, who function in isolation from their communities, even waging war against them. This has transformed politics into a game of adjusting and monopolising the means of violence and discipline.

The bureaucratisation of religion

Although neutrality should be a fundamental element in secularity's relationship with religion, secularists in the Middle East have been anti-religious on the whole. Attempting to impose full control over religious institutions and symbols, they have even tried to monopolise the right to interpret particular doctrines and texts. Thus, along with material power, the 'world of symbols' has been seized upon and submitted to the authority of the state elites, while the majority of the population has been excluded and marginalised.[67] As pointed out by Pierre Bourdieu, 'symbolic capital' is no less important than material capital. Not only have state elites attempted to limit and control religious practices, they have tried to present themselves as the sole representatives of modernity. In this process, notions of civil society, progress, rationalism, etc. have been deployed to hide the true despotic nature of these regimes.

The secularist states often found themselves playing a double game: to reinforce their legitimacy among the masses and weaken Islamist opposition, they turned into guardians of the faith; and to market themselves abroad, and to weaken their liberal and leftist opponents, the states claimed to be agents of modernity.

In the process, the elites recruited some who may once have been in the opposition, but who found themselves exhausted by tyranny and punishment. Recruitment became a game of bribery where elites were bought off by economic and political privileges that should remain the exclusive property of the state. The nature of the elites constantly changes skins, shifts camps and trades slogans in accordance with its despotic needs, and with the demands of the market. Such is the military junta in Algeria, which once declared itself the protector of socialism; but after the collapse of its communist allies, this same ruling elite began to portray itself as a guardian of 'democracy' and 'civil society'.

Most peculiar of all is the junta's censorship of the democratic process in the name of 'democracy'. Algeria seems to be following in the steps of the army in Turkey, which launched coups against elected governments, supposedly in support of the mighty cause of 'secularism' and 'democracy'.

In these ways, the concept of *laïcité* adopted in the Middle East – particularly in Turkey and North Africa – bears the stamps of Jacobin influence. State powers annexed religion for their own purposes. Islam was transformed into a state department, the *'ulama* its minor civil servants. Imams were appointed by the state, which administered their affairs and even dictated the content of Friday sermons.[68] The militant *laïcité* of Atatürk in Turkey and Bourguiba in Tunisia waged war against religious institutions and symbols in the name of 'progress' and 'enlightenment'. The state also began to intervene in the private sphere, at the very heart of individual freedoms, by imposing certain codes of conduct and dress by force and prohibiting others. For example, in clear violation of the fundamental principle of individual freedom, men were prohibited from wearing headgear and beards while veils were prohibited for women.

The major paradox in secularisation as it took hold in the land of Islam was its tendency to write off religious institutions and symbols as mere illusions and fantasies, all the while imposing itself as the official guardian of religion, and from which it claimed to derive its legitimacy. An excerpt from a speech Atatürk delivered in August 1925 illustrates the kind of militancy that was typical of the project: 'In any case, the superstitions dwelling in people's minds will be completely driven out, for as long as they are not expelled, it will not be possible to bring the light of truth into men's minds.'[69] To provide a more recent example, General Ben Ali, Tunisian president from 1987 to 2011, was head of one of the most radically secularist regimes in the Arab region. Ben Ali was designated by his ruling party and propaganda machine as the protector of the sanctuary of the nation and of religion (*'hami hima al-wattan wa ad-din'*), and insisted that the state was the only authority in charge of religion.

Militant secularism in North Africa and Turkey is highly puritan in nature. This has manifested in successive religious cleansing campaigns, trying to bring 'errant' populations in line with a solid and homogeneous secularity. Herein lies a clear contradiction: the secularist elites, while attacking Islam and its symbols, are adamant that religious activities or interpretations other than those ratified by state can never be tolerated, and must be targeted and punished in the name of heresy. What has emerged is a kind of autocracy or, to use a term coined by Rachid Ghannouchi, a 'secular theocracy'.[70]

The nationalisation of religion forms part of a wider project aimed at nationalising and constraining the whole of society within the control of an elitist state. In these conditions, the state is invariably reduced to generating blind violence while attempting to maintain a façade of pluralism and civil institutions. Civil society is incorporated and absorbed into the state machinery. Mosques, endowments, courts, religious institutes, trade unions, parties, charities, schools, the press, all are seized. In the end, the entire system tends to be reduced to the person of the leader. That is, the state becomes the private property of the leader who does not hesitate to declare, 'I am the state' in the fashion of absolute monarchies.[71]

The dominant trait of the post-colonial secular state in the Arab–Islamic world was that it attempted to harness religion and turn it into a political ideology. This resulted instead in the nationalisation of the religious sphere and the marginalisation of the masses. The pseudo-secularisation that went hand in hand with pseudo-modernisation meant nothing more than the systematic destruction of civil society – both its traditional and modern components – and the installation of despotic states. Not content with being just its manager and security guard, the state entered forcefully into society, penetrating the domestic sphere and invading citizens' privacy. According to one analyst, state strategy 'was to break the fabric of traditional society by taking away its monopoly of the cellular base. By changing family law, the state was reaching into the deepest and most hidden psycho-anthropological strata of society.'[72]

In my view, two key factors have linked secularism in modern Arab–Islamic history with exclusion rather than inclusion. First, as already explained, its anti-religious claims and strategies led to conflict between the secular elites who were armed with the tools of state repression and the vast majority of society and social institutions that were marginalised by the state. Second, secularism in the Middle East has been associated with fanatical nationalism that has great difficulty dealing with the region's ethnic and linguistic diversity.[73] The secular faces of Arab nationalism and Kemalist Turkism are essentially chauvinistic, having been influenced by race-riddled western tradition. Thus, religious cleansing has been deemed necessary to protect a closed secularism, and ethnic cleansing has often followed swiftly thereafter, having been legitimised as the only way of preserving the 'purity' of the nation in the face of otherness. The case of the Kurds and other ethnic minorities under the secular regimes in Turkey and Iraq are patent illustrations of this. What complicates the situation is that such exclusions take place in a region that accommodated a profusion of ethnic and religious diversity in the past. A simple comparison of religious and ethnic tolerance in the so-called modern secular national states and the traditional sultanates would favour the latter.

Of course, secularity in the west has not always been associated with religious and ethnic tolerance, or with democracy, but it has generally provided certain fundamental conditions for the integration and inclusion of segmental forces that religious monarchies had excluded. Thus the likes of the Jews in Poland and the Huguenots in France ceased to be legally inferior when 'citizens' replaced 'believers'. However, in the Middle East, secularisation has led to massive social disintegration and disarray, creating a deep dichotomy between the elites and the masses similar to those created by colonial administrations and the apartheid regime in South Africa. The frightening face of Middle Eastern secularism was not necessarily generated by secularity *per se* (if there is such a thing as secularity in itself), but by the region's religious and historical context and the way in which secularity came to function.

Generally speaking, the emergence of secularism in Europe and America was associated with the introduction of new political concepts such as religious tolerance, social concord, reconciliation and the neutrality of the state. This was related to the historical context in which these secularisms emerged, and which had been characterised by religious and sectarian schisms. In the Middle East, secularism did not represent a concrete solution to real problems experienced by a majority of citizens. Instead it was inherited from imperialism and imposed by the post-colonial political elite.

For Syrian sociologist Burhan Ghalioun, Arab secularities that are commonly described in the west as 'progressive' are dogmatic and politically despotic. He explained that, in the Arab world, *laïcité* has been 'transformed into a *sign* of modernity, assumed as a second identity by *minority* social groups. Laicism is increasingly used to justify exclusion and legitimise authoritarian power.'[74] Accordingly, Ghalioun declared that what is needed is to 'laïciser la laïcité'. He stated that

> when a state monopolises the right of reference to the divine word, assigns to itself the role of reforming religion, intervenes in the interpretation of the text, dictates to the imams of the mosques Friday sermons and claims itself protector of the true faith, it is the first to betray the *laïque* attitude.[75]

The solution, for Ghalioun, lies in adopting an open project of secularisation that goes beyond its anti-religious sentiments and reinforces the link between secularism and democratisation, because 'laicisation and secularisation without democratisation concretely signify confessionalisation and tribalisation of political life and power'.[76]

Ghalioun calls for 'la démocratisation de la laïcité' but, to my mind, *laïcité* holds within it many despotic elements that are not easily overcome. A more appropriate aim would be 'la de-laïcisation de la laïcité'. The democratisation of secularism may be attainable only if the latter relinquishes its radical inclinations and strong étatisme. But then it could hardly be called *laïcité*. One of the obvious symptoms of the rigidity of French secularism is its inability to adapt to the multiculturalism and multi-ethnicism that now characterise French society.

To address the hypocrisy of Arab secularists 'who claim the right to meddle with Islam under the guise of reform and progress, while they wish for its ruin', Tunisian scholar Hichem Djait proposed what he called an open secularity that is not anti-Islamic in its aspirations and attitudes.[77] However, Djait's proposal is controversial, even self-defeating. He suggested that Islam should remain the official religion of the state, and that the state should be responsible for its protection and maintenance – the state being historical self-consciousness in the Hegelian sense of the term – yet without interfering in religious affairs. Islam, he maintained, concerns the entire *ummah*, both past and present, and is thus greater than any state. Further, Djait said, 'Islam is still an active concrete force, deeply entangled in Muslim society, which it traverses from one edge to the other'.[78] In other words, Islam is a reality to which one cannot turn a blind eye, even though it is, in some ways, strangely unsuited to the spirit of our age. At the same time, Djait suggested that to enter the modern age, reason needs to liberate itself from religion, which he sees as the soul of a still-infant humanity. He argued, however, that reason cannot be freed from religion by glossing over it as positivists do, but by passing through its very own gates – that is, through a process of internal religious reform. This apparent contradiction is due to Djait's own veneration of, and devotion to, Islam (he is an expert on Islamic history) combined with his positivistic faith in secularism as the expression of history's destiny. But can any state reconcile its claim to having Islam as its official religion, and being its guardian, with the desire to emancipate itself from religion?

Aware of the inherent hostility of Muslims towards secularity, and of secularism's affinities with despotism, Moroccan philosopher Mohammed 'Abed al-Jabri called for the term 'secularity' to be forsaken in favour of the word 'democracy'. He argued that the defect in Middle Eastern secular states lies in the absence of political freedom and tolerance, and in the general climate of despotism. For him, the answers should be sought in democratisation. In his endeavour to avoid the negative connotations of secularity, al-Jabri appears to have overlooked the real issue. That is, his emphasis on democracy does not address the difficulty, since the problem is secularism itself.[79]

In my view, the principal problem confronting Muslim societies is not so much the emancipation of the state from the dominance of religious institutions. With the exception of Shia Islam, no official religious establishment proclaims itself the custodian of the faith. The problem is how to emancipate religion from the political body of the state and its elites. Contrary to Djait's proposal for the state to be religion's guardian and thereby gain the upper hand over it, I would argue that the solution lies in ensuring the neutrality of the state towards religion. What I understand by neutrality is the restriction of the state's jurisdiction over society, confining it to ensuring the well-being of its citizens. In my view, the state should have no authority over its citizens' beliefs, religious practices, interpretations, or institutions. Religion and symbolic culture should belong to society at large. This understanding of the state and society has greater potential to restrict the role of the state and free up the internal development of society. A state responsible for the governance of a Muslim society must respect all its citizens' religious commitments and beliefs, and refrain from sectarianism and fanaticism. The state's ideological identity can be determined by a society's historical evolution, as well as its embedded cultures, symbols and norms, which inevitably include reflections of the state's role in shaping these features.

Some might see this as a Jeffersonian solution to the problem of the relationship between the religious and the political, and my proposal might coincide with the American model of secularisation in some respects. However, I see it as being authentic to Islamic history – stretching back to the Abbasid dynasty's rebellion, when a large number of enlightened Muslim scholars stood up to the despotic tendencies of the Muslim state that was attempting to impose a particular school of thought as the official ideology. In that instance, scholars called on the state to abide by the restrictions of the *shari'ah* and entrust the religious sphere to the care of the *ummah* and its imams.

I also have deep reservations about using the term 'secular' in relation to my proposal, for two reasons. First, as I have shown, the term 'secular' is intensely controversial and haunted by dualisms inherited from the Christian tradition (the likes of worldly/otherworldly, spiritual/temporal, ecclesiastical/secular, etc.) that are incompatible with the Islamic worldview, and its founding principle of organic unity. Second, given the historical context from which political secularisation emerged, no state has ever been entirely neutral in relation to religion and many states have served as catalysts of secularisation. In fact, one of the contradictions inherent in secularism is its overwhelmingly anti-religious, even atheistic, tendencies, even as it calls for neutrality towards religion.

Secularism and democracy

Perhaps one of the most sacred equations in western academic circles is that no secularism means no democracy. For the west, 'secularity conventionally implies openness to reason, willingness to compromise, freedom from bigotry, and the institutional separation of church and state'.[80] However, the bitter reality that most secularists prefer to overlook is that some of the most despotic regimes in the Middle East are the most 'secular'. Regimes in Syria, Iraq, Turkey, Algeria and Tunisia testify to this. The more traditional regimes such as those in Morocco, Jordan, Yemen, Kuwait and Lebanon have largely been more capable of political openness and democratisation. This is not to say that these countries are democratic, but they are less despotic and more flexible in their relation to their citizens. It seems, therefore, that the choice open to Muslim states at present is not between democracy and despotism, but between full-scale and semi-despotism.

In the Islamic world, secularism is perceived as a generator of social disintegration and political disarray, and has proven itself unable to guarantee democratisation. Perceived as fostering fatalism and blind loyalty, Islamic culture is often condemned by writers such as Bernard Lewis and Samuel P Huntington as the principal obstacle to democratisation. This view is prevalent in the west not only because it seeks to establish the cultural essentialism that preaches the superiority of western culture, but because it also overlooks the real obstacles to democratisation. This thesis happily ignores the socio-political structure of Muslim societies, the role of regional and international stakeholders, and the fact that many of the political elites inherited their power and status from the roles they were given during the colonial and post-colonial eras.

Even if we accept that culture plays a central role in furthering or hindering democratisation in the Middle East, culture can never be static or closed *per se*; it always remains subject to legitimisation and interpretation. Nevertheless, many western intellectuals appear intent on labelling Islam as the source of all stagnation, as a culture that respects 'the sovereignty of God' while sacrificing 'the sovereignty of human beings'. Islamic resurgence is seen as anti-democratic *par excellence*, leaving followers to choose between being a Muslim or a democrat, as if the two camps are destined always to diverge.

The main weakness of this view is its disregard for the activation and renovation of modern Islamic thought, and for Islam's ability to find alternative ways of expressing political modernity. Islam is moulded by different strategies of interpretation and conduct, and these are fed by the different conditions in which its followers find themselves. If we consider the Islamic map as a whole, it is evident that anti-democratic movements are in the minority. Apart from marginal tendencies such as the Salafi movement or Hizb ut-Tahrir, mainstream Islamic revivalism is moving towards democracy.

As John Esposito and John Voll have noted, the two most important issues relating to this modern Islamic resurgence are the 'potential democratic resources of the Islamic tradition and the ability of the new Islamic movements to operate effectively to meet the demands of both Islamic authenticity and popular democratic participation'.[81] Since its encounter with western political liberalism, modern political Islamic thought has sought to revive those Islamic political traditions and notions that can be judged compatible with democracy. Among these are notions such as *shura* (consultation), *'adl* (justice) and *shari'ah* (legislation).

The nineteenth-century pioneers of this intellectual tradition range from al-Tahtawi, Khayr al-Din and Ibn Abi Diyaf to al-Afghani and 'Abduh. Its contemporary disciples have not been content with merely reconciling Islam with democracy, but are going as far as deconstructing liberalism, so as to be able to distinguish democracy as a mechanism for regulation from its ethical and philosophical roots. Democratic mechanisms, they have argued, have to be redesigned and synthesised with inherited local civil mechanisms. The product of this synthesis is referred to as 'Islamic democracy', and the leading figures behind this project are Tunisian intellectual Rachid Ghannouchi and Egyptian jurist Tariq al-Bishri.

Naturally, Islam's political functions have varied from one context to another. In Saudi Arabia, for example, Islam has been used as a means of legitimising a kind of 'religious monarchy'; in Malaysia it has been used to catalyse a process of democratisation. Indeed, even within the borders of one country, Islam can manifest in different ways. Such is the case in Iran where two political tendencies are polarised. A democratic Islamic tendency, led by President Mohammad Khatami, has called for individual and public liberties, political pluralism, power-sharing, and women's participation in public life; this exists side by side with a conservative movement that holds to the principle of *velayat-e-faqih* as the foundation of autocratic rule.

In western political and sociological discourse, the emergence of secularism is associated with what John Rawls describes as the setting up of 'overlapping consensus'.[82] Western secularity is linked, as Michael Sandel pointed out, to the neutrality of the state in relation to religious sectarianism, and the establishment of political consensus among the various religious and political forces. This creates a solid connection between secularity and democracy. However, what Rawls, Sandel and others have overlooked is that, in other historical and cultural circumstances, secularism can produce and support despotism instead of democratic change. This was and still is the case in the Middle East. Furthermore, rather than rational and civil consensus, secularism can, in certain conditions, generate socio-political fragmentation. Indeed, secularity as a phenomenon is probably just as complex as any religion, and the world would do well to be wary of simplistic stereotypes.

4

Max Weber on Islam

The Islam of today is substantially the Islam we have seen throughout history. Swathed in the bands of the Coran, the Moslem faith, unlike the Christian, is powerless to adapt…to varying time and place, keep pace with the march of humanity, direct and purify the social life and elevate mankind.

– Sir William Muir, *The Caliphate*, p. 598

Although Max Weber is not best known for his writings on Islam, his work on the subject, albeit fragmented and dispersed, continues to exert a powerful influence, and his views on the subject of world religions are often invoked both implicitly and explicitly in analyses of Islam and the Islamic world. Weber's perceptions of Islam and Muslim societies as resistant to modernisation because of their inherent rigidity, social stagnation, political despotism and a lack of intellectual rationalisation continue to dominate western intellectual, academic and popular discourse. Despite its striking superficiality, Weber's influence has been devastating. Weber's notions of cultural and comparative sociology shifted the Orientalist tradition (which until then had been confined to the margins of academia) into the very heart of the academy. This meant that even those entirely unfamiliar with Islam felt empowered to make use of the concepts that Weber placed at their disposal, and Weber's reading of Islam remains strongly active in the dominant 'narratives' in western academic, intellectual, political and cultural discourse. My aim in this chapter is to unveil the shortcomings in Weber's view of Islam, and to call into question the whole body of knowledge elaborated first by Orientalists and then institutionalised by Weber.

The first point to make is that Weber made no systematic study of Islam. He died before his project on the comparative sociology of religion was completed. His views on Islam remained fragmented and are dispersed throughout his work on comparative sociology. His ideas were deeply influenced by his preoccupation with the relationship between religious belief and the emergence of capitalism. Weber's thesis of the Protestant work ethic can be fully comprehended only if we place it in the context of his interest in the genealogy of western rationality. As he admitted, his first concern was 'to work out and to explain genetically the special peculiarity of Occidental rationalism, and within this field that of the modern Occidental form'.[1]

Underlying Weber's work is the notion that the modern west's peculiar success is encapsulated in the historical process of rationalisation, and that this finds its fullest expression in modern capitalism and the bureaucratic institutions of the modern state. Weber's interest in the east, therefore, was primarily directed towards what he viewed as the intellectual and historical failure of Oriental and, more specifically, Islamic culture. At the heart of Weber's reading of Islamic history lay the contrast between the 'rational and dynamic' Occident versus the arbitrary and unstable political and economic conditions of the Orient. By setting up this dualism, Weber simply echoed the view that dominated nineteenth-century discourse. By highlighting the failures of other cultures, Weber hoped to demonstrate, implicitly and explicitly, the triumph of the west.

What is astonishing is the contrast between his rigorous examination of western history, which reveals his cognition of the complexity of the subject, and the cursory, simplistic and essentialist treatment he gave the Islamic world. Weber seems to have merely accepted and endorsed medieval Christian and classical stereotypes, thereby bestowing a degree of 'scientific' legitimacy on these in the name of comparative sociology.

Rationalisation

Rationalisation is a key and complex term that infuses the bulk of Weber's writings. One of its crucial facets refers to the triumph of purposive and calculative rationality over religious and teleological worldviews. The rationalisation of a society's worldview and conduct denotes a process whereby everything becomes instrumentally calculated and anticipated, and is eventually stripped of any teleological significance. For Weber, rationalisation is also a crucial aspect of any process of change in modern societies, and cognition is, in turn, central to rationalisation. As Talcott Parsons pointed out, rationalisation is the key conception through which cultures define their religious situation, and through which the sociology of religion must understand cultural definitions of a given situation.[2] Within this analytical framework, Weber treated the development of modern western worldviews as the vanguard of a general evolutionary trend.

As Weber contended in *The Protestant Ethic and the Spirit of Capitalism*, capitalism has existed in various societies, from Babylon to ancient Egypt, China and India, as well as in medieval Europe. Only in the modern west, however, has capitalism become associated with the rational organisation of labour, which, according to Weber, implies the routinised, calculated administration of continuously functioning enterprises. Weber also noted that modern capitalism would also be impossible without the separation of households from enterprises, and the emergence of new forms of accountability related to this.[3]

Islam as a warrior religion

Weber argued that prophets and priests are the force behind the systematisation and rationalisation of religious ethics. The shift from mystagogue to prophet is the hallmark of rationalisation within religious development. By a prophet, Weber meant 'a purely individual bearer of charisma who, by virtue of his mission, proclaims a religious doctrine of divine commandment'.[4] Weber insisted that charisma is the principal catalyst of movement and change in traditional societies, and that the charismatic figure stands in the vanguard of any process of change. To this, Weber added another significant factor that he believed determined the evolution of religious ethics: 'the laity whom prophets and priests seek to influence in an ethical direction'. He argued that the transformation of religious messages by the laity, as 'social carriers of religion', heralds the institutionalisation of the spontaneous charismatic force of a prophet.[5] That is, a prophet's energy becomes objectified in the community of believers created by lay disciples. Weber described this process as the routinisation of religion, and added that charismatic leaders are successful only when their messages are spread by powerful social groups that have the ability to refashion religious doctrines in relation to their own social ties and interests. Weber stressed the importance of success as a necessary condition for the preservation of charismatic authority. If such leaders begin to fail, they tend to think their gods are abandoning them, or that their powers are failing, and their authority is subsequently reduced.[6]

Islam, Weber observed, was the product of Near Eastern monotheism in which Jewish and Christian elements played a significant part, but which accommodated itself to the world in a unique way. That is, in Makkah, Islam developed a pietistic urban eschatology but, following the migration of the Prophet Muhammad and his companions to Madinah, the religion transformed 'from its pristine form into a national Arabic warrior religion'.[7] Islam's deviation from a prophetic into a warrior religion, Weber contended, was largely due to its move from the commercial urban context of Makkah, to Madinah, which was surrounded by Bedouin warrior culture.

Weber argued that 'the class of warrior nobles, and indeed feudal powers generally, have not readily become the carriers of a rational religious ethic',[8] and noted that, in Islam, religious promises became connected with war, and that the motivation behind its religious commandments was not conversion but war. From this analysis, Weber identified Islam with war and material interests, placing considerable emphasis on Muslims' neglect of the notion of salvation. Weber went so far as to claim that Muslims accepted the principle of tolerance for other religions – and especially of Christians or the 'People of the Book' – only because they could derive benefits from this in the form of taxation and tributes.

In the development of these ideas, Weber was considerably influenced by the views of Carl Heinrich Becker, his colleague and close friend, whose views were broadly representative of classical nineteenth-century German Orientalism.[9] Ignác Goldziher, whose views can be classified within the same framework, proclaimed that the object of Muhammad's mission was to replace the basic *jahiliyyah* (pre-Islamic) morality of *muru'ah* (which included values such as courage, generosity and honour) with much broader religious ideals and teachings. Islam, he contended, availed itself of worldly means to fulfil its goal of establishing a kingdom in this world. Thus, Islam was seen as a secularised religion, primarily shaped by politics and worldly interests. According to Weber, Islam emerged first as a moral revolution against Arabian values, but later turned into a 'warrior religion'. Historically speaking, Islam was perceived to have swallowed the Arab mentality that prevailed during the Prophet's time, and which was based on aggression and conquest.[10]

Weber maintained that Islamic teachings on wealth, usury and work preclude economic development and the rational accumulation of wealth. He also argued that Islam did not form a basis for the formation of states, nor were its doctrines the source of its expansion and success. For Weber, the spread of Islam was driven by Arab tribesmen's yearnings for political and economic power, and their use of 'religion' to legitimise their interests. The conversion of conquered peoples was accounted for by their desire to join the ruling group and escape taxation.[11]

Weber also depicted Islam as a religion governed by a hedonistic spirit, and a love of luxury and property. According to him, Muslims view the luxuries of the material world with pleasure, and their attitude is to enjoy rather than accumulate wealth. Indeed, as Weber noted, the role wealth plays in Islam 'is the most opposite to the role played by wealth in the Puritan religion'.[12] Muhammad 'stands in the extreme opposition to any puritan economic ethic and thoroughly corresponds with the feudal conception of status'.[13]

Weber argued that two important social groups blocked the ascetic tendency that did emerge in Makkah. The first were warriors, who acted as the principal social carriers of Islam. The second group emerged later, and consisted largely of the Sufi brotherhoods who developed a mystical practice. For Weber, the warriors turned the religious quest for salvation into a territorial adventure, and tendencies towards Islamic asceticism were incorporated into a military caste. The Sufis later introduced magical and 'orgiastic' elements into Islam, which watered down its monotheistic features.[14] According to Weber, these two tendencies left their mark on Islam, turning it into little more than a weak and feeble cult.

Islam and Oriental despotism

Weber provided an account of what he described as 'the stagnation of pre-capitalistic Oriental societies' based on what he saw as their patrimonial political structure and stagnant mode of production. He held that while feudalism had generated the necessary conditions for capitalist development in Europe, Oriental societies were controlled by social structures that precluded any real historical change. For Weber, these societies lacked class struggle, private property, free cities and abstract legal structures. Patrimonial domination was said to make political, economic and legal relations unstable and arbitrary or, to use Weber's term, 'irrational'. Weber often contrasted the social condition of feudal Europe, which he argued had guaranteed proper rights, with the prebendal feudalism and patrimonialism of the Orient, which he said maximised arbitrariness. For Weber, the principal features of Islamic history are the absence of towns, arbitrary law, and state interference in trade.[15] For Weber, Islam 'stands in extreme opposition to any puritan economic ethic', and therefore, as incompatible with capitalism.[16]

It is worth noting that Weber and Karl Marx shared the view that Oriental society combined enduring social structures with periodic dynastic political change. Weber tended to identify the political history of Islam with the model of the 'sultanate state', which he deemed to be the epitome of absolutism, 'where patrimonial authority lays primary stress on the sphere of arbitrary will, free of traditional limitations, it will be called "Sultanism"'.[17] The problem with Sultanism, Weber claimed, is its patrimonial bureaucracy that monopolises land ownership and arbitrarily oppresses its subjects. In addition, he argued that this type of government is incapable of controlling the political encroachment of a mercenary army.

Islamic feudalism was referred to by Weber as 'prebendalism', because it lacks any notion of property rights and is associated with patrimony. For Weber, prebendalism implies that a set of territorial rights lie in the hands of landlords who lack a feudal ideology. This he contrasted with European feudalism, under which the concepts of freedom of the city and legal rationality apparently flourished. Implicit in this argument is the view that Islam's historical failure – represented in the shift from feudalism to prebendalism – is indistinguishable from its epistemological and ideological failures, and that both result from an absence of rationality.

This analysis of the sultanate state was indicative of Weber's profound ignorance of Islam's political history – his knowledge was confined to the Mamluk and Ottoman models of power. Even if we were to accept Weber's typology of a sultanate state as the most arbitrary type of rulership, it would still be deeply illogical to attempt a reading of the long and complex political history of Islam on the basis of the sultanate state, which was a relatively recent historical construct.

Weber and Marx both believed in the ever-increasing rationalisation and efficiency of the capitalist system, albeit for different reasons. While Weber considered capitalism to be humanity's inescapable destiny, he saw it as a dead-end, leading no further than the 'cage of bondage', arguing that freedom would be demolished by bureaucracy and that religious enthusiasm would destroy itself in a 'cold calculating rationality'.[18] Marx looked beyond capitalism, believing it to be a progressive yet transitory period. Nonetheless, Weber and Marx agreed that Oriental societies were socially 'reactionary', 'stagnant' and 'regressive'. There is a clear similarity between Weber's concept of prebendalism and Marx's theory of Asiatic modes of production. For Weber, western feudalism stimulated the development of capitalism, within which free cities, autonomous guilds, an independent legal profession, and free labour were able to flourish. In contrast, Oriental prebendalism inhibited, or at least slowed down, the pace of such development. Indeed, in *The Religion of India*, Weber merely recapitulated Marx's vision of Asian societies, where the absence of production, private ownership, and payment in kind were held accountable for their stagnation.[19]

Marx, on the other hand, commented on the contrast between the political instability of traditional Indian society and the massive 'unchangeableness' of its basic structures. He then extended this analysis to all of Asia. '*The simplicity of the organisation for production in these self-sufficing communities...supplies the key to the secret of the unchangeableness of Asiatic societies,*' Marx wrote in *Capital*.[20] Marx went so far as to conclude that 'Indian society has no history at all' and suggested that 'England has to fulfil a double mission in India: one destructive, the other regenerating the annihilation of old Asiatic society, and the laying of the material foundations of western society in Asia.'[21]

Of course, this view of Oriental socio-political structures as stagnant was not only held by Marx and Weber, but was prevalent in much western political thought. Hegel, for instance, believed that western political conditions – from the Greek period and the later emergence of Christianity – encouraged the development of self-consciousness and reflexivity while Oriental systems prevented the growth of individuality and freedom.[22]

It can be argued then that Weber simply invoked the classical Orientalist tradition, positing an ontological dualism between an Oriental world where despotism and social stagnation reigned, and an Occident filled with dynamism and democracy. Weber simply replicated the old western fiction of a despotic and irrational east vis-à-vis the solid, rational and free west, echoing the sharp dualism that can be traced back to the Greeks. The Aristotelian conception of 'Asiatic despotism' outlined in Chapter One was never relinquished. Instead, it was seized upon by modern Europe. Like Montesquieu, Mill, Hegel and Tocqueville, Weber divided the geographical map into a dynamic and progressive west and a stagnant east. Weber's approach to the east was very much in keeping with the general position on Orientalism, which directed its attention primarily to what was absent from eastern cultural systems so as to assert the singularity and superiority of the west.[23]

The city

Weber argued that to be a city in the full sense of the word, an urban area must possess the following five features: fortifications; markets; courts that administer a partially autonomous law; distinctively urban customs of association; and partial autonomy. Astonishingly, Weber then concluded that cities, in this sense, have existed only in Europe, never in Asia, and, in the Near East, only partially and for short periods of time.[24] In his analysis, Weber used European cities and the features they began to acquire in the fourteenth century as his model, and his definition is by no means value-free. His underlying preoccupation was to elucidate 'the western miracle', which he saw as being deeply connected to the emergence of 'rational', bureaucratic, industrial, modern Europe. He therefore accorded much significance to the kinds of bureaucratic organisation associated with the modern state, believing this to be an incarnation of rationality.

Muslim cities are indeed different from their European counterparts. Their order, although highly urbane in form, complex and varied in civil institutions, is not tightly associated with an overarching legislative core. Muslim cities also have distinctively urban forms of association, albeit without municipal institutions or municipal laws. This 'lack' does not signify stagnation or a lack of diversity. On the contrary, the source of the vitality and richness of traditional Muslim cities may lie in the very absence of such state apparatuses, which have allowed *ahli* (indigenous) societies to prosper, and to develop an array of diverse and efficient institutions.

Essentially, Weber attempted to accord universal validity to the Roman state as reproduced in its modern European form, and condemned Muslim and Asian cities for failing to conform to this idealised model. Weber paid no attention to the reality of Islamic cities or to their complex infrastructures and institutions. His primary preoccupation was with state bureaucracy as the historical incarnation of rationalism. This is apparent in his distinction between arbitrary law-making on the one hand and legal judgments that are logically derived from general laws on the other. In cases of what Weber termed 'substantively irrational law', that is where judgments are based on religion, emotion or politics, he maintained that judges do not abide by general abstract principles, but judge each case using their own purely individual and arbitrary criteria.[25]

In fact, the weak role of state apparatuses in Muslim societies can largely be accounted for by the Islamic worldview. Indeed, as Hourani and Stern noted in their book *The Islamic City*, no incorporate intermediary exists between an individual believer and the community of believers.[26] That is, all believers stand as equals before the religious text, with which they all hold an open relationship, and a spirit of inclusive solidarity therefore tends to dominate Islamic social thought. This is not to deny that, since the first centuries of Islamic history, scholars have emerged as central authorities within Islamic social structures. Of course, intellectuals have been a vital part of the fabric of Muslim society, playing key roles in the mosques and schools that form its vibrant heart. Arguably, therefore, scholars can be said to represent the true consciousness and voice of Muslim cities. Furthermore, in Islamic states, the functions of organisation, integration and incorporation, which are performed by the state in the modern western model, were largely undertaken by the *shari'ah*, and this formed the basis on which allegiance was given to the state.

What is utterly lacking in Weber's reading of Islam was any recognition of the *shari'ah*'s role in city life, both on a moral and religious level, as well as in terms of Islam's historical development. Contrary to Weber's view, the birth of Islam was strongly connected to urbanisation. The migration of the Prophet Muhammad, and early 'carriers of religion' – to use Weber's term – from Makkah to Madinah was part of their search for an urban base. It was no accident that the birth of the first Islamic state was associated with the renaming of a city. The change of name from Yathrib to Madinah was fully expressive of the shift from life in the desert and into an urban (and more urbane) existence. In Arabic, the word *madinah* means city, and is synonymous with *tamaddun,* which denotes civility, as opposed to *tawahush* (savagery). Contrary to the view adopted by Weber, at the time of the Prophet, the social and cultural environment of Madinah was infinitely richer and more cultivated than that of Makkah.

Sayed Muhammad al-Attas captured the intimate and profoundly significant connection between the concepts of *din* (religion) and *madinah* (city), as well as the role played by believers, individually in relation to the former, and collectively in relation to the latter. That is, religion at its best is practicable only in organised societies, where it can be intimately involved in commercial life. As al-Attas noted, Madinah was thus named because it was there that true *din* was realised. The city of the Prophet was where *din* was lived out under his authority and jurisdiction. The city epitomised the Islamic socio-political order, and for many Muslim believers, cities remain the domain of their physical and spiritual activities.[27]

Now let us return to Weber's reading of *shari'ah*. The main weakness of the *shari'ah* in his eyes is that it is 'transcendental', super-historical and outside society; something that believers cannot but implement. This view remains overwhelmingly prevalent in western circles; *shari'ah* is regarded as an oppressive authority that crushes the human will and lies outside historical contingency. According to this view, to be a 'true Muslim' is to blindly obey the superpower of a God immanent in a super-historical scripture, and Islam is thus a fundamentalist religion *par excellence.* However, this reading is heedless of both the historicity of the religious text and the contingency of its historical embodiment. True, all Muslims see the Qur'an as the word of God as revealed through the last of God's messengers, and they believe in the scriptures of earlier monotheistic religions. However, most Muslims also believe in the power of *ijtihad*; that is, they believe in the value of intellectual efforts directed towards opening up new perspectives and fresh interpretations of a given subject, and that history has a role to play in throwing light on the religious text and religious praxis. In other words, there is some distance for Muslims between the primary source (the text) and the activity of understanding and interpreting the source.

A feature of the Islamic episteme that clearly reflects the contingency characteristic of knowledge of the 'original' sources is the diversity of Islamic schools of jurisprudence (*madhahib*) and their general acceptance as different expressions of *ijtihad* within the Islamic framework. As Brinkley Messick noted, *shari'ah* texts live 'in social relations, in human embodiers and interpretive articulations'.[28] In other words, *shari'ah* is open to *ijtihadi* interpretations within specific socio-historical conditions; it is not a set of abstract transcendental commandments that have to be passively implemented.

In addition, the ideal of egalitarianism in Islam opens the religious text to the whole of Muslim society, which renders it immanent among individuals and groups. This means that, in a sense, *shari'ah* lives within different levels of worldly activity, forming the basis of a kind of 'contractualism' within the general discourse of Muslim society. As Marshall Hodgson explained, contractualism is characteristic of *shari'ah* and of Islamic society in general.[29] Thus, the project that early Islam aimed to realise was the establishing of an egalitarian community of the faithful who would stand in opposition to the tribal and town-centred hierarchies of seventh-century Arabia. As Messick noted, this egalitarianism, an 'insistence that all...[are] on the same level before God is a fundamental presupposition running through *shari'ah* discourse, and is conventionally considered a hallmark of Islam itself'.[30]

Islam and rationalisation

Weber often insisted that Judaism and Islam are both essentially monotheistic; in some writings he posited a unity between the great religions of the 'monotheistic family'. As Weber saw them, the monotheistic religions are distinguished by their assumption of universalism – a notion that he saw as being at odds with the religions of the Far East that revolve around local gods. It seems, however, that his perception of the 'bond' between the monotheistic religions was little more than a passing notion for Weber. His more lasting view seems to have been that, while Islam shared some commonalities with Judaism and Christianity, it remained distinct because of its deficiencies in the field of metaphysical rationality.

Weber maintained that the scope that Islam allows for intellectual activity is narrower than that provided by Christianity, and that the development of an internal metaphysics was precluded by the emergence of a 'military aristocracy', while the popular Dervish faith proved utterly lacking in any tendencies towards rationalism. He attributed these deficiencies to Islam's feudal and anti-rational character, suggesting that Islam has never possessed the ethical or epistemological conditions necessary for the development of modern capitalism.[31] For Muslims, however, Islam's deviation from Judeo-Christian monotheism occurred as early as its prophetic era, and allowed their faith to accommodate itself to the world in a unique way. What I hope to show is that it is impossible to separate Islam's 'historical deficiency' from its philological foundations, since the two consolidate and complement one another.

As I indicated in Chapter Two, for Weber the rationalisation of religion meant the systematisation and intellectualisation of religious doctrine. He argued that as intellectualisation suppresses popular belief in magic, the world's processes become 'disenchanted' and lose their magical connotations. They simply 'are' and 'happen', but no longer signify anything beyond themselves. Consequently, a demand grows for the world, and the total fabric of life, to be subjected to order in a process that can be called 'rationalisation'.

For Weber, prophets (especially ethical prophets) were crucial in the shift towards metaphysical rationalisation. In discussing this concept, Weber distinguished between prophets and mystagogues. The latter seek to legitimise their position and claims in magical terms, while the former construct their worldviews in ethical terms. As Weber put it, mystagogues are not agents of rationalisation but of escape from the enigmatic problems of this world.[32] According to Weber, for a religion to be fully rationalised, the following five conditions must be met:

- First, 'sorcery' in its magical connotation has to be broken with, in favour of a new relationship between believers and the supernatural. This relationship takes the form of prayer, sacrifice and worship in the context of what Weber called a 'cult'. He distinguished cults from sorcery, in that cults introduce the concept of 'gods' into their internal doctrine as an alternative to the concept of 'demons'.

- Second, the institution of the 'priesthood' as distinct from 'practitioners of magic' must arise. Weber defined the priesthood as the 'specialisation of a particular group of persons in the continuous operation of cultic enterprise, permanently associated with particular norms, places and times and related to a specific social group'.[33] The rationalisation of metaphysical beliefs, Weber insisted, is usually missing in cults that have no priests. He believed that the full development of metaphysical rationalisation and ethical religion 'requires an independent and professionally trained priesthood, permanently occupied with the cult and with the practical problems involved in the cure of the souls'.[34]

- Third, the concept of an ethical God must exist. The view that God possesses ethical qualities, as Weber pointed out, is not exclusive to monotheism; it exists in varying degrees in magical religions too. However, Weber argued that in monotheistic religions this development had far-reaching consequences – giving rise to the notion of an omnipotent legislator God, who reigns over the whole cosmos, who vanquishes primitive natural and localised religions.

- Fourth, the notion of taboo must be rationalised. Weber maintained that the emergence of religious ethics does not signify a total rupture with magic-oriented culture. Rather, magical norms and practices such as taboos undergo a process of rationalisation and incorporation into a newly developed ethical religion. This ultimately results in 'a system of norms according to which certain actions are permanently constructed as religious abominations subject to sanctions'.[35] While Weber insisted that the norm of taboos is a necessary feature of any religion, he also maintained that economic rationalisation is impossible where taboos achieve a strong power and presence in the consciousness of the believer.

- Finally, magical ethics have to be transformed into doctrines on conscience, sin and salvation. According to Weber, the concept of salvation in ethical religions is linked to the problem of theodicy, which is the problem of how to understand physical pain and sin in moral terms. The problem of theodicy is central to Weber's sociology of religion, since the contrast between an ethical omnipotent God and the overwhelming presence of evil in the world has proven acutely difficult to solve. Only in ethical religions has the problem of evil found a consistent answer. In this problem lie the distinctive devotional pathways of world-flight (mysticism) and world-mastery religion (asceticism). A horror of sin drives religious consciousness either towards 'presence in this world' or to 'a flight to the other world'. Weber noted that the claim of salvation emerged to resolve the tension between the perfect, sacred world and the imperfect, profane world. He argued that Christianity had only resolved this tension with the rise of ascetic Protestantism, but maintained that it had still always been an ethical religion because salvation forms part of its genealogical foundations. In fact, Weber argued that the notion of salvation was what made Christianity distinct from the religions of the Far and Near East, which had never known such a concept.

Perhaps it is not surprising that Weber's typology of ethical rationalisation matches Christianity and, even more specifically, Calvinism. For Weber, Calvinism was the epitome of the rationalisation that had been integral to Christianity since its inception. Although elements of rationalisation are present in other religions (including Islam and the religions of the Far East), Weber insisted that only in Calvinism were these elements consistently connected within a theological system.[36]

For Weber, the rationalisation of religion was essentially about what he called the intellectualisation of theology. He argued that the early marriage between Christian theology and Hellenistic tradition underlined the uniqueness of Christianity, stating that: 'the full development of a systematic theology must be credited to Christianity under the influence of Hellenism'.[37]

The specificity of western culture that served as the bedrock of Weber's theories lay in two key factors. The first relates to the epistemological sophistication of the west by virtue of its highly systematised and rational thought. According to Weber, this derived mainly from the doctrines of Hellenism that were later incorporated into Christian theology. Although other religions have their theologies and dogmas, not all have as systematic a theology. Christianity alone came to incorporate Greek thought and adopted it to serve the purposes of its own dogma.[38]

The second factor is the emergence of rationalised social structures and institutions. Of these, the institutions related to legislation and administration are of particular importance. Westerners are highly familiar with the rationalisation of bureaucracy, whereby the most fundamental functions of everyday life 'come to be in the hands of technically, commercially and above all legally trained government officials'.[39] Modern western bureaucracy – the hallmark of rationalisation, according to Weber – is truly unprecedented. Its fundamental novelty lies in its infiltration into a wide range of institutions and all areas of culture. Indeed, for Weber, the evolution of modern civilisation was virtually identical with the development of bureaucratic organisations.[40]

Only in the west is the affinity between religious ethics and economic rationalism so clear. The astonishing parallels between certain exigencies of Calvinist theological logic and the logic of modern capitalism, Weber contended, is almost unprecedented, although such affinities have also come to light outside the western sphere. For Weber, Christianity's contribution to the construct of western culture was crucial in shaping both western thinking and western history. A related issue that interested Weber was the urban nature of Christianity, and the fact that its importance grew in direct proportion to the size of the urban communities it generated. In European history since the Middle Ages, loyalty to the Church, including to various sectarian movements, essentially developed in cities.

Weber held the following three factors responsible for the singularity of western Christianity:

- From its inception, Christianity seized on certain concepts that destroyed taboo barriers between kin groups, and provided the moral ground for non-mechanical social relations.
- Christianity lies behind the emergence of the concept of 'office', as embodied in church structures and later in the economic and political fields.
- Only under Christianity has the norm of a community as a 'compulsory organisation' with a specific function flourished.

On the basis that these were prerequisites for rationalisation, and that Islam is devoid of such elements, Weber ruled out the possibility of the rationalisation of Islam. What he saw as positively present in Christianity, he also saw as lacking in Islam. Thus Islam was posited as the negation of Christianity, as an 'empty' religion in which rationality cannot exist. Weber also pointed to the emergence of social carriers of religious norms in Islam as an indication of the absence of rationalisation, prompting French sociologist Raymond Aron to describe Weber's method of comparative sociology as a 'method of absence'.

Weber also deemed Islam to be a non-intellectual religion, arguing that in Islam 'only a few heterodox sects that possessed considerable influence at certain times displayed a distinctly intellectualistic character'.[41] In comparison to Judaism, he argued, Islam lacked the requirements of comprehensive knowledge of the law and intellectual training in casuistry. This, Weber argued, was because the model or 'ideal type' in Islam is the warrior and not the scholarly scribe as is the case in Judaism.

When contrasted with Christianity, Islam appeared to Weber to be a sensual religion that knew no quest for salvation. The spirit of mysticism was neglected by the warrior in favour of wealth, power and glory. Even when Weber acknowledged the existence of ascetic sects amongst Muslims, he thought these were only temporarily influential, mostly turning into 'fatalism'. Weber held that pre-determination – a key concept in Protestantism, which opened the gate to rationalisation in the western context – was, in Islam, transformed into a fatalism that circumscribes human freedom.

For Weber, another obstacle on the path of rationalisation for Islam was its 'only required dogma': that is, its pronouncement that Allah is the only God and Muhammad His messenger. This emphasis on God's presence suffocated human freedom or, as Weber put it, 'The god it taught was a lord of unlimited power, although merciful, the fulfilment of whose commandments was not beyond human power.'[42]

To conclude, Weber classified Islam within the general category of the otherworldly religions of the Orient, connecting the Far and the Near East under the typology of Oriental despotism. Although he recognised the existence of common elements between the great monotheistic religions, he seemed to see only an occasional convergence between Islam on the one hand and Judaism and Christianity on the other.[43]

Weber's limiting assumptions

Terminological baggage

The emergence of sociology can be perceived as signalling a shift away from theological and towards purely secular conceptions of the world. While this overlooks the solid correlation between the history of sociology – including the sociology of religion – and the long process of secularisation that extends back to the Renaissance, it can be argued that the founders of sociology transferred the grounds of religious validation from transcendence to immanence – from God's word to God's work. This formed a part of a general shift in the order of knowledge from the realms beyond to the here and now.

In the general context of positivism, religion became a mirror of the social order, and the task of the sociologist became to grasp the image in this mirror. Auguste Compte (1798–1857) offered a telling example of this when he spoke of 'physical sociology' as a synonym of physical nature, analogising the function of the sociologist with that of the physician. Armando Salvatore described this as the shift from the 'politics of beyond' to the 'politics of behind'. My point here is that sociology as a whole – and notably the sociology of religion – is founded on a single western narrative that introspected the secularisation of Christian theology. In many ways, the sociology of religion reinvented existing Judeo-Christian terminology in a secular context.

This is evident in Weberian terminology, which remained theological and Christian *par excellence*, and includes such notions as sin, salvation, theodicy, priests, alienation and charisma, as well as dualisms such as sacred/profane, worldly/otherworldly, etc. While one might think that these concepts and terms were 'neutralised' and 'domesticated' by sociology, they still carry theological and existential connotations. For example, an analysis of the word 'charisma', which is one of the key concepts in Weber's sociology of religion, is used in the New Testament to describe the great variety of divine gifts bestowed on the faithful as an indication of their status before the supernatural. Weber transferred this key term from Christian theology to political sociology to denote 'a general category of authority'.[44]

Concepts such as 'anomie', 'alienation' and 'charisma' remain products of the interchange between theology, humanistic philosophy and sociology, regardless of attempts to neutralise their meanings.[45] What is more, the limitations of Weberian concepts and terms are often overlooked when they are applied to other religions, and to Islam in particular. I am not trying to deny any link between different religions in the name of specificity. No doubt, Islam shares many features with other monotheistic religions; but it also parts company with these in many respects. What I want to stress is that all religions can be better understood in terms of their own internal tenets and references.

Certain notions in Weber's terminological baggage, the likes of sin and salvation for example, simply don't apply to Islam. There is no concept of original sin from which human beings need redemption, nor is there any such thing as alienation or estrangement from God in an evil world. Humanity, in the Islamic view, is not the product of original sin but has an existential role as God's vicegerent on Earth. The world is not seen as an iron cage from which we have to escape, but as the natural site of human activity. Islam is a truly *jihadi* religion, meaning that it seeks not to escape the complexity of the world but to face all the controversies of worldly affairs in the spirit of the 'here and now'.[46] It follows that the notion of theodicy is absent from Islam and, if one frees oneself from the cage of Weberian rationale, it becomes clear that this is not necessarily a sign of deficiency or weakness.

Weber himself pointed out that there is no tension in Islam between the sacred world of transcendence and the profane world of human emotion and reason, since the Islamic order is devoid of the notion of original sin. The problem is that Weber went on to categorise salvation as the ideal condition of the 'rationalisation of religion'. Of course, his own Christian paradigm and bias played a role in this. The dogmas of Christianity may have meant little to him, but 'no one has yet doubted that he was a Protestant, a Lutheran with a keen eye for Calvinist competition and someone who suffered from the split between the ethics of conscience and of responsibility'.[47] Weber's atheism remained Protestant in essence, and his worldview a secular Christian one. So although Weber wanted to provide an objective understanding of Protestantism, he seems to have been caught in a 'hermeneutic circle' in the sense that, in his reading of world religions, he ended up reinterpreting his own interpretive and secularised Protestantism.

A primary influence in Weber's formative years was the pietism of his mother and aunt, so his interest in religion was, in part, 'a coming to terms with his own biography, and what he said about religion is an expression of his own beliefs'.[48] Weber viewed Catholicism, for example, from a largely Protestant vantage point, and he used this same yardstick in his reading of world religions and when developing his typology of religion. He seems to have internalised the Christian dualism between secular and profane, worldly and otherworldly so deeply that any faith that did not display this was, in his eyes, either a 'non religion' or 'deviant'.

Weber was also deeply influenced by Kantian philosophy, which along with Calvinist theology, is deeply embedded in modern German hermeneutics. Kant offered the German worldview a comprehensive vision that was adopted into German culture and framed its development in the nineteenth century. As a result, generations of academically educated professionals were filled with the Kantian ethos. Weber was one of them. Kant adopted Christian morality and language within a secular framework in the name of 'civil religion' or practical reason. It is true that Weber rarely referred to Kant directly, but his epistemology and philosophy were formulated in the context of a revival of neo-Kantianism, especially the German New Kantian School.

Like Kant, Weber saw reason as a force for unification and organisation. He saw the world as emerging out of chaos, ready to be shaped by the powers of understanding and reason (or what he referred to as 'the worldview'). However, unlike Kant, Weber did not accept that reason and order are in tune with the divine. I believe Martin Albrow was correct in describing Weber's theory of interpretation as follows: 'There could be no faith in religion, the task of construction had to be started all over again.'[49] That Weber began with a Kantian frame of mind is evident in his claims relating to the rationalisation of the world, but he hoped to see the world organised through the power of the intellect and purged of its religious connotations. Essentially, Weber was a secular Christian thinker who had lost faith in doctrinal Christianity. As I noted in Chapter One, Weber was also strongly influenced by Nietzsche, particularly by Nietzsche's 'perspectivist' theory of meaning and morality. In my view, however, the Kantian framework remained the dominant one.

As noted in Chapter Two, a form of the word 'religion' is generally common to all the languages of European Christendom, and it derives from the Latin *religio*. This pre-Christian term for the cults and rituals of pagan Rome was Christianised by St Jerome in his Latin translation of the Bible.[50] The antinomy lies in Weber's adoption of a Roman Christian term to read world religions, heedless of the limits of this paradigm. For Weber, the Roman religion could be classified as a mature form of religiosity. As he put it, 'Roman religion remained *religio* (whether the word is derived etymologically from *religare* (to tie) or from *religere* (to consider), it denoted a tie with tested cultic formulae and a "consideration" of spirits (*numina*) of all types which are everywhere.'[51] This clearly revealed the limits of Weber's conceptual dictionary in dealing with other world religions. The typology *religio* is not necessarily applicable to other religions, and certainly not to the *din* of Islam. However, the typology was firmly established in Weber's mind and introspected in his heart; and all that remained was to evaluate other religions in terms of this model.

In the case of Islam, Weber seems to have faced acute difficulties with his categories. On the one hand, he classified Islam with Judaism and Christianity within the typology of monotheistic religion, but saw it as a very particular case, and as being clearly distinct from Roman *religio*. On the other hand, although Weber ended up labelling Islam as one of the Far Eastern 'world religions', he saw it as taking a very different form from other faiths in the category.

Weber's predicament underlines the general problem that confronts western thinkers when seeking suitable religious categories for Islam. Islam can be seen as neither 'eastern' nor 'western', neither Christian nor unequivocally non-Christian and, wherever it was placed, it remained bound to Europe by a long intimate, ambiguous and usually painful relationship.[52]

The dualism of east and west

Weber's comparative sociology of religion was not 'value-free', and the dichotomy between 'Occident' and 'Orient', between 'the worldly religions' of the west and the 'otherworldly religions' of the east governed and directed his work from beginning to end. This led him to contrast Islam with Judaism and Christianity, and to judge Islam as being inferior to Judaism and Christianity in decisive ways. In his cultural and geographical comparative studies, Weber posited an Occident imbued with rationality and 'order' against an Orient haunted with irrationality and political despotism linked to patrimonialism. Weber's approach was thus to emphasise the elements of rupture and discontinuity between world cultures and religions.

Weber's firm belief in the west's intellectual and geographical uniqueness, which he ascribed to the Greek intellectual tradition it inherited, is highly contentious. In Weber's work, Europe appears to be fully formed and fixed – 'metaphysically' determined as the location of reason and order in opposition to the world beyond it. Although Weber's approach was by no means straightforward or simple, its complexity and rigour is clearer in relation to his analysis of Europe.

What Weber failed to question was i) whether Europe is really an objective and fixed fact, or simply an amalgam of history, imagination and phantasm, without which there can be no such thing as identity, and ii) whether any geographical determination, with its bid to delineate definitive borders, can ever be isolated from the polarisation involved in politics and power play.

To less biased eyes, the notion of Europe is a historical construction, with its own particular narratives and development path. Europe was once little more than a noblewoman in Greek mythology (Europa) and later a vague geographical location. As Tomaz Mastinak showed, the concept of Europe developed through a slow historical process, in which the holy war waged by Latin Christians against Muslims was of crucial importance. Mastinak saw the Crusades as a key formative element in what was to become Europe, and judged them to have had a profound impact on western ideas and institutions by signalling 'the first western union' and the creation of a crusading army as a 'spectacular advance toward peace and unity'.[53]

It can be argued, therefore, that the image of the 'Muslim other' was necessary for the construction of the 'European self'. What is more, this image was never revisited and was reduced to mere medieval curiosity, but persists to the present day as a key element in the articulation and preservation of European identity. After Constantinople, the capital of the Byzantine Empire, fell into the hands of the Turks in 1453, Europe began to articulate its identity through the practice and imagination of ridding itself of the Turkish presence. This concept and process of cleansing seems to have been integral to the emergence of the notion of Europe. What emerged from its confrontation with the Ottoman Empire was a profound awareness of the fact that although its power was fragmented, a new collective entity, Europe, was coming into being, and its identity was in the process of formation.

Weber seems to have been unaware that the notions of the Occident and the Orient cannot be isolated from cultural imagination. They are ideas that have a history as well as a social and traditional imaginary. The two entities support and, to some extent, reflect one another so that without the 'Orient', the 'Occident' can have no meaning, and vice versa. As Edward Said noted, the 'Occidentalisation of the Occident', based on its geographical and cultural distinctiveness, occurred alongside the 'Orientalisation of the Orient'. We can conclude, therefore, that within the 'Orientalisation of the Orient' is the 'essentialisation' and 'ethno-centralisation' of the Occident.

Obviously politics and power struggles play crucial roles in moulding cultural identities and delineating geographical borders. For instance, geographically and culturally, Russia is part of Europe, but, within the climate of the Cold War, it was excluded from the European sphere and, as such, was designated part of 'the east'. Similarly, as heir to Constantinople – one of the greatest centres of power in European consciousness – Turkey has always been part of the European sphere, yet it remains decisively excluded from the European circle and cast as a purely Asiatic country.

While Weber recognised the long and labyrinthine roots of rationalisation in different world religions and diverse cultural spheres, he ended up reducing this process to a teleological march from the Greek miracle, via Christianity, to the modern secular west. True, he highlighted the part played by historical contingency in defining the face of the modern west, but for him, historical conditions seemed to unveil their efficacy only in relation to the Greek and Christian traditions. What Weber overlooked is that civilisations and cultures – including world religions – are never isolated. Their emergence and development testify to a complex movement of correlation and interaction, so that no culture emerges from a *tabula rasa*, and at any particular point in time, every culture is the product of an ongoing process of accumulation of symbolic heritage, much of which it shares with other cultures. In his *Muqaddimah*, Ibn Khaldun highlighted this general perspective by stressing the cyclical nature of human development.

If nothing exceptional and no cultural distinctiveness stands behind the ascendance of the modern west, what lies at the root of the power that it holds over the contemporary imagination? Hodgson attributed 'the great western transmutation' to the emergence and marriage of technology to an international hegemonic system that has been shaped by ascending European powers. In making his argument, he drew attention to the 'accidental character' of the process. Western technology has played a crucial role in transforming the world's economic, intellectual and social milieus. On the economic level, the technologies invented by modern Europeans led to the industrial revolution and later the 'agricultural revolution', which enabled a massive increase in productivity. On an intellectual level, the experimental science that began with Kepler and Galileo opened the infinite horizons of time and space, and led to the independent and exploratory philosophical culture of the Enlightenment. Socially, the ousting of feudalism led to the rise of bourgeois financial power.[54] Thus, from the beginning of the nineteenth century, and as a result of these developments, the modern west found itself in a position to dominate the whole globe, not only militarily, but politically and commercially as well. As Hodgson put it:

> European hegemony did not mean direct European world rule. What mattered was that both occupied ('colonial' or 'settled') areas and unoccupied (independent) areas were fairly rapidly caught up in a worldwide political and commercial system, the rules of which were made by, and for the advantage of, the Europeans and their overseas settlers.[55]

Weber's evolutionism

Although Weber clearly departed from evolutionism, he never rejected the idea of progress. That is, he shared the evolutionist conception of history as a gradual progress towards 'rationalisation', while rejecting its belief in progress. While Kant, for example, argued that 'the public use of one's reason must all times be free, and it alone can bring about enlightenment',[56] for Weber, only a few 'overgrown children' still believe this.[57] He argued that modernity, which implies a rationalisation of all personal and public conduct, is synonymous with bureaucratisation, and implicit in this is the pervasive institutionalisation of an 'iron cage'. Weber wrote that 'everywhere, houses of bureaucratic serfdom are being constructed and finished, the advance of bureaucracy seems irreversible'.[58] According to Weber, the 'iron cage' is a necessary condition of modernity and can be resisted only by resignation. Ultimately, therefore, Weber dismantled the connection between rationalisation and emancipation, which had long been entangled in the discourse of modernity. His pessimistic outlook on history drove him to see mechanical machinery as a metaphor for socio-political restriction and control. His own writings are dominated by mechanical terms such as 'cages', 'clogs' 'switch men' and 'tracks'. He noted also that in modernity, each individual becomes a 'little cog in the machine', and their only aspiration is to become 'a bigger cog':

> As terrible as the idea seems that the world might be full of nothing but professors – we would flee to the desert if that should happen – so much the more terrible is the idea that the world should be filled with nothing but those cogs who cling to a little post and strive for a somewhat greater one.

Weber concluded that 'this passion for bureaucratisation…is enough to drive one to despair'.[59] However, while his pessimism about modernity drove him to forsake the great 'aspirations' of the Enlightenment, he did not entirely abandon its teleological ideology of progress. Weber cherished the Enlightenment philosophers' and intellectuals' belief in the ever-increasing rationalisation and efficiency of social systems, even though he saw this as a dead-end that leads only to the 'cage of bondage'. In this sense, most of the philosophers, sociologists and political thinkers of the nineteenth century were Hegel's descendants, and this includes Weber. Even though the concepts he addressed developed in many different ways, Weber's vision of history was primarily a pessimistic form of Hegelianism.

Weber offered an interpretation of the anthropology of religion in terms of its evolution from a purely magical effort to deal with supernatural forces to a gradual attempt to comprehend gods in a cosmological order. The history of religion is generally perceived as an evolution from 'sorcery' to 'religious practice', from 'demons' to 'gods', from 'magicians' to 'priests', from 'taboo' to 'prophecy', from 'polytheism' to 'monotheism' and from 'enchanted garden' to 'disenchanted world'. All this reflects Weber's attempt to view religious development in terms of rational progress. Weber acknowledged, however, that the break from magic to *religio* is never definitive or linear. The marks of magic are still present and active in *religio*. These are clearly perceptible in aspects of 'paganism' that remain vividly present in Catholicism, as well as in the continuing influence of taboos and magic on monotheistic religions. However, this does not negate the internal logic of progress in the general direction of religion and rationalisation. Thus Weber read the internal logic of religious consciousness as a teleological movement towards gradual 'rationalisation', and for him, religious history reached maturity in Puritan asceticism.

We all know that the idea of progress was the great discovery of the eighteenth century, and ultimately reflects the secularised Christian view of salvation taking place in this world instead of the other. Indeed, since the eighteenth century, European thought has come to see the ideal of progress as 'permitting ordinary thought being built into its assumptions and language'.[60] However, the idea of progress is based on a crude dichotomy between a present time that slopes upwards towards enlightenment, while traditional societies cling to their enchanted pasts. This is yet another harsh dualism that permeates Weberian sociology.

As Gianni Vattimo pointed out, the idea of progress requires an ideal human being towards which humanity must evolve. He also argued that in modernity, however, the criterion has always been that of the modern European, 'as if to say we Europeans are the best form of humanity and the entire course of history is directed towards the more or less complete realisation of this ideal'.[61] This is precisely the spirit that dominates Weber's comparative sociology: an unquestioned faith in the superiority of the model of the modern west.

The origins of Weber's approach to Islam

In previous sections of this chapter, I uncovered some of the general assumptions underlying Weber's conception of Islam as a deficient and irrational religion and of its political history as a model of despotism. In this section, I explore the intellectual and political background supporting Weber's portrayal of Islam in a little more detail. How did it emerge, and what forms does it assume as it functions today?

Weber's work covered most great religions, including Christianity, Judaism, Confucianism and Hinduism, and it is not easy to explain why Islam was excluded from this list, as Weber never explicitly justified his decision. There appear to be three possible reasons for this peculiar gap in his studies.

First, from an examination of the cursory fragments Weber wrote on Islam, it seems likely that his views were based on the still-prevalent medieval Christian portrayal of 'Muhammadism' as a false religion. From this perspective, Weber may have seen Islam as little more than a minor sect or simple religion unworthy of systematic and specialised study.

Second, Weber's knowledge of Islam was very limited in comparison to what he knew about other world religions. It is often argued that he was acutely aware of his intellectual weakness concerning Islam, but died before he could overcome it. However, this does not explain why he gave precedence to other world religions that are arguably no less intellectually intriguing than Islam.

A third explanation may be sought in Weber's sociology. It is well known that he constructed a general paradigm, with the aim of systematising a comparative sociology of religion. Since Islam did not neatly fit into this paradigm, it came to be excluded from the fields of knowledge that attracted his interest. The general rationale he constructed is that Islam stands apart from the great monotheistic religions, even though they meet on a number of common points that Islam inherited from the Judeo-Christian tradition. As noted earlier in the chapter, for Weber, Christianity alone was capable of furnishing a 'rational answer' to the enigma of theodicy through the notion of redemption. However, the notion of original sin and the quest for salvation are both absent from Islam.

Medieval Christian understandings of Islam

As discussed, Weber described Islam as a deficient religion on account of its warrior values and hedonistic tendencies. The origin of this view is, in fact, not Weberian, but derives from a long intellectual and religious European tradition that first took root in medieval Christendom.

Generally speaking, Weber's reading of Islam was governed by two overlapping tendencies. First, medieval Christianity portrayed Islam as a warmongering, hedonistic religion that aimed to conquer the world through the force of the sword and the power of fear. During the Crusades, the Church reflected itself in the mirror of Islam, which was stigmatised as a brutal, bloodthirsty religion that glorified war and slaughter.

Second, Islam was not perceived as an independent revelation, but as the worst of all heresies, a terrible perversion of Christianity focused specifically on the psychology of the Prophet Muhammad. Muhammad was widely regarded as an impostor and a charlatan who feigned prophecy to deceive the world and as a magician with no real miracles.[62] In the eyes of medieval Europe, all of Muhammad's teachings were spurious. He performed no miracles, and his life was devoid of virtue. At worst, he was a fraudulent demoniac or a magician; at best, an imposter who claimed prophetic gifts in order to obtain power: 'an immoral hypocritical man who exploited religious claims to justify his immorality'.[63]

Although Islam was not cast as sheer unbelief or blind paganism, it was not seen as a 'real religion'. It was perceived to be a species of Christian heresy, a schism falsely claiming to have a revelation of its own, and even to reflect something of the true revelation of Judaism and Christianity. In the eyes of medieval Christianity, Islam was merely a distorted copy of the true religion.[64] In an age fraught with the tragedy of religious schisms that fuelled countless political conflicts, Islam was not only perceived as merely a deviant sect, but as a perverted and, indeed, dangerous enemy.

Of course, as shown earlier, this image of Islam did not arise purely from the Crusades, but also from the Christian world's own gradually developing ideological identity. This process generated a sharper image of the enemy's features, and helped to focus the west's energy on marshalling its forces for the Crusades.[65] For example, medieval Christianity saw worldly activity as an expression of 'original sin', so it reconstructed an imaginary view of Islam as a purely materialistic religion, driven by worldly interests. Similarly, the general climate of political and military confrontation between Islam and medieval Christendom, particularly during the Crusades, resurrected the image of Islam as an aggressive warrior religion. Later on, during the Renaissance, when European consciousness became more critical of the monopoly of the papacy, Islam became synonymous with papal deviance and moral corruption, including pride, greed, violence, and the lust for power and possession. Within Reformist Protestantism, Islam was associated with the unbearable evil of the Catholic Church. To undermine Protestantism's attacks on papacy, the Catholic Church too designated Muhammadism as its rival.

Of course, the image of Islam constructed by Europe during and after the Middle Ages was both polemical and apologetic. Historically speaking, the Christian world lagged far behind Islam in all fields of knowledge, and the Muslim social order seems to have been more open and dynamic than its Christian counterpart. To my mind, Hichem Djait was correct when he noted that medieval Christianity's vision of Islam was polemical, historically indicative, and

> for that very reason, it exhibits a sense of inferiority. Every question about the other masks an obsession with the other. And if classical Islam was indifferent toward the West, it was not due to a lack of curiosity on its part, but because it had nothing to gain from the West and so ignored it. Still, those medieval prejudices crept so deeply into the collective

unconscious of the West that one fears they may never be uprooted.[66]

An enduring distortion

A stable and solid line of continuity runs between medieval Christian portrayals of Islam and those propagated by its modern secularists. As Rodinson pointed out, 'The worldview remained monolithic, but the authoritarianism of Christianity was replaced by the rationalist, progressive, and secular philosophy of the Enlightenment.'[67] In a time marked by emancipation from the monopoly of the Church, some western scholars saw Islam as a rational religion whose championing of science and rational thought contrasted with the Christian Church that was openly hostile to both. To such scholars, Islam seemed to strike a balance between the demands of morality and the needs of the flesh, between the senses and social interaction.

This perception, however, remained restricted to a mere handful, for when it came to the subject of Islam, secular Europe has remained deeply entrenched within the medieval Christian framework. The medieval characterisation of 'Muhammadism' persists, even though it is now articulated within an immanent secularised language. Moreover, when the west accomplished its transition from stagnation and decadence to cultural, economic and military modernity, it reinvented Islam as the antithesis of all its achievements. If modern Europe is dynamic, the world of Islam is stagnant. If the west is governed democratically and honours self-ownership, Islam is plagued by a despotism that crushes the individual. If the west is rigorously rational, the world of Islam is the embodiment of raving instinct and wild emotionalism.

Generally speaking, modern western discourse inherited the medieval characterisation of Islam, consolidated this and came to identify Islam entirely with the image it had created. The early image was of a religion of wild hedonism, licentiousness and the exuberant savagery of animal instinct. Along with this, Islam was identified with aggression, force and violence, and by implication, was unable to engage in rational or peaceful debate.

Ironically, for a Christian theologian in the Middle Ages, the main questions were about the sources of this religion's power and success. How had it succeeded in conquering regions that had long been Christian, and was the Islamic value system in some way accountable for its rapid spread? The answers varied in accordance with the perspectives and outlooks of those who offered them. Theologians, traders and intellectuals, as well as travellers, artists, philosophers and soldiers developed their own outlooks on Islam. However, instead of constructing a unified framework, and bringing all these diverse positions together, Christian theologians came to define Europe's stance vis-à-vis Islam in the climate of the Crusades against the Islamic world.

For such theologians no link between Islam's worldview and its historical conditions could be considered. Islam's accomplishments could not validate its claim to be a true religion since Christianity was believed to be the one and only path to God. St Augustine's understanding of history expressed this conception. His view was that no earthly city abides, the righteous may wither away and still be righteous, worldly catastrophes and glories have no essential link with truthfulness, or indeed with falsehood. The historical achievements of Islam could not prove its legitimacy. Its triumphs were no evidence of its truth, but a challenge to the truth insofar as God in his impenetrable wisdom had predicted and assured the victory of evil and lies in a sinful world.[68]

Islam's intellectual and mathematical superiority over medieval Europe meant that Islamic scholars were acknowledged as key contributors to the history of thought, but Islam was never acknowledged as a religion or as an ethical system. The west simply denied that the accomplishments of Arab thinkers reflected on Islam in any way, and Islam's historical record was thus dissociated from its doctrines and its value as a religion was refused judgement.

In modern times, the key questions for western philosophers, and later for sociologists, have altered dramatically, focusing on the decadence rather than the ascendance of Islam. Paradoxically, while medieval Christians dissociated the historical success of Islam from its doctrinal and philological sources – which they deemed false and indeed fraudulent – modern western intellectuals have tended to attribute Islam's decadent historical condition to those same beliefs and value system. The ideology of progress that saw the modern west identified with 'rationalisation' and 'progress' on the ladder of history has played a major role in constructing this conception of Islam. The implicit question, which at times becomes explicit, is about the 'stagnation' and 'backwardness' of the cultural and geographical spheres that exist outside modern Europe, and particularly the world of Islam. Weber's outlook on Islam fell within this general context, and indicated his unqualified acceptance of traditional medieval Christian as well as common nineteenth-century interpretations of Islam.

German Orientalism, and more particularly the scholars from whom Weber sought an insight into Islam, invoked the general Orientalist representation of Islam as a 'bleak, bare, parasitic compound of Christian and Jewish monotheism'.[69] Weber merely reactivated and institutionalised this view within the framework of the sociology of religion. Indeed, the power of textualisation played a crucial part in shaping Weber's contributions on the subject. When Weber spoke of Islam, his language and cultural repository spoke for him. Beneath his identification of Islam with hostility and hedonism – in opposition to Calvinist Puritanism – is a distinctly medieval Christian perspective.

Weber's view of Islam was obviously reductionist and simplistic, even though his perspectives are still widely accepted in western academic and political discourse, and in the western media. As noted, Weber's very simple view of Islam seems to have been largely derived from classical German Orientalism, and his typology never took account of Islam's specific features. Weber was also adamant that one of the main reasons for the historical failure of Islam and its inability to flourish in modern times was its lack of rationality and the absence of the internal energy of what he called 'intellectualisation'. According to Weber, Islam lacks the genealogical foundations for rationalisation, and more precisely Greek conceptualisation.

Allama Muhammad Iqbal's writings on Islamic thought shatter Weber's approach. For Iqbal, the problem of Islam lies in the over-intellectualisation of its doctrine, not in the absence of doctrine. Islam, he contended, exhausted a great deal of its energy in an abstract metaphysical engagement with the intellectual heritage of Hellenism, which is incompatible with the realistic and 'pragmatic' nature of Islamic thought. Contrary to the view that rationalisation is a concomitant of Greek philosophy, Iqbal attributed the crisis of certain schools of thought (such as the Ash'arite and the Mu'tazilite Schools) and of Muslim philosophers, including al-Farabi, Ibn Sina (Avicenna), Ibn Bajah, Ibn Rushd (Averroes) and others, to the formality of Greek thought. Iqbal argued that classical speculation is incompatible with the spirit of the Qur'an, which directs human thought to *al-anfus* (the self), and *al-afaq* (the world). According to the Qur'an, inner experience is but one source of human knowledge; nature and history are two other such sources, and it is 'in tapping these sources of knowledge that the spirit of Islam is seen at its best'.[70]

The revolt of *tajdid* (renovation) against classical scholasticism, which started with al-Ghazali, who shook the foundations of Greek metaphysics, was fully elaborated by Ibn Taymiyyah and Ibn Khaldun, the great pioneers of reform in the history of Islam. Before Kant, al-Ghazali discovered the limits of reason, reducing metaphysics to no more than a heap of rhetorical illusions. Ibn Taymiyyah linked religious consciousness with spiritual and intellectual revolt against all religious illusions and fantasies. The essence of his intellectual construction is found in the theory of *istikhlaf* (vicegerency). Ibn Khaldun redirected Islamic reason from scholastic abstraction to the domain of history and *'umran* (sociology) centuries before sociology developed as a field of study in the west. The views of some of these scholars are discussed in more detail in later chapters of this book.

5

Habermas's theory of modernity and secularity

This chapter is devoted to a critical assessment of Jürgen Habermas's theory of modernity. I aim both to lay bare the limits of his theoretical framework and to extend his view of modernity.

Generally speaking, Habermas remained committed to the Weberian approach to secularity, and his theory of communicative action recycled Weber's reading of modernity. Habermas maintained that the spirit of modernity (as embodied in the modern structure of consciousness, social sphere and personal conduct) is not only incompatible with religious worldviews, but is in conflict with them. He argued that religious ethics are irreconcilable with the economic and administrative rationality found in the modern capitalist economy, and that the transition from pre-modernity to modernity corresponds to the shift from sacred to profane, from religious to secular, from enchanted garden to disenchanted world.

Habermas reconstructed the Weberian theory of rationalisation referring to the rationalisation of worldview, social life and personal conduct. The modern structure of consciousness, he maintained, presupposes a life-world that allows for the possibility of a rationally conducted life.[1] He argued that that structure of modern consciousness is the result of a long process of rationalisation, rooted in the internal rationalisation of world religions.[2] Drawing on the Weberian paradigm of the evolution of worldviews, Habermas saw these as evidence of a learning process through which an internally reconstructable growth of knowledge can be traced. Habermas insisted that the dynamics of development are not continuous or linear but do reflect a structural learning progress. For him, worldviews undergo four evolutionary steps that are similar to those we experience in the course of ego development. Thus:

1. Just as pre-operational children look at the world with reference to themselves alone, in a sociomorphic worldview, the phenomena of the world are seen in relation to the tribal group.

2. As sociomorphic traits persist, myths develop that establish a sense that a kind of unity holds the diversity of appearances together. Formally, this resembles the sociocentric–objectivistic world conception of a child at the stage of concrete operations.

3. Mythological thought gives way to cosmological worldviews, philosophy and higher religion. As Habermas put it: 'the cosmologically or monotheistically conceived totality of the world corresponds formally to the unity that youths can establish at the stage of universalism'.[3]

4. Finally, the unified worldview that was preserved by cosmology and high religion breaks down into subjectivist views. From this point, the universalistic potential contained in rationalised worldviews can be set free, and the rationalisation process that began with the rise of capitalism and the modern state is no longer restricted by religious principles.

Habermas then applied this pattern of evolution to civilisations, arguing that civilisations also proceed through four stages of development. He proposed that the first stage is reflected in 'Neolithic societies', where mythological worldviews are still intimately entangled with systems of action. The second stage is apparently evident the 'early civilisations' that were characterised by a conventionally structured system of action and a mythological worldview that 'take on legitimating functions for the occupants of positions of authority'. The third phase is linked to the rise of 'developed civilisations' that have a conventionally structured system of action, and develop a rationalised worldview that breaks with mythological thought. The fourth and final phase that Habermas suggested is that of the 'Modern Age', which is characterised by a post-conventionally structured domain of action, a universalistically developed doctrine of legitimation and diverse value spheres.[4]

Thus Habermas made use of Weber's reading of the rationalisation of worldviews as related to secularisation. The general rationale of modernity that Habermas outlined is one of a cumulative drive towards a secular rationalisation that reaches maturity in post-conventional morality. To substantiate this argument, Habermas also cited Jean Piaget's work on cognitive psychology, arguing that Piaget had correctly distinguished between different stages of cognitive development – less in terms of a cumulative and quantitative acquisition of knowledge, and more in terms of structural shifts in the system of knowledge.[5] Thus, for Habermas, Piaget's theory was useful not only in mapping learning processes, but in providing a conceptual model that could be extended to the development of worldviews as well. Piaget suggested that as cognitive development is primarily about the evolution of intelligence in relation to the structure of thought and action, as well as something children acquire via an active engagement with their external environment, this leads to the reconstruction of external and internal universes. For Habermas, worldviews undergo the same process, such that the modern structure of consciousness can be seen as the outcome of the dissolution of mythological–narrative figures of thought as well as the breakdown of religious and metaphysical views. It is, therefore, possible to see stages in the normative development of social structures (as well as the structure worldviews) as being generally equivalent to the ontogenesis of individual moral consciousness.[6]

According to Habermas, mythical worldviews tend to recognise no dividing line between language and nature or between objects that can be manipulated and agent-subjects who are capable of speaking and acting in this world. In contrast to this, modern worldviews tend to be fully aware of the distance between culture and nature, subject and object. As he put it:

> The de-mythologisation of worldviews means the de-socialisation of nature and de-naturalisation of society.

This process – which is easily accessible on an intuitive level and often treated in descriptive terms, but which lacks good elaborate examination – apparently leads to a basic conceptual differentiation between the object domains of nature and culture.[7]

Thus, Habermas saw secularisation as structurally synonymous with a child's cognitive development from 'egocentric' consciousness to a 'decentred' form of consciousness. In other words:

Disenchantment thus signifies a breakdown of a 'socio-centric' consciousness of a seamless magical-mythical world and the construction of a decentred consciousness which recognises clear demarcations between the natural, social, and subjective worlds.[8]

To consolidate the contradiction between the modern and pre-modern world, Habermas shifted sociology's emphasis away from classical anthropology (as focused on by Lucien Lévy-Bruhl), and towards the work of more contemporary social anthropologists (such as Claude Lévi-Strauss, Ernest Gellner and others). When comparing the mythical views of primitive tribes to modern structures of consciousness, Habermas insisted that worldviews 'are comparable only in respect to their potency for conferring meaning. They throw light on existential themes recurrent in every culture, birth and death, sickness and need, guilt, love, solidarity, and loneliness.'[9]

With the aim of proving the symmetrical differences between modern and pre-modern structures of consciousness (along with the social action inherent in them), Habermas used the paradigm of 'open' versus 'closed' societies[10] to suggest that the point of divergence between modern and traditional worldviews and societies is based on their distribution of the sacred. He argued that whereas the sacred is widely and haphazardly dispersed and pervasive in primitive and traditional societies, it is highly restricted and controlled in modern societies, and not allowed to diffuse into every aspect of life. Habermas then went on to argue that modern structures of consciousness and forms of life are open while pre-modern ones are closed. Thus, for Habermas, the more the 'sacred' is confined, the more the worldviews and modes of societies become open and flexible. Secularisation for him implies an automatic increase in levels of both rationalism and openness.

The limits of Habermas's theory of consciousness

Habermas's theory was constructed on a network of symmetrical dualisms such as open/closed, modern/pre-modern, secular/religious and communicative/pre-conventional morality. That is, secular, communicative and open modernity opposes religious, closed and non-conventional pre-modernity. As noted, Habermas also drew on Piaget's theory of cognitive development to develop a typology of consciousness.[11] It is possible to take issue with these basic premises.

In terms of dualism, Habermas clearly preserved the Enlightenment view that linked the pre-modern with superstition, dogma and intolerance, and modernity with openness, reflexivity and scientific empiricism. Thus, he contrasted *les ombres* of the past with *les lumières* of the present times. While Habermas's vivid awareness of the complexity of modernity helped ensure that his analysis was not nearly as superficial or simple as most Enlightenment thinkers, his discourse was as profoundly immersed in the Enlightenment utopia of emancipation and a will to overcome what was designated as pre-modern.

Yet, as Edward Shills observed, traditionalism does not rely on intolerance or dogmatism any more than scientism, rationalism and secularism does. In fact, in the twentieth and twenty-first centuries, the most destructive acts of intolerance have been committed by secular revolutionary regimes – progressive revolutionaries proving themselves scarcely more tolerant than reactionary ones. In essence, dogma is just as common among revolutionaries as it is among those who prefer to give tradition the benefit of the doubt.[12]

In certain historical conditions, secularity can be arrogant and despotic, as was the case under Jacobinism, fascism, Stalinism, and as it does in certain contemporary Middle Eastern states. This rules out any claim to the existence of a uniform model of secularity or secularism *per se*, just as it does the existence of any single, homogeneous religious paradigm. Of course, religion is as complex and diverse as secularism. However, tolerance is not necessarily a secular characteristic, just as dogmatism and fanaticism are not necessarily close allies of religion. It is true that many atrocities have been perpetrated in the name of the sacred, but just as many have hidden behind the banners of secularism and progress. In the Middle East, for example, religious and ethnic diversity were protected and preserved under various Islamic authorities at various times in history, but post-colonial secular regimes have since sought to tear this apart. Indeed, the norm of social homogeneity and uniformity might well be more common under secular nationalism than under other forms of governance.

Then, one must ask whether it is acceptable to equate Piaget's cognitive development with the development of worldviews. We must also question whether Piaget's learning theory (or Lawrence Kohlberg's ideas about the stages of moral consciousnesses) are value-free and universally valid. Thomas McCarthy has shown that Piaget developed his model on the basis of research carried out with urban middle-class schoolchildren in Switzerland, and subsequently in several other advanced western societies, but did little cross-cultural research.[13] It follows then that his results can be considered incomplete and inconclusive. McCarthy has also noted that it was with the aim of claiming universality that many western scholars unquestioningly assert that

> the Western middle-class child is the norm and 'time lag'
> discovered for development of other cultures seen as 'deficit'
> or 'retardation'. That is, human reason is viewed as following
> the same course of development in different societies but at
> a faster or slower pace, and with a more or less early arrest
> depending on the social environment.[14]

However, even if we accept Piaget's cognitive theory, and overlook our reservations about its limits, a number of questions remain concerning the validity of applying a thesis on cognitive psychology to the development of worldviews. Can cognitive psychology, as embodied in the distinction of the self and the object, ever really be synonymous with the secularisation of worldviews? Are non-secular views necessarily stuck in an immature stage of worldview development? Is a disenchanted worldview in the Weberian sense necessarily more rational and mature than a non-secular one?

It seems to me that the development of human consciousness and human civilisation is not necessarily comparable with the yardstick of cognitive or ego development. Theoretically speaking, human consciousness is not necessarily a cumulative march towards rationalisation or secularisation. Human history reveals a multiplicity of gateways, directions and forms of rationalisation. On a purely practical level, there are no serious indications that secularisation is progressively marching across the globe. In fact, while secularisation is undeniable in places, de-secularisation is just as real in others, and it assumes different forms in different parts of the world.

Habermas started with a pre-existing model, which he employed as the basis for a study of different fields of knowledge and simultaneously of its own legitimacy. He armed himself with a Weberian reading of modernity and then sought various means of confirming its validity. In my view, it is legitimate to argue from inside the theory of communication itself, that a life-world is a background perspective, mediated and reproduced through communicative reason. Thus, in the sense that a life-world is both its own producer and a product,[15] Habermas's model of rationalised life-world reflects his own secularised life-world. Using his own hermeneutics and historical conditions, Habermas presupposed their universal validity and subsequently argued that all previous development led to them. What he derived from this was what he had already put into it.[16]

This begs the question of whether so-called formal and universal structures of consciousness are merely an abstraction and sublimation of a specific historical structure of consciousness. We could overlook such relativist and hermeneutical critiques, including their obsessions with the circularity of language, if we eventually saw Habermas making an attempt at openness or a willingness to learn from other 'structures of consciousness'. However, it seems that, in the end, the broad outline of his thesis was the tale of a pre-modern versus a modern world (represented respectively by his analysis of EE Evans Pritchard's work on the Azande people of Central Africa and western modernity), and that, for him, little more than a vacuum lay between the two.

What Habermas regarded as the primary components of the learning process in a modern structure of consciousness (such as competence, distinction between the subject and object, communicative action, flexibility etc.) do not necessarily require secularism. They can and do function just as well in a non-secular context. A more useful comparison, in my view, is not between a unified model of modern consciousness versus a pre-modern consciousness, but between different modes and forms of modern consciousness.

The limits of Habermas's theory of modernity

Habermas's theory of modernity is based on a distinction between cultural modernity, that goes back to the Enlightenment tradition, and social modernity, as primarily embodied in the processes of rationalised capitalism and the modern bureaucratic state. This dualism derived from new Kantianism, which distinguished between values and facts. Habermas mostly agreed with radical critics of modernity in the Nietzschean tradition, and argued that the paradigm of self-centred subjectivity and self-centred reason had been exhausted and was indefensible.

Habermas also maintained that reason is 'a thing of this world', and is concretised in history, society, body and language. He parted company with this tradition, however, when he insisted that the defects of the Enlightenment would be cured only within a broader, more extended Enlightenment, that is, when communicative reason and strategic action prevail over the selective processes of modernity and instrumental rationality.[17] Habermas drew a distinction between the character of modernity, as embodied mainly in the power and wealth of capitalism, and the great achievements of modernity expressed in civil society and the public sphere, in which communicative action takes place. Modernisation, for

Habermas, was a march of emancipation overlaid with the distortions of reason, and he stressed the need for a distinction between the rationalisation of systems and the rationalisation of the life-world as a whole. The latter denotes an increase in potential morality and a rationality that would not be exhausted by the selective processes of modernisation. Thus, for Habermas, the destructive and distorted aspects of modern capitalism must be rejected, but not the broader rationalisation of the life-world. However, unlike the post-structuralists, who evoked the power of the extraordinary and the aesthetic, Habermas remained within 'the ground of reason' and the Hegelian tradition, seeing dialectical reason as a force of reconciliation and unification, capable of overcoming the diremption of modernity through the internal potentiality of reason:

> Hence, Enlightenment can only make good its deficits by radicalised Enlightenment; this is why Hegel and his disciples had to place their hope in a dialectic of Enlightenment in which reason was validated as an equivalent for the unifying power of religion.[18]

Habermas purged the Hegelian absolute of its metaphysical undertones and reintroduced it into language and history in the guise of the 'life-world'. Unlike Nietzsche's followers, who condemned reason from beyond the horizon of reason, Habermas sought to reactivate a counter-discourse that he saw as inherent in modernity, so as to remain within the tradition of modernity, or as he put it, without jumping outside the 'boundaries of reason'.

> Modernity can and will no longer borrow the criteria by which it takes its orientation from the models supplied by another epoch; it has to create its normativity out of itself. Modernity sees itself cast back upon itself without any possibility of escape.[19]

For Habermas, the infantile optimism of the project of modernity had evaporated, but its great problem and dilemma still lingered, and he asked:

> Should we continue to hold fast to the intentions of the
> Enlightenment, however fractured they may be, or should we
> relinquish the entire project of modernity?[20]

In response, Habermas's main strategy was to shift the grounds of philosophical discourse from a centralised subjectivity to the philosophy of language where his communicative theory could flourish, but he still clung to modern philosophy's bid to formulate and defend rationality and universality.[21] He seems to have believed that if the potentiality of modernity is menaced and deformed, it is by the wrong sort of reason, not by reason itself.[22]

The principal task Habermas set himself was to find a middle path between three conflicting approaches to modernity, namely:

- The old conservatives, who looked to the pre-modern phase with nostalgia and reverence, while holding the break with substantial reason and the differentiation of value spheres in contempt.
- The new conservatives, who welcomed the socio-economic achievements of modernity – especially those relating to the market – but remain sceptical of the explosive elements of cultural modernity.
- The young conservatives, who were committed to the extraordinary power of aesthetic modernity, and who had 'liberated' themselves from all the constraints of cultural modernity. (This tendency hovers in the spirit of Nietzsche, and is explicit in the work of French intellectuals from Georges Bataille to Foucault and Derrida.)

Habermas stood firmly opposed to what he saw as the nihilistic character of post-modernism, which he saw as having fallen 'outside the horizon of reason', in its rejection of all distinctions between truth and falsity, communication and distortion, reason and unreason.[23] In fact, post-modernist discourse constantly invokes archaic times, and the forgotten forces buried therein, favouring the magical powers of aesthetics. What Habermas seems to have found threatening, however, was the possibility of an alliance between anti-modernist and post-modernist ideas, since these both aim to shake up the tradition of modernity.

What remains alive and valid after attempts to deconstruct the project of modernity is its cultural tradition. This is why Habermas insisted, 'I believe that we should learn from the aberrations which have accompanied the project of modernity and from the mistakes of those extravagant proposals of sublations, rather than abandoning modernity and its project.'[24]

The main dilemma haunting Habermas's approach to modernity was the solid categorical model derived from within modernity itself. He condemned any 'radical critique' of the tradition of modernity as a deviation from the dialectic of modernity, and dismissed any 'totalising critique of reason' as having exited from the horizon of reason. That is why he was of the view that Nietzsche and his heirs brushed aside 'the two hundred year-old counter-discourse implicit in modernity itself'. For Habermas, to reject modern ontological thinking and Kantian language was to succumb to the 'irrational' and the mystic, but the question asked by the American philosopher Fred Dallmayr remains relevant here: 'How can this rationality be corrected if every step beyond its confines is immediately branded as irrational or mystical?'[25]

Alas, Habermas's theory thrives on symmetrical syllogisms such as the claim that the 'non-logical' is synonymous with the mystical non-rational and, hence, irrational. Underlying this critique is a defence of the concept of reason that is deeply entrenched in western tradition, and stretches back to the Greek notion of *logos*. While Habermas claimed to have surpassed the transcendental Aristotelian conception of reason (along with Kantian self-enclosed reason), reason for him remained a thing of this world, embodied and mediated in a worldly language. This is not to say that Habermas had moved beyond the Aristotelian characterisation of reason as *ratio* or the Hegelian determination of reason as a power of universal sublimation and unification. *Logos* has many meanings within the philosophical context. At the forefront of these are the rational, the intelligible, pervasive order and the source of that order, or the principle accountable for that order.

The adjective 'rational', as articulated in modern times, has been used to characterise agents and beliefs since the time of the Greek philosophers, who defined the term as the negation of non-rationality or irrationality. One can argue that Habermas preserved the Greek deter-mination of reason as *ratio*, as well as the polar oppositions between the 'rational' and 'non-rational', safeguarding the 'rational' with a set of borders and fences borrowed from modern epistemology. It seems Dallmayr was correct in saying that

> despite the 'essentially' incarnate (and impure) character of reason, pure rationality continues to serve as yardstick of opaque or 'real' elements – in a manner relegating the latter to a level of imperfection or inferiority with which we may have to 'make do'…More generally, only traditional epistemology provides the basis for subordinating the meaning-disclosing potency of world (or language) to factual or pragmatic claims.[26]

What banished Nietzsche and his followers from the province of reason was Hegel's 'inclusive model of reason' and the antinomy of the 'exclusive model of reason', from which, as Habermas explained, otherness is ex-cluded altogether. However, what was unthinkable for Habermas was the possibility of an alternative vision of the 'rational' and the 'irrational', that is, of crossing the rigid line that separates the internal from the external.[27]

The position Habermas adopted in his polemic with Nietzschean tradition is reminiscent of Ibn Rushd's response to al-Ghazali's project to deconstruct Greek metaphysics. Al-Ghazali regarded philosophers' arguments in favour of metaphysics as nothing more than rhetoric, and therefore as entitled to no claims of rational necessity. Contrary to philosophical assertions, no correspondence exists between philosoph-ical categories and ontological objects. In order to shatter the arsenal of categories that philosophers had erected, al-Ghazali used various argu-ments devised by diverse schools of thought, arming himself with the discourses of his opponents, from Muslim theologians to the *mutasaw-wifah* (Sufis), in a quest to reveal their internal contradictions.

Ibn Rushd viewed al-Ghazali's approach, which broke with Greek metaphysics and Aristotelian doctrine, as an exit from the circle of rea-son as a whole, reason for him being exclusively contained in the Greek perspective, and Aristotelianism being its most mature configuration. Just as Ibn Rushd deemed al-Ghazali to be a 'heretic of the non-rational', so too was Nietzsche excommunicated from the tradition of reason for advocating a non-Kantian, non-Hegelian form of reason. The only difference is that Ibn Rushd defended the Aristotelian model, while Habermas pleaded for the Hegelian synthetical one. While Ibn Rushd saw any non-Aristotelian 'understanding' of reason as little more than irrational nonsense, Habermas declared all post-Hegelian forms of reason to be the very reverse of reason.

Just as nothing compels one to endorse the Nietzschean response to Platonism with its emphasis on the power of the aesthetic, we are not obliged to wholeheartedly accept al-Ghazali's response to the philosophers, and might object to his inclinations towards Sufism. Nonetheless, one cannot but acknowledge the validity of the deconstructive drive shared by al-Ghazali and Nietzsche, which remains largely unchallenged. Both philosophers shook the borders of reason, and unveiled the fragility of the 'rational'. With these two pioneers and, indeed, to the horror of 'the philosophers', rhetoric and the non-rational are revealed as key components and active players within the sphere of philosophical reason.

In addition, the Ghazalite and Nietzschean traditions expose the error of Aristotelian and Hegelian claims to the uniqueness of the model of reason that they champion. That model is declared to be merely one historical possibility amongst countless other possibilities. Using different 'discourses' and their own particular strategies, al-Ghazali and Nietzsche revealed that Greek *logos* and Hegelian reason are mere forms or modes of 'reason', not reason itself, and that the notion of reason is simply a figment of philosophical imagination – a myth, a tale and a phantasm.

Although Habermas insisted on different occasions and in different ways that modernity is an unfinished project, he ended up limiting the unlimited by implying that the project is to be pursued within the confines of the Enlightenment tradition. He considered any movement outside this tradition to be either a return to the archaic and pre-modern or a step outside the circle of modernity in the direction of the non-rational or the anarchism of post-modernity. He aimed to preserve the old theme of unity and plurality, and the question of 'how these two aspects are to be brought into relation with each other'.[28]

It is neither an exaggeration nor a travesty to submit that underlying this reading is a kind of unconscious egocentrism. It is true that Habermas, particularly in his later work, insisted on the overlapping relation of self and other, but he located the self in the position of a speaker more than a hearer. The structures he employed were based mainly on an idealised form of western liberalism raised to the status of the universal. However, his theory of communication reflected the influence of all the epistemological and ontological problems inherent in the western philosophical tradition. Thus Habermas spoke the language of universalism by sublimating his own hermeneutics to universal claims, but without the will to listen to the voices of 'others'. No trace of Chinese, Indian or Islamic elements are to be found in his writings, the presence of which might have done much to embody the spirit of his much-invoked 'inter-communication'. It is legitimate to ask, as McCarthy did, 'whether the model succeeds in capturing *universal* conditions of reaching understanding in language, that is, *general* and *unavoidable* presuppositions of communicative action, or whether it represents instead a thinly disguised Eurocentrism'.[29]

Although (in *The Theory of Communicative Action*) Habermas projected the 'other' in the image of the primitive tribe, in order to reflect the specificity of modern consciousness, he later adopted a view based on reciprocal and mutual learning, arguing that the 'other' should not be a simple mirror through which 'we' reflect 'our' perspectives, but a means of improving our knowledge:

> In a situation of profound disagreement, it is not only necessary for 'them' to try to understand things from 'our' perspective, we have to try in the same manner to grasp things from 'their' perspective. They would never seriously get a chance to learn from us if we did not have the chance to learn from them,

and we only become aware of the limits of 'our' knowledge through the faltering of 'their' learning processes.[30]

Nevertheless, there remained a huge gap between what Habermas's theory of communicative action proclaimed and what it practised. The 'other' left no identifiable traces in his texts, and the humble spirit he called for in 'our' dealings with the 'other' is seldom, if at all, evident in his theory of modernity.

Habermas rearticulated Weber's model of modernity, elaborating it theoretically and arming it with a claim to universal validity. The only difference between Habermas and Weber is that the former tried to universalise western modernity with a greater degree of flexibility than the latter. We know that, in his later works, Weber faced a dilemma concerning the possibility of compromising the specificity of western modernity with its universal validity, noting that

> The son of the modern European cultural world will examine the problems of universal history, unavoidably and justifiably, from the perspective of the following question: which chain of circumstances has led to the fact that exactly in the West, and in the West alone, cultural phenomena have appeared, which nonetheless – or at least as we like to think – lay a line of development having universal significance and validity.[31]

In the Weberian context, the universality of modernity was viewed in two ways. First, although modernity was marked by western cultural specificity, it was seen as capable of expanding beyond its European and North American origins, adapting to different contexts and finding new forms of legitimacy. At the core of this notion of modernity was the 'rationalisation' of the market via capitalism, and of public life through the extension of modern bureaucracy. Second, modernity was seen as naturally asserting its superiority over all pre-modern and pre-disenchanted cultures by virtue of its 'brilliant moral accomplishments' that were believed to be universally applicable, transformative of all cultures that remain overwhelmed by tradition.

It is obvious that there is a tension if not a contradiction between the perspectivist view, based on the intellectual and historical specificity of the modern west, and the universalistic claim, based on a belief in the universal validity of the historical experience of the modern west.[32] Weber here, as Habermas rightly remarked, dissociated modernity from its modern European origins, and styled it as a spatially and temporally neutral model for all of humanity. He further broke the internal links binding modernity to the historical context of western rationalism, thereby exposing it to the horizons of universality.

Weber's pervasive influence meant that many questions remained unthinkable in Habermas's theory of modernity. At the forefront of these are the following:

- Is it possible to sever the bond between rationalisation and secularisation?
- Is the convergence between secularisation and modern rationalism merely a historical and epistemological development, or does it establish a unique and necessary framework that precludes the possibility of the emergence of models with different characteristics?
- Is the connection between modernity and secular rationality only *a* narrative and not necessarily the last word in the 'great narrative' of modernity?

Habermas and Weber were both firmly committed to the view that the affinity between secularism and modernism is self-evident. In fact, most western philosophers and sociologists consider this alliance to be undeniable, and see secularisation as both a conclusive and necessary process. Nevertheless, non-secular cultures are not necessarily anti-modern or pre-modern, and can display many characteristics that are often seen as essentially secular. Religious pluralism, tolerance and civil politics can all function within a religious and moral framework. In fact, religious tolerance is not necessarily the child of modern secularism at all, and has a long history in various religious contexts.

Secularism and disenchantment, as Weber maintained, manifest a rupture with the conclusiveness of the religious. Modernity expels God from the centre of society and places science there instead. The religious is thereby relegated to the internal and private sphere of individuals' souls.[33]

At the forefront of the large array of dilemmas confronting any intellectual effort aimed at grasping the meaning of the concept of secularism is the ambiguity inherent in the term 'secular' within socio-philosophical discourse. The adjective 'secular', in Latin *secularis* and in French *seculier*, denotes:

- Not spiritual, relating to affairs of the present world, not holy, worldly.
- Not bound by monastic rules.
- (In French, *séculaire*) age-old.

'Secularity' (the noun) means worldliness, and attention to the things of the present life. Meanwhile, the verb 'to secularise' (*séculariser* in French) means to transfer from ecclesiastical to civil or lay use, possession or control, and to make secular.[34] Generally speaking, three meanings are associated with the terms 'secular', 'secularity' and 'secularism'.

The first relates to the distinction between worldly institutions and modes of action and otherworldly or religious activity. This is the far-reaching semantic definition conferred on the term when the Christian Church designated non-ecclesiastical activity as secular or worldly. At the time, the term had an obviously pejorative connotation. In modern usage, the word still carries the traditional Christian notion of a rigid separation of the worldly from the religious, but the term has been purged of its negative connotations. The second meaning relates to demystification in the Weberian sense of the term disenchantment, meaning that the world is no longer a dwelling place for hidden sacred spirits, but a purely physical domain subject to instrumental calculation. This leads to the third meaning of the term, which posits a universe stripped of religious significance and all forms of teleological understanding. Morality is conceived as a subjective preference in the midst of warring gods (value spheres), not an expression of objective choice.

Two possibilities need to be considered here. The first is of effecting some kind of disengagement between the concepts of secularisation and demystification. The second is of severing the bond (revered by many western intellectuals) between rationality and secularity.

Although secularisation and demystification share several features, the former is much broader and more controversial than the latter. All forms of secularisation entail demystification perforce, but not all forms of demystification require secularisation, as may well occur within a religious context. That is, the world can be demystified, as can personal and social activities, while still preserving religious meaning. Worldviews and social conduct may well be rendered rational – in the sense of forsaking all sorts of mythology and magic – without necessarily leaping into an altogether secular framework. However, what remains truly inconceivable in modern western discourse is that religion may be conducive to rationalisation without drifting into secularism, as Weber insisted would be the case.

In my view, a line needs to be drawn between rationalisation and secularisation. Rationalisation is broader than secularisation, and may function in secular and non-secular contexts. What I understand by rationalisation is the procedural investment of reason's potential in the construction of different historical structures, embedded language, and culture. Rationality may assume a number of historical forms, and may or may not have secular connotations. Even if modern rationalism, as expressed in western modernisation, had always overlapped and converged with secularisation, this would still not imply any necessary connection between the two. What Weber and Habermas saw as expressions of secularisation in modern western society not only operate and flourish in religious contexts, but can even be seen as forming the very essence of religion. Included here are the disenchantment of nature, rational modes of conduct, and consciousness of the distinction between the self and the world. Accordingly, modernity and secularisation require demystification, but modernity does not necessarily require secularisation. In other words, the close alliance between secularisation and modernisation propagated by western intellectuals is not a necessary one.

Weber described the disenchantment of the world as necessary for modernisation, but this is only partially true. Weber, I submit, was correct to argue that modernity disenchants the world in the sense that it relieves it of its mythical burdens. However, I believe he was mistaken in perceiving this plausible claim as entailing the elimination of religious meaning and presence from worldly institutions and activities in favour of nihilism. Thus, the various subtypes of modernity discussed in much of the sociological, political and philosophical literature, and that are active in western socio-political contexts, are merely different modes of *western* modernity. These do not exhaust the notion of modernity *per se*, nor do they constitute modernity itself, which is, as Habermas memorably noted, 'unfinished'. Indeed, for this notion to express its true significance, Habermas's paradigm needs to be broadened to accommodate the possibility of non-secular forms of modernity.

If we adopt a functional definition of modernity – as Alain Touraine often did – as 'the diffusion of the products of rational, scientific, technological and administrative activity',[35] these 'products' are clearly workable across a range of cultural and historical contexts. Of course, when nations outside the European sphere, and particularly in South-East Asia, embarked on their march towards modernisation, they did not swallow any ready-made models, but stamped their own cultures and indigenous traditions on the whole process. A great many Asian sociologists, thinkers and politicians credit the Asian values at the root of the Asian renaissance for birthing and sustaining that renaissance. It is clear that modernisation in that part of the globe overlapped with local socio-cultural traditions. The binding of tradition with the modern in the Asian context has led to a clear disarticulation of modernisation and westernisation.

However, nowhere has the European face of modernisation experienced such radical transformations and challenges as it has in the world of Islam. Some of these challenges have tended towards outright rejection of the project, particularly in the more outlying Islamic lands. The most obvious example of this was Afghanistan, which was under constant military threat from Russia, and shaken by the race between international powers (the European nations in the eighteenth and nineteenth centuries, with the United States joining in from the twentieth) to gain greater influence in the geo-politics of Central Asia. Ultimately Afghan leaders sought refuge in utter closure and total isolation from the outside world.

Nowadays, it seems that the two poles of radical rejectionism – that is, the brutal secularism of Kemalist Turkey or Bourguibist Tunisia, and the opposite camp in Wahhabi Saudi Arabia or early revolutionary Iran – find they have no choice but to move to the middle ground if they are to survive. Meanwhile, the vast majority of Muslim societies, including Indonesia, Malaysia, Egypt and Morocco, to name but a few, made no objection to the notion of modernisation as such, but did express major reservations about the European model. They therefore attempted to reconcile aspects of western modernisation with Islamic tradition, showing that any modernisation project in a Muslim country that turns its back on Islam's vibrant heritage will sow the seeds of its own destruction. No modernisation is possible without a firm alliance and constant interaction with Islam. Neither, indeed, is there any hope of continuity for those who erect high walls to shield themselves from the accomplishments of the modern age in the hope of safeguarding their own utopian visions.

Of course, messianic preachers of modernisation tend to see any steps towards modernisation as an actualisation of the Hegelian prophecy, a triumph of the western model, and as another step towards the annihilation of the 'traditional'. It is, however, much safer to steer clear of sorcery and prophecies, and leave history's unpredictable and labyrinthine course to deliver its verdict. Nevertheless, it may come as a shock to preachers of secularity that some of the most modernised parts of the Muslim world have become the most fertile grounds for Islamic revivalism, and that some of the most modernised sectors of Islamic society are among the least secular ones. Contrary to western paradigms and prophecies, de-secularisation appears to be the perfect accessory to modernisation in the Islamic world.

The real obstacle to democratisation in Muslim countries lies in the realisation by the secular elites of their own marginality. Any free election without state interference would almost certainly be catastrophic for those secular forces that are pushing for modernisation. The binding relationship between secularism and modernism is, indeed, infinitely more abstruse and controversial, and certainly nothing like as indubitable as Habermas and Weber and many others in the west's academic and political establishment have tended to think.

John Gray's observation that modernisation and westernisation – including secularisation – are not necessary concomitants is praiseworthy.[36] The notion of modernisation as necessarily involving the reproduction of the western experience of modernity is among the most erroneous myths and delusions of the modern age. As Gray pointed out, the disenchantment that accompanied the European Enlightenment could perhaps have been tempered but not overcome. However, non-western cultures that remain substantially intact have the option of retaining their own conceptions and adapting western technology 'without succumbing wholly to Western humanism and nihilism'.

Gray held the view that the Enlightenment project is self-defeating, and that its self-destructive elements find their clearest expression in Nietzsche's nihilism. However, unlike Alasdair MacIntyre, who tried to overcome the nihilism of modernity by recovering the Aristotelian intellectual tradition,[37] Gray sees Nietzsche's nihilism as the natural outcome of the Enlightenment tradition and the necessary fate of western modernity in its later stages of development. Gray has, therefore, called on liberal regimes to accommodate themselves to the idea of sharing the earth with others who do not partake in their political culture or adopt their institutions.

The spread of secularism, and the nihilism that accompanies it, is distinctive of industrialised European societies, although perhaps not their most prominent characteristic. Indeed, the sacred, in all its diverse expressions, is still vividly present in European consciousness as well as in public life, in spite of the reduced role played by institutionalised religion. However, in other parts of the globe, there are very few indications that such nihilism is likely to take hold. In Muslim society, tendencies towards nihilism and atheism are still confined to the margins, and have proven unpopular among the Muslim elite.

Islam's rigorously transcendental monotheism, along with the absence of the notion of theodicy, which caused great torment to religious consciousness in the west, presents its followers with an ever-flowing source of meaning and teleology. The religious text that occupies a central position in both the private and public lives of Muslims, and the endlessly varied forms of its interpretation, provides a solid foundation of value and meaning.

Ultimately, few civilisations have been passive receivers of externally developed models of modernity. Great civilisations breathe their own spirits into historical experience, refashioning modernity anew, and casting it into as yet untrodden fields. This both encapsulates the notion of novelty that is concomitant with modernity and the Sufi understanding of a 'moment' as a flow and a renewal in accordance with the believer's psychological state. It would be absurd to assume that China, with its ancient heritage and profoundly nationalist trajectory, its wide geographical extension and dense population, would be a passive recipient of any imported model. The same is true of Islam. Its profound and still active symbolic capital stands as an insurmountable obstacle before any attempt to transform it into a carbon copy of western modernity. The world's civilisations possess enormous capacities for continual rejuvenation and reinvestment of their symbolic heritage. Many Muslims' attitudes towards modernity seem to indicate a simultaneously wilful and involuntary bid to submit it to their own religious realities and perspectives. This attempt to religionise modernity assumes a variety of forms, ranging from reconciliation and adaptation to the radical reactionary rejectionism shown by extremists.

There is, however, a real need to give Habermas's characterisation of modernity as an unfinished project its full significance in ways that transcend his own narrow understanding of the term. Modernity's unfinished nature exposes it to the potentials within various historical possibilities and strategies, and to a diversity of models and configurations.

It is thus not a question of adjusting to its 'western form' or of modifying an ideal; it is about shattering the sublimated model entirely. This is a requirement for any project that aims to thrust modernity into the adventures of universality.

Habermas left us with a list of alternatives consisting of a single, double-faceted option, to choose to be pre-modern and a prisoner of the traditional, or to be anti-modern and to preach nihilism.[38] What Habermas failed to consider was the possibility of confronting modernity from outside the stringent dualism that held him prisoner. That is, the conceivability of engaging in a critique of modernity from within those (alien but modern) voices that resonate outside the Habermasian model with its pre- and post-modern fatalist determinism. The hegemony of western modernity, owing to a set of historical factors that have much to do with monopolising the instruments of power, does not divest history of its Hegelian cunning or its abrupt detours. The diversity of historical embodiments and expressions of reason clearly testifies to the possibility of a plurality of expressions and experiences of modernity.

To dismiss secularity as an unnecessary component of modernity does not imply clinging to an unsecularised but still-western model – a kind of modernity minus secularity. Nor is it an attempt merely to reconcile a religious heritage with all the remaining constituents of modernity. What I have in mind are yet-unexplored forms of modernity that western consciousness might find novel or strange. For example, al-Ghazali's ontological approach can be adapted for this purpose by shifting it from the sphere of metaphysics to the philosophy of history. Al-Ghazali sought to refute the ontological determinism of Muslim philosophers who were influenced by (dry-as-dust) Greek philosophy. Al-Ghazali's guiding principle was the notion of possible worlds, which has since become a central idea in contemporary philosophy of logic. Al-Ghazali conjectured that the world in which we live, albeit perhaps the best of all possible ones, does not preclude the possibility of other worlds.[39] This notion forms the backbone of al-Ghazali's refutation of logical determinism, and his assertion that 'our world' is not governed by the principle of necessity, but by that of habit. We have always witnessed the sun rise from the east and set in the west but, al-Ghazali insists, this is an expression of the cosmological order laid down by the free will of God, who remains above order. This goes against the contentions of Aristotelian Muslim philosophers such as al-Farabi,[40] Ibn Sina[41] and later Ibn Rushd,[42] as well as theologians of the Mutazilite School, who all developed a notion of God as stern and rigid by submitting God to the principle of necessity.[43] The only difference between Aristotle and his Muslim followers is that while Aristotle held the unmoving prime mover to be redundant, his Muslim students, while holding fast to their belief in logical necessity, saw God as an active Creator operating within the constraints of a necessary cosmological order that had been created. In other words, God had willingly submitted to the order that had been created. God, for the Mu'tazilis, for instance, *is* absolute justice, but also wills this quality of justice, so that God and all that abides in the universe is just.

Of concern here are not the intricacies of metaphysics debated by al-Ghazali or his opponents, or al-Ghazali's quest to create space for the possibility of miracles through his refutation of determinism. What is of greater interest was his bid to provide for the conceivability of diverse ontological and, accordingly, historical possibilities. Even if we bow to the contention that modernity, as we know it, is the most eminent model thinkable, there is still room to consider whether other forms of modernity might exist, and whether history, despite those who cry of its end, remains replete with rigour and vitality, pregnant with fresh potential.

The spread of certain institutions or models of organisation from one cultural realm to another by no means indicates the superiority of the exporting culture over its importing counterpart. Civilisations are not isolated islands, but coterminous spheres engaged in constant flows of interaction and exchange. The more capable a culture is of continuity and prosperity, the greater its capacity for incorporation and adaptation. The modern west has incorporated Chinese bureaucratic institutions, making them more efficient and pervasive throughout the entire social and economic fabric, to the point of rendering the whole of the modern world blandly bureaucratic. The west has also made extensive use of the empirical scientific spirit of Islamic culture, which thrived on repudiating Greek scholasticism's penchant for abstraction and its resentment of the concrete and the mutable.

It has always been the case that efficient institutions possess great potential for universalisation. The modern west is a case in point; it has shown a real ability to embody rationality in active institutions and to cure 'the political malady' (an expression I borrowed from Paul Ricœur),[44] by stumbling upon democracy amidst terrible religious wars and sectarianism. These accomplishments are ripe for expansion, but since living creatures populate civilisations, people will undoubtedly breathe their spirit, symbolic capital and historical expertise into such instruments and institutions, developing and even refashioning them anew.

Arab–Islamic culture, born in the arid zones of the Arabian Peninsula, was truly impoverished in relation to institutions and instrumental expertise. It has always, however, by virtue of the richness of its value system, been capable of absorbing the expertise of the great civilisations that preceded it – from the Babylonians in Iraq, the Pharaohs of Egypt, the Persians in Iran, the Romans in North Africa, and from the Turks of Constantinople and Eastern Europe. As Ira Lapidus asserted in his *History of Islamic Societies*:

> In all Muslim societies, the prevailing culture was a mixture
> of Islamic concepts and symbols and non-Islamic institutions
> and identities. However important, Islam was still but one
> aspect of a more complex society.[45]

Weber and Habermas's secularised Christian backgrounds had an overwhelming influence on their thinking. Perhaps this is why they both perceive any convergence between the religious and the secular as a merely transitory moment in the life of secular modernity. They witnessed Protestantism's attempt to reconcile the religious with the secular spirit of the modern world in the capitalist system. Then they saw the worldliness of Protestantism conquer religion and cast it to the fringes of tormented consciences vainly seeking salvation.

The direct opposite seems to be occurring in the Islamic world to-day; it is shifting away from a momentary secularism to a modernity imbued with faith – transitioning from a secular worldliness to a religious worldliness. The deep entanglement between the religious and the worldly that is intrinsic to Islam would be utterly unthinkable for Habermas and Weber, since to them worldliness is secular *per se*.

The dominant view among western intellectuals is that the shift from 'secular' to 'religious' consciousness and conduct is regressive – a movement from modern to pre-modern, from secular Enlightenment to religious backwardness. At best, it is hoped that the phenomenon is limited to the ranks of reactionary movements seeking refuge from the stifling burdens of modern times. Of course this is not the case, but even if we were to concede that the process of de-secularisation was a reversal of history, we still have to question why the past is being invoked, what it might be invested with, and, indeed, to what kinds of interpretive activities it will be subjected. It must be remembered that the past can be used as a means of legitimising a status quo and its continuity, but also as a catalyst for change and dynamism. It is useful to recall Hannah Arendt's astute observation on the success of the American Revolution (as compared to its French antecedent), which she ascribed to the bid by its founders to invite the past into the very act of nation building:

> When they turned to the ancients, it was because they discovered in them a dimension which was not handed down by tradition – neither by traditions of customs and institutions, nor by the great tradition of Western thought and concept. Hence it was not tradition that bound them back to the beginnings of Western history but, on the contrary, their own experiences, for which they needed models and precedents.[46]

America's founders used the glory of ancient Athens and Rome with the aim of establishing a new body politic; that is, they activated the past to respond to the needs and concerns of the present.

At this stage I wish to draw attention to two essential features that make Islam unique, and in which worldview and religion conjoin to form what may be termed an 'Islamic modernity'.

The first feature is the worldly nature of Islam, which renders vacuous any attempt to establish a dualism between the scared and the temporal. Of course, this is not to say that in the history of Islam a distinction between the religious and the political, or, on certain levels, between the temporal and the spiritual, has never been suggested. However, no moral or theoretical legitimacy has ever been accorded to these distinctions, largely due to the repudiation within Islamic consciousness and thought of any Augustinian-type separation of 'the city of God' from the human city. In brief, what we have witnessed and experienced in western modernity thus far is a species of secular worldliness with materialist, even nihilist, tendencies. This was elaborately depicted and philosophically articulated by Heidegger, who looked on Nietzsche's mourning of the death of God as an intense expression of a tendency inherent in western history and consciousness for thousands of years. Islam, on the other hand, has established a type of non-secular worldliness that is capable of co-existing with and even incorporating the modern world, thus breathing spirituality into what may be deemed material and secular *par excellence*, including the political and economic spheres. To contrast Islam with secularity is not to hold the religious against the secular or the spiritual against the temporal. The difference is one of secular worldliness versus spiritual worldliness, of transcendental secularity versus immanent secularity.

The second feature of Islam centres on the fundamental part played by the reformist movement in bridging the gap between the traditional Islamic world and modern times. The reformists did not seek merely to accommodate Islam to the needs of secularity, but to incorporate modern developments creatively within Islamic discourse. Historically, this intellectual phase – irrespective of the soundness of the proposals it put forward – heralded the dawn of a modern Islamic discourse. It stands distinct from traditional Islamic discourse, although it remains in intimate contact with the past.

Western readers, overwhelmed with the trajectory of modernity in the west, might see Islamic reformism as a copy of Protestantism, and as a mere prelude to secularisation. However, we must try to steer clear of existing models and preconceptions if we are to gain some insight into this complex intellectual and historical phenomenon, and this is the task I tackle in the next chapter.

6

Islamic reformism and modernity

Islam reformed is Islam no longer
— Lord Cromer, *Modern Egypt*, 1908

It is well known that modern Islamic reformism was pioneered by eminent scholars from distinguished Islamic institutions such as those in Najaf, Iraq, al-Azhar University in Egypt, al-Zaytouna University in Tunisia and the University of al-Qarawiyyin in Morocco. The turbulence that followed the Muslim world's subjection to western dominance was a major incentive for scholars to seek guidance from the fundamental tenets of Islam and to attempt to reconcile certain European notions with Islamic tradition.

My aims in this chapter are threefold. First, to emphasise the internal dynamism of Islamic thought as manifest in the various movements of reform and revivalism that have emerged throughout Islamic history, in the prominent figures who pioneered these movements, and in the key terms and concepts on which the Islamic order of knowledge rests. Second, to outline the general features of modern Islamic reformism, revealing the elements that were derived from Islam's own long traditions of revival and reform and those that were selected and internalised from outside Islam. Third, to explore some of the new perspectives that have been made possible by modern Islamic reformism. Throughout the chapter, I seek to shed some light on the kinds of questions that were generated by the tumultuous conditions within which various reformers found themselves, and to explore some of the strategies they developed to deal with these conditions.

Early reform traditions

There is no doubt that modern Islamic reformism exhibits varying degrees of continuity with Islamic history and incorporates certain elements from the outside world. It is therefore a simplification to see contemporary Islam as a reaction to recent history, and to overlook the chains of continuity that bind the faith to its own long history of self-revivalism.

The Islamic lexicon clearly bears the hallmarks of its past even when fresh new layers of meaning are added to words that have long existed. Two terms are key in the Islamic vocabulary of resurgence: *tajdid* and *islah*. *Tajdid* can be translated as 'renewal' and *islah* as 'reform', but while a unifying continuity is evident beneath a range of ever-changing usages, their primary meanings tend to vary from one Islamic intellectual and historical context to another. What is certain is that both reflect the long history of revivalism within Islamic faith and practice.[1] *Tajdid* tends to be used more often since Arabic etymology presents it as the opposite of the term *taqlid*. *Taqlid* is an Islamic legal term that literally means 'to imitate' or 'to follow (someone)'. As an Islamic jurisprudential term it means to follow the rulings of one particular jurisprudent on religious laws and commandments uncritically, and without requesting or offering any explanations. The word encourages the opening of religious faith to fresh perspectives to ensure that faith remains current and ready to respond to new challenges and needs. The ideal model of the city of the Prophet and the examples set by the Rightly Guided Caliphs are often referenced here to challenge all forms of *taqlid* (religious imitation and social stagnation).[2] *Islah*, on the other hand, refers to the endeavour to address what are often seen as deviations from the true principles of the faith.

Ibn Khaldun, in his seminal work *al-Muqaddimah*, emphasised that all the political transformations in Islamic history can be traced to the emergence of religious reformist movements that have condemned rulers for betraying the ideals of Islam and for failing to follow the example of the Prophet and his companions. In the history of Islam, most opposition movements have begun by advocating social reform, and have then transformed into political groupings with radical agendas. It is important to note that, far from being a mere symbol or myth, the political ideal of *'adl* (justice) and the example set by the Prophet and the Rightly Guided Caliphs provided Muslims with a vision of an active utopia – proving that it is possible for humans to bridge the gap between lived reality and the ideals of Islam.[3]

Reform and renewal in Islam can be said to derive legitimacy from three principal drivers. The first is that religious faith, as characterised in the original texts, can be overwhelmed by social customs and traditions. Reform thus acts as a bridge between 'standard Islam' and 'social Islam'. The principal task for a reformer is to bring socialised or ritualised forms of Islam back to the level of the religious ideal; that is, to elevate religiosity to the level of religion and to redeem the authority of the text over tradition. Noteworthy here is the dualism that exists between religiosity as a socio-historical phenomenon and religion as a super-historical system of values and symbols. It follows that the role of the reformer is to religionise history and historicise religion by drawing clear lines of distinction between the ritualistic and the authentic forms of religion as embodied in the original texts and the example of the Prophet.[4]

The second driver is the recognition that religious *consciousness* may be afflicted with conservatism and stagnation as a result of the pervasiveness of *taqlid* and of the accumulation of doctrine. Reform then becomes about returning to the 'fundamentals', with the aim of exploring these in new ways, and adding fresh *ijtihad* or interpretations to them. In this context, the role of a reformer is to dig through the hard crust of interpretive tradition, and to go beyond historical religion to uncover 'canonical religion' *per se*.

The third is the acknowledgement that religious *spirit* can weaken under the influence of formal doctrines and religious abstractionism if these become devoid of inner spirituality. If this occurs, a revivalist educational and spiritual effort is required to reactivate and strengthen religious values in the psyches of believers. In the Islamic tradition Abu Hamid al-Ghazali was the most prominent champion of spiritual revivalism. His aim, as outlined in his famous work *Ihya' 'Ulum al-Din* (Revival of religious science),[5] was to turn the Islamic mind away from rigorous legalism and towards a softer kind of spirituality. Thus al-Ghazali, with his Sufi doctrines, provided a reference point to which much Sufi revivalism, whether traditional or modern, tends to turn.[6]

The emergence of various other Islamic reformist movements has often been linked to major internal and external challenges that have confronted Islam. As Richard Hrair Dekmejian aptly put it: 'The pattern of successive waves of resurgence in response to crisis situations constitutes an in-built sociopolitical mechanism that has enabled Islam to renew and reassert itself against internal decay and external threat.'[7]

Two principal features can be said to be characteristic of Islamic reformism. The first is an irrevocable condemnation and profound mistrust of *taqlid*; this often manifests in a vehement rejection of scholasticism. The second is a profound commitment to the authority of the canonical sources, the Qur'an and the Sunnah.[8] However, to champions of reformism, this commitment does not preclude the possibility of rethinking the ways in which these sources should be interpreted and understood, and these two features have given rise to a continual repudiation of esoteric and mythical interpretations of the Qur'an, and the revival of formal, straightforward *ta'wil* (interpretation). The expectation that believers uphold the fundamentals of the religion and the original texts implies a continual moving beyond the confines of scholastic traditions. Calls for a return to the 'original texts' do not encourage a return to ready-made postulates but promote fresh interpretations of clear and solid texts. Thus, while reformist efforts to encourage *tajdid* refer back to 'standard norms', and aim to bring society in line with the Qur'an and the prophetic tradition, they are primarily movements of revivalism and reinvention that generate fresh *ijtihad* and condemn *taqlid*.

Some might see reformism as a kind of idealisation of the past, since the Prophet, his tradition, and his rightly guided successors remain the reformists' primary inspirations. However, to fully appreciate the reality of religious reformism in Islam, we must free ourselves from the 'ideology of progress' that views history as a cumulative teleological movement, the tangible ends of which are realisable only in the future. Islam sees history as a process of syntheses, wherein the future is inseparable from the past, and from the morality of the community of believers. By engaging in authentic *ijtihad*, and refuting *taqlid*, Islam's great pioneers of reform have often invoked the example set by the first generation of Muslims, using this as a vital tool in their struggle against stagnation and decay. In this way, the past has proven a catalyst for creativity and renovation, a unique gateway to the future.[9] Some of the great reformers are discussed in the next section, along with brief overviews of their contributions.

Abu Hamid al-Ghazali

Al-Ghazali was born in the ancient city of Tus in Persia (near Mashhad in what is now Iran) in 1058 and received his early education there.[10] By the age of 33, al-Ghazali had shown himself to be endowed with great genius, and had made significant contributions to Islamic law and theology. He was therefore appointed as professor and director of the al-Nizamiyya institute in Baghdad.

Al-Ghazali is one of the most controversial and complex intellectuals in post-classical Islam. Seeking to place him within a specific school of thought is a daunting task. Readers of his work are often struck by the intricate and labyrinthine nature of his texts; although he constantly shifted from one school to another, he never broke completely from one before embracing the next. His thought is, in effect, a synthesis of all the intellectual tendencies to which he subscribed throughout the various stages of his career. In his autobiographical work, *al-Munqidh min al-Dalal* (Deliverance from error),[11] al-Ghazali described his intellectual journey as a rejection of philosophy, theology and jurisprudence, leading towards spiritual Sufism, which he presented as the most consistent and convincing mode of truth.[12] He recounted how, after a period of psychological turmoil and sheer scepticism, he set out in search of truth. This led him to examine the claims made by the great thinkers of his time, including philosophers, theologians, Ismaili Gnostics and

Sufis.[13] Although al-Ghazali sought to present his intellectual life as tracing a clear linear path from theology and philosophy to Sufism, this account is not entirely accurate. As Louis Gardet noted, what al-Ghazali did was synthesise the different aspects of Islamic tradition.[14] Thus, when he claimed that he had abandoned philosophy in favour of a Sunni form of Sufism, he did so using the language of philosophers and theologians. Furthermore, even when al-Ghazali rejected philosophy and theology in favour of Sufism, he never completely renounced either one. Instead he became vividly aware of their limits, arguing that it is only through what he termed 'knowledge through experience', and knowledge 'attained through a warm heart' that believers attain closeness to God. To him, what remained valid within philosophy was logic, or more precisely Aristotelian syllogism, as an instrumental tool for the religious mind. Similarly, he saw theology as an essential guardian of religious belief.[15]

There is no doubt that many elements within his system of thought seem to stand in sharp contrast to one another – a fact substantiated by the convoluted and even incoherent nature of his texts, in which one passage can be contradicted by another on the same page. Some have explained this incoherence by pointing to al-Ghazali's tendency to speak differently to different audiences. Ibn Tufayl (d. 1185) for instance, who drew attention to such contradictions in al-Ghazali's discourse, argued that al-Ghazali used one approach for ordinary people and another for the elite, as well as an esoteric approach that was made available only to a select few.[16] This claim seems to be borne out in al-Ghazali's *Iljam al-'Awam 'an 'Ilm al-Kalam* (The restraining of the common people from the science of theology),[17] in which he proposed that ordinary people should be forbidden to discuss the complex and controversial subjects of Islamic theology, thus separating the discourse of the elite from that of the lay community.

To my mind, these explanations are too superficial to account for the intensely complex nature of al-Ghazali's thought. Certainly, the contradictions in his texts mirror his mutable intellectual personality, but he lived in an age when Islamic culture was massively diverse and complex. There is no doubt that al-Ghazali lived his convictions with integrity and great enthusiasm, and his inner life was bound up with his work. This explains why, when critiquing al-Ghazali's *Tahafut al-Fala-sifah* (The incoherence of the philosophers), Ibn Rushd titled his critique *Tahafut at-Tahafut* (The incoherence of the incoherence)[18] in deference to al-Ghazali's work, and concluded almost every argument by referring to him with the words 'God bless the sheikh of *al-Islam*'.

This deference is not unusual among Islamic scholars. Ibn Taymiyyah, who was firmly opposed to al-Ghazali's agnostic Sufism, still placed much emphasis on the latter's sincerity, intellectual brilliance and 'ocean-like wisdom'.[19] Ibn Khaldun saw al-Ghazali's discourse as indicative of a new tendency in Islamic theology, noting that 'The first [scholar] to write in accordance with the new theological approach was al-Ghazali, who was later to be joined by the imam Ibn al-Khatib. A large number of scholars followed in their footsteps and adhered to their tradition.'[20] For Ibn Khaldun, al-Ghazali expressed the shift from what he called the method of the ancients to that of the moderns. Although it is widely accepted that al-Ghazali added nothing new to *doctrinal* theology (largely because it had by then been systematically constructed by the Ash'arites[21] and the Mu'tazilis[22]), it was through him that Greek logic was introduced into Islamic jurisprudence and theology, and thus successfully integrated into the learning institutions of the *'ulama*. In addition, to make logic more accessible to jurists, al-Ghazali wrote two books on the subject entitled *Mi'yar al-'Ilm* (Criterion of knowledge) and *Mihak al-Nadhar fi al-Mantiq* (Touchstone of reasoning in logic).[23]

While the dominant western view characterises Islam a deficient, irrational religion that fostered a relatively simple and primitive culture, what prompted al-Ghazali's shift towards Sufism was his perception that Islam's legal and theological systems had become 'over rationalised'. The inner spirituality of Sufism seems to have offered him a refuge from the dry and rigorous stolidity of many Muslim philosophers, theologians and jurists. However, in reconciling Sunni Ash'arism with Sufism, al-Ghazali shook the very foundations of the fortress of mainstream Sunni Islam. Before al-Ghazali, scholarly Islam was sceptical and even antagonistic towards Sufism, but, in his later work, al-Ghazali clearly showed how mainstream canonical Islam can be blended with spiritual Sufism. Al-Ghazali seems to have tried to dissolve Islamic legalism into the realm of mystical Sufism, while enrobing canonical Islam and Ash'arite theology in Sunni Sufism. In this process, al-Ghazali conferred on the law a moral and religious status that he saw as purely instrumental, while arguing that the law can have complete validity only within a mystical context.

In terms of Islamic philosophy, al-Ghazali's influence has been even more pervasive. He wrote the *Maqasid al-Falasifah* (Objectives of the philosophers),[24] in which he examined the views of Muslim philosophers (particularly those of al-Farabi and Ibn Sina) in a profound, systematic and neutral way, advancing no criticism of their arguments. However, in his later work, the *Tahafut al-Falasifah*, al-Ghazali attempted and, in my view, succeeded in demonstrating their internal contradictions and inconsistencies.

At a broader level, al-Ghazali's philosophical work performed a dual function. On the one hand, his radical critique of philosophical discourse unveiled the limits and contradictions in Greek metaphysics, thereby redirecting Islamic culture towards the concrete and the mutable, and shifting Islamic thought from meta-history to history. On the other hand, his mystical Sufism undermined the power of reason and his radical critiques of Islam's philosophical heritage weakened the foundations of 'Islamic rationalism'. Ultimately, however, the most significant impact of al-Ghazali's work is evident in popular Sufi orders that claim to draw inspiration from his teachings but tend to promote fatalism and human passivity.

Ibn Taymiyyah

Since early times, the object of Muslim reformers has been to derive a moral model from the past and reactivate it in the present. Among these, Ibn Taymiyyah (1292–1357), whose intellectual imprint continues to influence the modern reformist movement, is a prominent figure. Born in Mamluk-ruled Syria in the wake of the first Mongol invasion – times that were fraught with tragedy – he called for a return to early Islamic traditions. Through his Hanbali School,[25] Ibn Taymiyyah launched a serious attack on what he regarded as intellectual and practical deviations from the path of Islam.[26]

He founded his intellectual system on the three main concepts.

The first is the unity and inter-correlation of the Qur'an, the tradition of the Prophet and the consensus of the Prophet's companions – the main sources of Islamic legislation and authority. Ibn Taymiyyah's primary goal was to redeem the authority of the original sources of Islam over that of various sects and schools of thought. Ibn Taymiyyah's main objection to the jurists of his time was their lack of originality and creativity. The early imams and founders of schools of *fiqh* (jurisprudence) had become enslaved to specific *madhahib* (schools of jurisprudence). While life in Ibn Taymiyyah's times had become intensely complicated, and creative *ijtihad* was clearly called for, the *fuqaha* had become silent, stagnant and narrow-minded.

As Ibn Taymiyyah put it,

> Most jurists know only the school of law of their founder, of which they at best have only cursory knowledge. Thus they are not able to distinguish between issues that have been firmly resolved by clear scriptural texts and consensus *(ijma)* on the one hand, and the peculiarities of the school or instances where juridical discretion *(ijtihad)* flourishes…such jurists are like donkeys that merely transport old books.[27]

The second concept is that the rational and the religious (*shar'a*) are complementary. Ibn Taymiyyah stood against theologians who held the view that an external distinction exists between reason and revelation; instead he insisted on the internal unity of reason and faith. The general theory championed by the Mu'tazilah and the Ash'arites alike was that their internal propositions and rational postulates enjoyed the status of certainty, while the principles of the *fuqaha* were mere conjectures, and therefore dubitable, since they dealt with the mutable and suffered the pitfalls of *ijtihad*. Pitting himself against such theologians and philosophers, Ibn Taymiyyah rejected the dichotomy between reason and revelation, proclaiming that revelation is itself founded on reason. Furthermore, he argued that revelation not only requires the exercise of reason, but incorporates a number of rational principles.[28] For him, the *shari'ah* and reason ('aql) are essentially congruent, and that which contradicts one contradicts the other.[29]

Ibn Taymiyyah's third major contribution was to emphasise the unity between the will of God and the freedom of the human ego. He took a strong position against mainstream Ash'arite Sunni theology, which sought to safeguard divine omnipotence and absoluteness by sacrificing human beings and declaring us powerless. For Ibn Taymiyyah, there was no contradiction between God's will and human will. He distinguished, however, between the *existential* will of God and the *legislative* will of God, and held that God's existential or creative will refers to the creation of everything in this world, both good and evil, and that this is a subject for belief. God's legislative or moral will, as enshrined in revelation and embodied by successive prophets, reveals that good and evil are sharply distinct and antithetically opposed. Individuals have the rational capacity and freedom to obey God's legislative will or to reject it, to do good as enjoined by God or commit evil and disregard God's will.

For Ibn Taymiyyah, to deny the human capability to act is to destroy the norm of responsibility and, thus, to erase the norm of justice itself. For this reason, he saw the notion of *fana* (which relates to the breaking down of the ego and recognition of unity with God) as advocated in Sufism as detrimental to the foundations of social order.

Ibn Taymiyyah's reformism had two primary dimensions: firstly, to reform Islamic thought through recovering 'Islamic authenticity'; and secondly, to refute Sufi esotericism, along with its insistence on inner mystical meanings within the text that can be revealed only to a limited circle of enlightened and pious followers.

These two aspects of his thinking embroiled him in polemical disputes with various Islamic schools of thought. In Ibn Taymiyyah's time, Sufism had developed a highly elaborate degree of 'rational' construction, incorporating elements from different intellectual traditions (ranging from the philosophy of the Indians and the Greeks to Islamic theology and *fiqh*), all of which were reformulated in poetic and metaphorical language. The principal shift in the history of Sufism occurred in the thirteenth century with the master of pantheistic Sufism Muhyiddin Ibn 'Arabi, whose philosophical genius turned Sufism into a thoroughly rigorous philosophical discourse, with its own system of terms and concepts.[30] Late Sufism, as propagated by Mansur al-Hallaj (c. 858–922),[31] Abu Muhammad 'Abd al-Haqq Ibn Sab'in and Ibn 'Arabi, was not based merely on mystical or Gnostic personal experience. It was a synthetic philosophy that highlighted the complex and sophisticated nature of Islamic culture, which reached the pinnacle of its vitality in Andalusia and the surrounding region. Intellectual Sufism laid special emphasis on the personal element of faith, revealing the incommunicability of religious experience and a tendency to dissolve all existential and moral dualism in the unity of being. Since the twelfth century, this school had attracted followers from all sections of Muslim society, turning into a massive social movement with a far-reaching network of organisations (*turuq*).[32]

Ibn Taymiyyah distinguished between the early 'authentic' form of Sufism, which he saw as driven by a love of piety and asceticism, and Gnosticism, which he argued was indifferent to spirituality. He was unequivocally opposed to over-indulgence in ecstasy that aims at nothing more than yielding pleasure, and claimed instead that religion is essentially a worldly affair. He held that any act of worship that alienates believers from their immediate mundane concerns had been marked by the practices of Christian hermits and passive Sufism. According to Ibn Taymiyyah, worshipping God is essentially a worldly activity, not a flight from social life. It is a *jihad* in the broad sense of the term.[33]

Ibn Taymiyyah also rejected the pervasive influence of Aristotelian logic on Islamic theology and philosophy. In this vein, he may be said to have completed al-Ghazali's work of discrediting the Greek philosophers through exposing the contradictions in their work on metaphysics. Al-Ghazali excluded Aristotelian logic from his general attack, hailing it instead as a neutral tool that protects the mind from succumbing to falsity and as a notion that had already been incorporated into Islamic theology and jurisprudence. He was adamant that anyone who had not mastered logic was not entitled to make any claims to knowledge. Ibn Taymiyyah, on the other hand, insisted on the contingency of Aristotelian syllogism, and maintained that syllogism is inseparable from the language of the Greeks and from their metaphysical polytheistic vision. Greek logic, Ibn Taymiyyah argued, was as narrow and limited as the 'narrowness of their language'. He insisted instead on the possibility of various forms of logic.[34]

By emphasising the primacy of the original texts, Ibn Taymiyyah called for the opening of the gates of *ijtihad*, and challenged scholasticism and sectarianism.

Ibn Taymiyyah's reformist project also had a political dimension. Here we witness him arguing political theory against the Shia imamate, and stressing the value of *ijma'* (consensus within the politico-religious community) over that of hereditary rule.[35] Although Ibn Taymiyyah – like his predecessors, the Sunni jurists – accepted the legitimacy of 'de facto rulers' to avoid the perils of *fitnah* (civil disorder), which threatened to destroy the Muslim community, he called for the reform of the political institutions so that they would embody the value of *'adl* (justice) and express the unity of the Muslim *ummah*. While insisting that justice is the basis of moral governance, he rejected the use of violence to displace tyrannical rulers, and argued that removing one form of despotism only gives rise to another – or, worse, to social disarray.

This radicalism led to Ibn Taymiyyah's imprisonment, and eventually to his death in captivity. His views threatened to disrupt a system that was firmly established. His views and efforts clashed with the well-organised networks of the *mutasarrif*s (administrative elite) and the *'ulama*, making him an 'organic intellectual' in the Gramcsian sense. During his own lifetime, manuscripts of his books and treatises circulated among his disciples, particularly in Damascus and some parts of the Arabian Peninsula. Since then, revivalist movements in classical and modern Islam have often returned to Ibn Taymiyyah's writings for guidance and inspiration.[36]

Late reformism

The decline of the Ottoman Empire from the seventeenth century generated a wave of Islamic resurgence throughout the Muslim world. Movements for revival and religious purification emerged from the margins and 'arid zones' of the Empire, all attempting to put an end to the political corruption and widespread moral decline prevalent among the Ottoman rulers. The Wahhabi in the Arabian Peninsula, the Senussi in Libya and the Mahdists in Sudan are all examples of such reformist movements.

Of these, the most prominent was the Wahhabi movement, led by Muhammad Ibn 'Abd al-Wahhab (1703–1792), who came from a family of established *'ulama*. Ibn 'Abd al-Wahhab reactivated the Hanbali School as understood by Ibn Taymiyyah in the thirteenth century. Ibn 'Abd al-Wahhab's teachings lack Ibn Taymiyyah's sharp analysis, and are altogether more rigid and straightforward than his predecessor's, perhaps reflecting something of the arid climate of the Najd, the central area of Arabian Peninsula. The Wahhabi movement is indeed primarily the product of the ascetic life lived by people in the Najd and the influence of the puritanically inclined Hanbali teachings. Pre-eminent for Ibn 'Abd al-Wahhab was the purity of religious doctrine over concerns for social unity and consensus. This was evident in his unreserved attacks on the Ottomans, the *mutasarrif*s and the *'ulama*.[37] Fazlur Rahman was, to my mind, correct to note that

> Ibn Taymiyyah's message lay dormant through the centuries, and even when it was 'discovered' by 'Abd al-Wahhab and his followers in the eighteenth century, it was miserably truncated. The Wahhabi version totally lost the vision of an integrally reconstituted Muslim community that lies at the centre of Ibn Taymiyyah's endeavour, even though Wahhabi in its own right it became seminally influential in modern Islam.[38]

Ibn 'Abd al-Wahhab's rigorous Salafism remains the most influential intermediary through which Ibn Taymiyyah's thought is understood and interpreted in the Islamic world, and in some ways this has been an obstacle to the deeper understanding and wider dissemination of Ibn Taymiyyah's thought.

On the Indian subcontinent, Shah Waliullah (1703–1762), a distinguished *'alim* from the Hanafi School of *fiqh*, with its deep-rooted tradition of Islamic scholarship, opened up the reformist project with his pragmatic and flexible approach. Vividly conscious of the decay within the ruling Mughal dynasty, Waliullah's reformist agenda saw the preservation of the unity of the Muslim community, and the consensus of its various constitutive factions, as one of its first priorities. In fact, his main aim was to reconcile Sunni and Shia Muslims by reframing their differences within Islam's wider boundaries.[39]

In his major and truly insightful work, *al-Insaf fi Bayan Sabab al-Ikhtilaf* (A rational explanation of difference of opinion [in *fiqh*]), Waliullah followed in Ibn Taymiyyah's footsteps by recognising the legitimacy of vastly different schools of thought and interpretations within Islam. Waliullah placed much emphasis on the view that differences between the founders of *fiqh* had arisen as a result of diverging methodological positions and rationales. He took this to mean that truth does not always lie within the boundaries of one school or another, but can be shared between different *ijtihad*s. The rigorous monotheism insisted upon by Ibn 'Abd al-Wahhab (as a means of purging Islam of what he saw as the 'paganism' and 'polytheism' prevalent in the Arabian Peninsula in the eighteenth century) was directed by Waliullah into the attainment of a united Muslim community that accepts the differences and diversity of various *ijtihad*s and schools. That is, while Ibn 'Abd al-Wahhab took monotheism as the basis for a sharp and rigorous purification of religious doctrine, the oneness of God provided a foundation for diversity and flexibility for Waliullah. If God is one, then everything in his boundless creation might be diverse and distinct but these differences are ontological in nature, and pertain to the determination of that which emanates from the ultimate One and Only. For

Waliullah, all that was indubitably true was the Qur'an and the Sunnah of the final Prophet. All else necessarily requires *ijtihad*, and the two sources of legislation form solid foundations for diverse forms of social organisation and intricate social processes.

The various movements of revivalism and reform in Islamic history described above all grew from within Islam's own frames of reference and ideals. In other words, they developed largely without being influenced by the world outside Islam. What all these movements share is a commitment to returning to the origins of the faith and a willingness to overcome certain heavily influential scholastic traditions, and an appeal for fresh *ijtihad* combined with a ruthless condemnation of blind imitation and an insistence on the need to be open to new perspectives on the primary texts. In effect, they all distanced themselves from the relatively recent past through a return to the chronologically more distant but also more authentic past.

Modern reformism

The reformist project represented by the Salafi movement that was born in the nineteenth century, and which has grown substantially since then, can be distinguished from earlier reformist projects by three characteristics. First, it took root in the heart of great urban centres rather than on the margins of the Islamic world, and by the second half of the nineteenth century, circles of Islamic reformism had emerged in the most vibrant of Arab cities: Baghdad, Damascus and Cairo. Second, it showed an intense awareness of the decline of Islamic influence vis-à-vis its historical and intellectual achievements and of the ascendancy of the modern west. Third, modern reformism emerged during the imperialist era, and was therefore compelled to introduce an 'external' element into its process of self-assessment.

As noted in Chapter Three, the modern reformist movement emerged during the Tanzimat era. In terms of maturity and openness, it far exceeded its predecessors. The question of modernisation and its legitimacy can be traced back to this era, when the sultan and his entourage felt a need to build a powerful modern Ottoman army, capable of responding to the challenges of European expansionism. This included setting up a new administration that would be capable of centralising government authority over the provinces.[40]

Until the eighteenth century, the Ottoman Empire had been a potent power, with outstanding military capacities and vast geographical reach across most of Eastern Europe and the whole of the Middle East. As the eighteenth century drew to a close, it became clear that the Empire was declining and rapidly losing ground to the rising European powers. By the dawn of the nineteenth century, the Muslim world had been shaken by consecutive imperialist invasions. From Napoleon's destruction of Cairo, to the later massacres of Algerian villagers by the French, the sound of western gunpowder had reverberated in almost every corner of the Muslim world.

A vivid consciousness of the west's military superiority pressed heavily on Muslims. In his detailed documentation of the Napoleonic campaign in Egypt, 'Abd al-Rahman al-Jabarti explained that this brought Muslims face to face with the painful realisation that the 'Nazarenes' were militarily superior to them.[41] The supremacy of the modern west was felt not only by the elites in the sultan's court or on the battlefields, but also by lay Muslims in the streets of Cairo. Only later did Muslim intellectuals begin to acquaint themselves with Enlightenment literature preaching western superiority, and it was only when the global balance of power shifted that the Muslim world came to see the west as a superior adversary.

Two tendencies emerged within the Muslim elite at this time. Advocates of the first (referred to as Rijal al-Tanzimat or people of reorganisation) called on Muslims to learn from the west in the military, political and administrative spheres. Proponents of the second tendency pushed for a kind of religious revivalism, seeing in the reactivation of Islamic heritage a remedy to the declining influence of Muslim states.[42] The second tendency took its starting point from the fundamental values of Islam, which it endeavoured to reinterpret in the light of contemporary conditions. The strategy embraced by the first camp was virtually the opposite in that it began with a set of western philosophical principles and attempted to adapt the Muslim worldview accordingly.[43] The principal aim of both camps was to bolster Islam internally, to safeguard its integrity against western encroachment, and to provide a general paradigm or baseline from which any process of adaptation or assimilation could proceed. Nevertheless, the western challenge gave birth to an acute dichotomy within the Muslim elite.

The bulk of Muslim masses, and a great number of 'ulama, took a third path, and reacted to the assault of imperialism by holding fast to tradition. They viewed the west with suspicion and doubt, regarding it as a force of aggression and destruction. Most Muslims first encountered the modern west through the sound of rifles and gunpowder pulverising their cities and conquering their lands. It quickly became clear, however, that the conflict was not only to be a military one, but also a struggle between two imaginations, two sets of sublimated memories. Thus while European intellectuals, travellers and anthropologists laboured to construct Islam as stagnant, non-rational and despotic, their Muslim counterparts were characterising 'the west' as run by brutal, ruthless and aggressive unbelievers. While a tiny fraction of the Muslim elite – particularly the leaders of the Tanzimat – looked to the west as 'a centre of enlightenment', creativity and freedom, the majority of Muslims saw Napoleon – violent, vindictive and imperialist – as the personification of western values.

Just as Islam was (and still is) deemed by many westerners to symbolise all that is strange, morally perverse, grotesque and savage, so too did many Muslims perceive Europe as satanic – evil, vicious and inhumane. Thus, while the modern reformers were keenly aware of the need to learn from western administrative expertise and modern techniques, these were seen as essentially institutional and organisational tools, rather than as intellectually or philosophically challenging. Despite the ongoing shift in the balance of power in favour of European forces, Muslim elites remained fully convinced of the 'superiority' of Islamic civilisation over any external forces. As the American historian Marshall Hodgson noted:

Despite the general Occidental florescence associated with the Renaissance, the West Europeans were, politically, receding even before the Ottoman Empire, while commercially the Muslims were still at least their equals in most parts of Oikoumene. Culturally too, the Muslims were in one of their most brilliant periods. This occurrence in world history reflects European history in that the renaissance florescence did not yet, in itself, transcend the limitations of agrarianate-level society.[44]

What set the modern west apart from the rest of the world, and what accounts for the notorious 'great western transmutation', is what Hodgson referred to as 'technicalism', whereby 'specialised technical considerations tended to take precedence over all others'.[45] Contrary to the notion popular among earlier generations of Middle Eastern historians, that Muslim societies were overwhelmingly stagnant, decadent, backward, and altogether powerless to withstand externally imposed changes, the Middle East had never ceased to activate its energies to meet external challenges or to try to respond to the demands of changing circumstances. The Middle East, with its rich cultural heritage and intricate history, came to be viewed by the west primarily as a political problem, but as Albert Hourani put it:

> It would be better, however, to see the history of this period as that of a complex interaction: of the will of the ancient and stable societies to reconstitute themselves, preserving what they have of their own while making the necessary changes in order to survive in a modern world increasingly organised on other principles, and where the centres of world power have lain for long, and still lie, outside the Middle East.[46]

In fact, as European armies marched into the heart of the Middle East, the region was already undergoing a process of internal reassessment and reform aimed at overcoming the military and political dangers posed by the west. Examples of this include the Ottoman reforms of

1880, the draft parliamentary constitution for Tunisia developed by Khayr al-Din in 1864, and the proclamation of the Egyptian constitution in 1879.[47] These reform processes all came to a grinding halt at the end of the nineteenth century.

Of course, Muslims had faced external challenges and military invasion before, but none that had presented a real threat to their values and moral standards. The Mughal and Tatar invasions, which reached the centre of the caliphate in Baghdad, were military threats that Muslims not only overcame but reversed, establishing their own great empires on the Indian subcontinent and on the borders of Russia. It can therefore be argued that their intense awareness of the west's hegemony led the elites in Islam's great urban centres to try to adapt western concepts and institutions as a means of strengthening and bolstering Islam in the face of encroaching western imperialism.

What concerned the Salafi reformists was not the philosophical and moral values that lie at the root of western institutions so much as their social and political functions, which, they argued, might serve as models for the renovation and reactivation of Islamic thought as well as Muslim political and civic institutions. Muslim reformists also accorded the natural sciences and the modern socio-political institutions of the west a universal status, so that they could be integrated within an Islamic cultural context. Thus, modern reformism aimed to reconstruct and reactivate Islam by endowing it with new content that merged internal and external elements. As to the mechanism used, it was mostly an adaptive borrowing that reformists hoped would help them to control western influence and integrate it within a Muslim frame of reference.

As the reformists' vision of Islam was readily affected by their perceptions of the demands of the times, Islamic concepts were adapted to respond to the contemporary questions of the day rather than remaining aloof or detached.[48] The main strategy of modern reformism was to uncover what it called the 'secrets' of the modern west's ascendancy, and to incorporate these into Islamic systems of thought. Thus, in the discourse of modern reformism, the idea of democracy became *shura*, parliament into *majlis al-hall wa-l-'aqd*, and constitutional law into *shari'ah*. Modern Salafism also revived some theories and schools of thought that were not prominent at the time. For example, 'Abduh focused on Mu'tazilah rationality, and Khayr al-Din al-Tunsi did the same with al-Shatibi's *Maqasid ash-Shari'ah* (Objectives of the *shari'ah*) and Ibn Khaldun's historical perspectives.[49]

Thus, the new reform movement was the outcome of the amalgamation of two principal elements. The first was the revival of the mechanism of reform inherent within Islamic history and thought, and manifest in the weight that Salafism placed on returning to the basic tenets of the faith, activating *ijtihad* and rejecting of all forms of *taqlid* and social conservatism. This call for a return to pristine Islam was associated with a condemnation of Sufism and customary religion. Modern reformism is often also associated with attacks on mysticism and on cults of saints, which are seen as having driven Muslims away from the 'true path'. The second element was the attempt to adapt western institutions to Islamic values and to incorporate them therein.[50] Thus, what distinguished the reform movement of the nineteenth and twentieth centuries from older reformism was the syncretism of internal symbolic language with the traditions of the modern west. Early reformists appealed to religious revivalism by condemning conduct that did not comply with the example set by the Prophet and his companions, while their modern heirs married internal Islamic perspectives with the external western paradigms.

Any reader of modern reformism who is sufficiently acquainted with Weber's analysis of Islam will find striking agreements between the two in terms of their basic premises. Where the two part company is in the conclusions they reached. Both agreed on the stagnant condition of Muslim society, and identified Sufism as epitomising this decay. But while Weber attributed the cause of the decline to its morality as a warrior Oriental religion, modern reformism judged Islam's decrepit condition against the doctrines in its original sources and in the historical ideals lived by the Prophet and his companions. At various times, Muslim history has failed to live up to the Islamic moral paradigm. For the reformists, this failure lay at the root of the civilisational decline they were experiencing. Their view was that the situation could be remedied only by rejuvenating Islam's founding principles and reviving its historical model.

Did the two poles of reformism, modern Salafism and the revivalism of the Rijal at-Tanzimat, converge, and how far apart did they stand? As separate endeavours attempting to end Islam's decline and restore its historical prominence, the two were bound to share a space of commonality. This is evident in the work of its pioneers, notably Jamal al-din al-Afghani and his disciples Muhammad 'Abduh and Rashid Rida (1865–1935), as well as that of leaders in Istanbul and the other Arab provinces. To my mind, this shared perspective is what lies behind the numerous alliances the two poles forged at various times. However, the 'marriages' between Islamic reformists and the advocates of the Tanzimat were generally unstable and short lived – like, for instance, the alliance between al-Afghani and Sultan Abdul-Hamid II. The common ground they shared should not blind us to the vast differences between the two camps. They met at the level of modernisation and reform, but whereas the Tanzimat elite, as pragmatic bureaucrats, were seeking the means of enhancing their own military and political power, the reformists saw improved efficiency as a means of reviving and strengthening Islam.[51]

From its early days, the Tanzimat struggled to contain the complex forces contained within it. Above all, their project lacked internal coherence, and this eventually led Abdul-Hamid II's rule to its logical conclusion. The Tanzimat project was nurtured alongside a massive drive towards statism and the destruction of traditional ties of loyalty. Efforts were made to improve military capabilities, to rationalise administrative systems, and to consolidate the authority of the Ottoman rulers by subordinating the provinces. This gave rise to a technically skilled elite who stood to gain status by 'modernising' the state and centralising state power. The aim of the Tanzimat was to create a state that would function as a superstructural device of social modernisation, and before which traditional social structures would crumble. Tanzimat reformism was essentially a policy that aimed to destroy the Islamic educational and legal system, and it shook Islam to the core.[52]

Historically, the Ottoman rulers had long tended towards a policy of assimilation that encouraged ethnic and religious diversity, believing that this was in the interests of a strong state. By contrast, the Tanzimat regime was based on a threefold hierarchy comprising the sultan, who was deemed the head of Islam; the administrative bureaucracy; and the state-security apparatuses, which include the army and the police.[53] The modernisation of the Ottoman state quickly became arbitrary and oppressive, initiating a new form of theocracy, and weakening the social elements within Islam that had served to quell the state's drive to absolutism.[54]

The Tanzimat introduced a form of despotism that reached a peak with the rule of Abdul-Hamid II. He armed his regime with an extensive network of bureaucrats and security officers, trained in modern means of holding on to power, such as the centralised and highly trained gendarmerie who replaced the janissaries and local guards. In addition, modern forms of transport and communication made it possible to locate these military and bureaucratic cadres in every corner of the Empire. Abdul-Hamid II also proclaimed himself caliph, according himself spiritual authority over all Muslims on the globe in an effort to lend symbolic legitimacy to his tyrannical rule.[55]

Not surprisingly, animosity developed between those Islamic reformists around whom the populace rallied, and supporters of the Tanzimat, who were empowered by the state, and a split occurred. Indeed, al-Afghani, who was a close aide to Abdul-Hamid II for a considerable length of time, was expelled from Istanbul, and his fellow reformists were repressed throughout the Arab provinces.

Muhammad Ali of Egypt (1769–1849), who came to power after the departure of the French from Cairo in 1805, was a good example of the spirit of the Tanzimat. Having proven himself a charismatic, capable leader during the Egyptian popular resistance against French occupation, Ali proclaimed himself the ruler of Egypt, and was acknowledged by the Porte in Istanbul as such. Ali was a self-educated man who learnt to read in his forties and showed an interest only in those fragments of political literature that might be relevant to him in his tasks as a governor. He generally discouraged a popular interest in public affairs and politics. For example, during one of Ali's state visits to Paris, an Egyptian student remarked that he was studying civil administration. Ali reportedly replied, 'It is I who govern. You had much better go to Cairo and translate military literature.' Similarly, when one of his ministers presented a translation of Machiavelli's *The Prince*, he is said to have listened with very little enthusiasm, remarking, 'I know more tricks than he does.'[56]

By contrast, most of the modern reformists were *'ulama* who had long histories of learning. Confronted with the turbulent conditions facing Muslim society, they felt compelled to forsake the comforts of their schools and mosques, and engage in the controversial realm of politics (in its narrow sense), which they had long shunned.

The one exception who managed to straddle both camps was Khayr al-Din al-Tunsi, prime minister of Tunisia from 1873 to 1877. At that time, Tunisia was one of the Ottoman provinces, and Khayr al-Din endorsed the Tanzimat both intellectually and morally before being appointed as Grand Vizier of Istanbul from 1878 to 1879. Khayr al-Din seems to have embodied the harmony and strength that is possible when the pragmatism of a political leader combines with the utopian vision of social reform. In his reform programme, Khayr al-Din sought out the sources of European wealth and power and located these in Europe's political institutions, which he perceived as securing freedom and social justice for society. He referred to these two ideals in the following passage:

> The one who recalls these two remarks, that the Islamic *shari 'ah* is intended to ensure happiness in both lives (present and future) and that good organisation in the present life strengthens religion, observes with sorrow that certain *'ulama* who should take into consideration the situation of the times, neglect the study of facts both internal and external, they do not have a full understanding of the relevant conditions and this constitutes the greatest of handicaps.[57]

Khayr al-Din was vividly conscious of the need for reform and re-organisation, and wished to carry this out within an Islamic framework. In many ways, his aims were closer to those of the Muslim reformists than to the instrumental vision of the Tanzimat's state bureaucrats.

Given the oppressiveness of the Tanzimat project and the pervasiveness of western liberalism, the reformist movement acquired a clear awareness of the value of political freedom, of the limitations of power, and of the vitality of a national constitution. This is evident even in the writings of its early leaders (including al-Tahtawi and Khayr al-Din), and in the later work of 'Abd al-Rahman al-Kawakibi, who did much to problematise Islamic reformism in his major work, *Taba'i al-Istibdad wa Masari' al-Isti'bad* (The nature of despotism).[58]

It is important to remember that the modern reformists were not a homogeneous group. Among them were liberals such as Rifa'a al-Tahtawi, author and teacher (1801–1873), and Egyptian jurist Qasim Amin (1863–1908), who admired the socio-cultural model of western liberalism and devoted much of their energy to reproducing the 'original model'. Others were radicals who condemned the modern west's military aggression as blind violence, but believed that Muslims could learn from the west in the domains of science and administration, and use this to address injustice and preserve the unity and integrity of the world of Islam. Some reformists also changed their socio-political views over time. For instance, some have argued that Muhammad 'Abduh became more 'liberal' in his outlook, after the defeat of the 'Urabi Revolution in Egypt from 1879 to 1882 (which caused him to be exiled to Beirut and Paris). Following his return home to Egypt, 'Abduh moved away from al-Afghani's anti-imperialism and pan-Islamism and focused on quieter, more conciliatory educational reforms.[59] Similarly, Rashid Rida shifted his views towards the end of his life, but he moved towards a more radical Salafism, assuming a more critical attitude towards western modernity following the First World War.

The rise of the modern west was attended by monstrous crises and great internal disarray. Yet, it is undeniable that, in the eighteenth century, western modernity, by virtue of its massive military power and vast expansion throughout the globe, was able to universalise its self-confident narrative of emancipation and progress.[60] The first generation of Islamic reformists were forced to enter into a theological polemic with a culture still overwhelmed by Christianity and identifying itself as the product of Greco-Christian history. While there were a few voices of criticism from inside the west, mostly echoing from the domain of Romantic art, Islamic reformists had no real access to this. To them, western modernity appeared unquestionable, its crises unheard of, its shortcomings well concealed. This explains why the early reformists attempted to recycle Enlightenment values within an Islamic framework.[61]

The philosophical basis of modern reformism

The vast geographical reach of Islamic reformism, and its widely diverse concerns and priorities, means that seeking commonalities that unite all its varied expressions would be an arduous task, and exploring the movement's various configurations might prove equally arduous. However, underlying this grand and intensely colourful canvas lies a common element that unites modern Islamic reformism from North Africa to the Indian subcontinent. This I call 'the philosophical discourse of modern reformism', and I briefly outline its major elements below.

Monotheism

Monotheism is the moral and philosophical bedrock of all reformist discourse. Monotheism exercises a dual function. On the one hand, it stands against all forms of superstition, irrationality and myth. The modern reformists' commitment to the values of monotheism explains the attacks launched against popular Sufism and esoteric religion. For reformists, the prevalence of popular Sufism was the main reason for Muslim societies' decline in the face of western imperialism. Its beliefs and practices related to saint worship, miracles and intercession led reformists to view Sufism as imbued with an ideology of fatalism and passivity. The reformists also condemned the traditional *'ulama* for their lack of creativity, and for blindly following tradition.

At the same time, monotheism was also recruited into the battle against modern materialism and positivist attacks on religious belief. Al-Afghani, in his brilliant work *al-Radd 'Ala al-Dahriyyin* (Refutation of the materialists), argued that religion is the foundation of civility and culture, hence to dissolve religion is to demolish the bases of civility. As he put it, 'There is no doubt that religion as a whole is the factor that maintains the social order. Civility cannot possibly flourish without religion' (my translation).[62]

What might surprise readers of al-Afghani is his profound understanding of the problem of secularity. He used the Qur'anic term *dahriyyah* to show that secularism is a form of materialism; that is, an immanent philosophy with no reference to transcendence.[63] Accordingly, al-Afghani devoted much of his intellectual energy to combating materialism, which he saw as the germ causing the corruption of society and the destruction of religion. He considered Islam and its moral foundations to be the pivots of the power and prosperity of Muslim *ummah* as well as the primary protectors of Muslim society.[64] For al-Afghani, Islam was the intellectual and social basis from which all renovation and reform must be derived. In line with this, he argued that eastern materialists were nothing but the frontline of western imperialist forces, and in fact worse than any western secularist. For him, 'the secularist of the Orient is distinguished from the secularist of the west by virtue of his baseness, vileness, disbelief, and heresy'.[65]

Al-Afghani combined philosophy with religious morality, seeing both as necessary for human civility and for liberating human beings from the wilderness of barbarism and ignorance.[66] His philosophy was not of the ontological sort; it was pragmatic and moral, capable of stimulating scientific research, enhancing individuals' personal and social conduct, as well as diagnosing the ills within Muslim society and seeking to remedy them. Similarly, the religion he championed was an enlightened one, *ijtihadi* in nature, that stood against all forms of stagnation as well as social and ritual *taqlid*. In addition, al-Afghani insisted on unity between the principles of reason and those of religion. He maintained that to negate reason is to destroy the basis of religion itself, arguing that 'The laws of nature, proofs of geometry, and philosophical arguments can only be considered as primary evidence,' and that anyone who pretends that religion refutes evidence has to admit the falsity of religion.[67] For al-Afghani, revelation was the source that awakened the spirit, while reason and philosophy set the framework and methodology for 'rational religion'. Thus, in the discourse of al-Afghani and his disciples, religion, philosophy and science are inseparable.[68] To readers unfamiliar with al-Afghani, this may seem to mirror the Enlightenment dream of rational or natural religion. However, many Muslim readers will recognise that this approach has a long history within Islamic thought. Al-Afghani was simply recalling the perspectives of Ibn Rushd, Ibn Taymiyyah and the Mu'tazilah on the issue of the religious and the rational.

Modern reformists argued that civilisation and 'progress' could be achieved only within the fold of monotheism. They called for a rational social order that remains strongly tied to religious morality. They often cited the Khaldunian view of civility as the embodiment of rational religiosity or, to use Ibn Khaldun's terminology, as 'reason guided by the light of God'.[69]

Although the notion of *tawhid* (the oneness of God) played a central part in Ibn Taymiyyah's work (especially in his polemics with pantheistic Sufism and Judeo-Christian theology), and later in Muhammad Ibn 'Abd al-Wahhab's writings (albeit more narrowly and simplistically), it was in the work of 'Abduh and Iqbal that the concept acquired a rigorously systematic theoretical articulation. 'Abduh maintained that Islam's monotheism uproots all sorts of polytheism and 'purges' reason from the illusion of polytheism.[70] He also asserted that monotheism is the basis of the unity of all religions, and that the *ratio* behind all monotheistic religions is obedience to one God. In addition, he argued that monotheism serves to bind together all Islamic schools and sects, being the bedrock or the 'origin of origins' from which all interpretations derive their roots.[71]

Free will

The oneness of God is the ontological condition for human freedom. It is the ultimate will of God that urges human beings to implement free will on earth and submit only to the creator. For 'Abduh, to witness the oneness of God was to shed all shackles keeping the human will from asserting itself, no matter whether these shackles take the form of another human will or of a set of fantasies and illusions. The true meaning of monotheism requires submission to one real God only.[72] In other words, 'Abduh based the freedom of the individual upon monotheism, noting that 'It follows that what is realised to human beings through religion are two great things, which they were deprived of for a long time: the autonomy of the will and the autonomy of thought and expression.'[73] In this 'Abduh followed in the footsteps of the Mu'tazilah, deriving the principle of free will from the primordial principle of divine justice. Thus, the reformists were openly dismissive of Sufi and Ash'arite conceptualisations of the relations between *tawhid* and the human subject. Sufism tends to regard the human subject as little more than a parasite, constantly overwhelmed by God's presence. For the Ash'arites, humans can only be considered to be agents or actors in a metaphorical sense, because the real actor is the free will of God. For reformists, *tawhid* does not deprive the human subject of its presence and activity; in fact, it does the opposite.[74] Where God's power is universal and God's will is eternally ordained, the reformists maintained, human beings are not deprived of free will, nor are they prisoners of predestination.[75] The Mu'tazilah rejected deterministic interpretations of Islam and regarded humans as fully responsible for their actions, arguing that it is only through accepting authorship of our actions that notions of reward and punishment by a just and rational God become intelligible.

Three ideas conjoin to form the Qur'anic view of human freedom, according to Iqbal. They stipulate that human beings are the chosen of God; that humans, with all their faults, are meant to represent God on earth; and that human beings are trustees of free personalities, which we accept at our peril.[76]

Although Iqbal advocated the freedom and free will of the human ego, he adamantly rejected the Cartesian dualistic characterisation of the subject, by embracing a dynamic view that emphasises the intersection of subject and object. Ego, for him, was essentially a unity of inner experience, in which

> the life of the ego is a kind of tension caused by the ego invading the environment and an environment invading the ego. The ego does not stand outside this arena of mutual invasion. It is present in it as directive energy and is formed and disciplined by its own experience.[77]

The real personality of the ego, Iqbal held, is not a thing but an act, and its reality lies in its directive attitude. The ego for Iqbal was primarily a kind of free personal agency that shares in the life and freedom of the Ultimate Ego (God), who, by permitting the emergence of a finite ego that is capable of private initiative, limited the freedom of his own will.[78] Iqbal interpreted the Qur'anic story of the 'fall of Adam' as a parable of humanity's 'rise from a primitive state of instinctive appetite to the conscious possession of a free self, capable of doubt and disobedience'.[79] This was the signal of the emergence of a finite ego that had the power to make choices.

Iqbal stood against passive theology that did much to deprive the human ego of the capacity of acting and judging. A famous saying of his was that 'the weak believer seeks excuses in God's predestination. The strong believer is God's very will, His predestination.' Sufism with its fervent spirituality and emphasis on the principle of unity still figured heavily in the Iqbali discourse, and remained prominent amidst the other influences from within Islamic culture. In fact, it can be argued that what lay behind Iqbal's philosophy was a reformed version of Sufism, that rebelled against the Sufi ethic of submissiveness, passivity and resignation.

Two philosophical features are implicit in the norm of monotheism as understood by Islamic reformists. The first is the emphasis on the oneness of God and God's rigorous autonomy from all creatures in favour of a dual ontology. This explains the firm stand reformists assumed against Sufi pantheism, which they saw as a mere polytheism that was unaware of the separation between the metaphysical and the physical world, and constantly confused one with the other. In contrast, Ibn Taymiyyah emphasised the distinction between the 'world of creation' (*'alam al-khalq*) and 'the world of command' (*'alam al-amr*). He insisted that if the unseen world of God (*'alam al-amr*) is ruled by the free will of the ultimate creator, the physical or material world (*'alam al-khalq*) must be governed by the principle of necessity, and a rational chain of cause and effect, or what has been referred to in Islamic philosophy as 'the world of causes' (*'alam al-asbab*) must exist.

The second element stressed by reformists is the value of the existential equality between human beings. God created human beings as equal, endowed them with reason and free will and sent successive revelations and prophets to shepherd us through our time on earth. The reformists argued that, since Muhammad was the final prophet, the main source of guidance for humans is reason directed by revelation.

Reformist discourse also accorded a political dimension to monotheism, which reformers saw as undermining the moral foundations of political and religious despotism. Thus, they argued that monotheism precludes rulers from appealing to any form of theocracy, and refers rulers back to their nature as human beings who stand before the transcendental authority of God. *Tawhid*, argued 'Abduh, deconstructs the power of official and institutional religion, since it frees believers from all intermediaries and lays the written book, as well as the book of existence, wide open for believers to dwell within; no authority exists above God and His revelation.

Muslim modernists have used *tawhid* to denounce submissiveness to any authority other than God and to delegitimise obedience to tyranny. This transformed *tawhid* from a theological formula into a comprehensive system of faith and political action.[80] In his book *Tabai' al-Istibdad*, al-Kawakibi constructed a synthetic view of political and religious despotism more clearly than any other reformist.

Readers might find the Islamic reformists' commitment to a Cartesian-like rational subjectivity somewhat surprising. Apart from Iqbal, who was inclined towards a more spiritual and emotional active subject within a 'rationalised' form of Sufism, most of the reformists have accepted the notion of the rational intentional subject, and had no qualms about assimilating modern subjectivity into the Islamic framework. Citing the rational tradition within Islamic theology and philosophy, they have infused it with the modern notion of subjectivity. It is striking that reformists see Mu'tazilite theology, and the philosophy of Ibn Taymiyyah, to which they are firmly committed and constantly refer, as largely compatible with the Cartesian subject. Much Islamic discourse is based around the concept of 'the rational actor', the responsible *mustakhlaf*. Most jurists hold that at the basis of all religious obligation is the mature, rational and responsible believer.[81]

In fact, the secret behind the convergence between the two lines of thought lies in the theological basis from which the modern philosophy of the subject was derived. It can be argued that the philosophy of subjectivity is merely a rationalised and reformed expression of Christian theology. Muslim reformists – consciously or unconsciously – referred to a monotheistic theology based on the idea of the creation of the human subject. This philosophy, in one sense or another, is close to the idea of creation and the theory of viceregency in Islamic theology. It is thus fair to assert that Protestant reformism actually brought Christian theology closer to Islamic doctrine. In fact, this observation is not entirely novel in that the Protestant reformers' rivals often sought to undermine them by labelling them 'heretical' or 'Mohammedan'. As Gibb noted:

> Now it seems to be a general rule of history that when two civilisations come into contact, and a transmission of ideas is effected, the recipients are attracted to those elements in the other civilisation which are most congenial to their own habits of thought, and on the whole neglect or reject the other elements which they find difficult to assimilate.[82]

We must, however, take care not to reduce the notion of rationality in Islamic reformism to the external influence of modern philosophy. There is no doubt that the reformists borrowed the norm of rationality and the glorification of rationalism from modern philosophy, along with the positivistic tendency inherent in it. However, the sharing of a term does not necessarily imply common terms of reference or meaning. The pioneers of Islamic reformism used the term rationality, and its derivatives, within an entirely different epistemological and moral framework.

What is surprising, however, is the convergence between Habermas's theory of the evolution of worldviews in terms of learning processes and 'Abduh's *The Theology of Unity*,[83] despite the fact that the two thinkers derived different conclusions from their theories. Habermas drew an analogy between cognitive evolution and the progressive trajectory of worldviews to reach the Weberian end of a 'free' secular rationality. 'Abduh, on the other hand, established a kind of parallelism between child development and the evolution of worldviews, leading to the Islamic stage of development as the embodiment of 'free religious rationality'. That is, 'Abduh saw the development of world religions as revealing a cumulative process of evolution, arguing that, initially, religion led humanity as parents lead a child. At the earliest stages of human consciousness, religion spoke to specific sections of humanity in direct and sensible ways, laying down rigid and clear obligations. The laws of Moses, for instance, are, according to 'Abduh, the hallmark of this early stage of monotheistic religion, as they appeal to common sense.

The next phase, according to 'Abduh, was Christianity, with its overwhelming inclinations towards pure spirituality and its longings for redemption in a transcendental kingdom. To his mind, Christianity offered humanity the dramatic and terrible fate that is embodied in the contradiction between reason and religion, science and faith.

For 'Abduh, Islam was unveiled to the eye of history as the ultimate phase of humanity's journey. He saw Islam as the final step in monotheism's arduous and labyrinthine march, and as heralding the maturity of the human mind. For him, the revelation of Islam emancipated religion from all forms of superstition and myth, while also liberating reason from all binds and constraints. As 'Abduh put it, through Islam, the authority of reason was liberated from all that held it bound and from every kind of *taqlid* enslaving it, and thus restored to its proper dignity, to do its proper work in judgement and wisdom, always in humble submission to God alone and in conformity to His sacred law. Within its bounds there are no limits to its activity and no end to the researches it may pursue.[84]

It goes without saying that the *shar'i* (religious) and the *'aqli* (rational) were intimately intertwined in 'Abduh's discourse. The s*hari'ah*, for 'Abduh, provided a framework within which a liberated mind can find both legitimacy and guidance. What was sacred for him, and for his teacher al-Afghani, were the Qur'an and the Sunnah, which lay down the general principles and guidelines to which every age has to address itself in a spirit of active flexibility.[85]

Religion and reason, he often said, are complementary, and as such no contradiction can possibly arise between religion and science, which he saw as Islam's twin sources.[86] This position has a long history in Islamic theology and philosophy. Ibn Rushd (Averroes) saw philosophy (or wisdom) and religion (or *shar'*) as 'milk sisters'.[87] Although each concept has its internal logic and postulates, they are intensely close, and it can be argued that the sole difference between them lies in the fact that religion speaks to a wide circle of believers in a reasonable and metaphorical language, while *hikmah* (philosophy) addresses a more narrowly circumscribed circle of like-minded individuals using a more argumentative and rigorous form of discourse.

On this issue, the Mu'tazilites stressed that the rational and the religious are not only compatible, but non-contradictory. Were a contradiction between reason and religion to arise, however, they argued that religion would have to be interpreted in the light of rational considerations.

In my view, the most systematic response to this question was developed by Ibn Taymiyyah, who internalised reason within religion, and religion within reason. Ibn Taymiyyah's aim was to salvage 'Islamic rationality' from mystical introspection and the Greek scholasticism advocated by many of the Muslim philosophers of his time. For him, to undermine reason is nothing short of attempting to destroy religion.[88]

When 'Abduh used the term 'reason', he invoked the epistemological significance of the term; that is, he referenced the ethical meaning of the term in an Islamic context. The Arabic term *'aql* (reason) derives from the noun *'iqal*, which refers to a camel's binding cord. Thus the term *'aql* is linked to notions of 'restraint' and to the allied notions of 'being kept from harm', and 'refuge'.[89] Just as a rope stops a camel from straying away, reason prevents human beings from succumbing to moral decay.

There are undoubtedly positivist features in the rationalism of Islamic reformism. 'Abduh, like al-Afghani, was convinced that the 'tool of reason' is transparent and neutral when it is purged of illusions, efficiently used and well invested. In this context, reason is apt to attain ultimate truth. Al-Afghani and 'Abduh were both adamant that reason is impotent when confronted with metaphysics, but they insisted that all else may be laid bare for reason to explore and unveil. Thus it can be argued that reformist discourse laid as much emphasis as Cartesian philosophy on the distinction between 'science' and 'illusion' (*doxa*).

Pragmatic ijtihad and challenges to the authority of tradition

> The underlying bases of *taqlid* in the beliefs of the nations have been shattered by Islam. In the same cause, it has alerted and aroused the powers of reason, out of long sleep…Islam raised its voice against these unworthy whisperings and boldly declared that man was not created to be led by a bridle. He was endowed with intelligence to take his guidance with knowledge and to con the signs and tokens in the universe and in events…Islam encouraged men to move away from their clinging attachment to the world of their fathers and their legacies.[90]

While *shari'ah* was seen by the reformists as providing the blueprint for an Islamic social order, no limits were placed on how wide its framework could be. The reformists extended the concept of *ijtihad* far beyond the legal connotations it had in traditional doctrine. *Ijtihad* makes it incumbent upon Muslims to adapt to the 'spirit of their time'. Thus the reformists saw *ijtihad* as a primary means of responding to the demands of ever-changing culture, and to the idea of progress.[91] Accordingly, they called on the Muslim masses to practise *ijtihad* and to renounce *taqlid*.[92]

Two other concepts from early Islamic jurisprudence were important to the reformists. The first is *maslahah* (public interest), which they borrowed from the Maliki School, and the second is the *maqasid* (aims) of *shari'ah* as established by the Andalusian jurist Abu Ishaq al-Shatibi. Rashid Rida, another of the great pioneers of Islamic reformism and a disciple of 'Abduh, added the Maliki principle of public interest to the doctrine *ijtihad*. In classical schools of jurisprudence, *maslahah* was strictly a legal principle used by jurists when deducing a new decree *(fatwa)* by analogy, based on the textual sources of Islam. The reformists extended the term and used it to help them formulate regulations where no clear scriptural text was available. Abu Ishaq al-Shatibi then judged the whole body of *shari'ah* as revolving around five ultimate objectives: the protection of religion, the self, reason, property and honour.[93] Reformist discourse extended these five principles beyond the limits of individuals and applied to them the extended socio-political context. In this way, *ijtihad* and its two pillars, *maslahah* and *maqasid*, equipped modern reformists with great flexibility, and the ability to selectively incorporate modern ideas and institutions.

Most reformists distinguished between the immutable core, or the fundamentals of religion, and the mutable elements of doctrine, which have to be adjusted to the historical contingencies of the time and place. The rituals of worship (praying, fasting, almsgiving, pilgrimage, performing ablutions, etc.), they all agreed, are fixed and clearly defined. However, most matters relating to social legislation are mutable, and change in accordance with historical conditions.

As explained, reformists used *ijtihad* to help them to manage changing and turbulent times, and to provide the intellectual and moral grounds within which modern ideas and institutions could be assimilated and function. The goal modern reformists set for themselves was to ascribe Islamic legitimacy to the modern world that they were brutally and suddenly confronted with. In other words, *ijtihad* allowed Muslims the possibility of entering modernity through the legitimate gate of Islamic hermeneutics. Although reformist discourse is no longer homogeneous or indigenous, given ongoing 'acculturation', it has retained Islamic terminology and systems of reference. That is, even now, when reformists borrow a European element, they imprint it within an Islamic framework and legitimacy.

The achievements and limitations of Islamic reformism

To evaluate the discourse of Islamic reformism we must consider to what extent the modern reformist movement has succeeded in constructing an internally consistent project, and to what extent it has attained its objective of rejuvenating Islam and rendering it compatible with the needs of modern times.

Those who read the modern Islamic reformists' work are often amazed by their limited experience and the narrow body of concepts they dealt with. Reformists can be seen to waver between a set of indigenous concepts and terminology and an imported one, with seemingly little awareness of the parameters of either. Their principal concern was to strike a balance between the native discourse of high, scholarly Islam and modern liberalism. As discussed, this process coincided with chaos within the Muslim world: the dissolution of the Ottoman caliphate – which represented the political centre of Islam – and the ascension of the west, which was intoxicated with its own vigorous utopias and aspirations that were then still untested by experience and undamaged by failure or crisis.

Modern reformists faced a modern west puffed up with self-confidence and equipped with advanced instruments of power and violence. The reformists had little choice but to seek mechanisms that could incorporate and accommodate western concepts and terms within the Islamic order, and to adopt a posture of self-defence to safeguard their very existence. In this process, the modern reformist movement attempted to impose a degree of control over foreign concepts and terms by referring them to their counterparts in the Islamic dictionary. Thus, democracy became *shura*, election became *bay'ah* (oath of fealty) and constitution was translated as *shari'ah*. This reflects, to some extent, the instability and lack of coherence that marked Islamic reformist discourse. Few of its leaders were entirely familiar with European texts and terms (the exceptions being al-Tahtawi and 'Abduh, who both mastered French). It follows, therefore, that the modern west was discovered via Islam's own language and philosophical lenses.

While a conciliatory tendency characterised nineteenth-century reformism, a split occurred between its later followers. One side was represented by Rashid Rida, one of 'Abduh's closest disciples, who did much to further his teacher's project. However, Rida's Salafism was not only more indigenous than his teacher's, but also more radical and hostile to the west.[94] The First World War, with its terrible record of atrocities, did much to shape his stance towards the Occident, revealing the incivility of its supposedly civilising mission.[95] The other side was led by Qasim Amin, whose reformism was of a more liberal variety, and more receptive to European liberalism. Amin may indeed be viewed as the first proponent of liberalism not only in Egypt but in the Arab world as a whole.

Obviously Islam's interaction with 'foreign civilisations' and new intellectual horizons in the twentieth century was by no means a new phenomenon, nor indeed was it born out of its recent conflict with Europe. Historically few Muslims have deemed openness to other cultures to be a threat. From its early history, Islam was open to other cultures and intellectual traditions, be they Indian, Persian, Chinese, Greek or Roman. In fact, Islam proved capable of incorporating various traditions within its fold, thanks to its claim to universality, its insistence on its continuity with previous revelations, and its adherence to the principle of the unity of the 'Adamic race'.

The conditions that characterised Islam's openness to other cultural and intellectual spheres were, however, very different from those that marked its experience with western imperialism. In the process of its own expansion to new territories, Islam engaged in a process of peaceful acculturation with the peoples it came into contact with. Muslims formed part of a civilisation that rose to prominence over vast geographical areas in which rich traditions prevailed. These traditions were subsequently eclipsed, but were at no point in confrontation with Islam.

When the west imposed its dominance over the Islamic world, Muslims proved unequal to the strident forces that came to conquer their lands and undermine their culture. Unlike its earlier encounters with other cultural milieus, Islam did not meet the west voluntarily, but was driven to confrontation at gunpoint, its lands devoured by imperialism, its world shrinking before the hegemony of the western socio-political model. The process of modernisation, whether in Istanbul or in the other provinces of the Ottoman Empire, was imposed either through the direct intervention of European diplomats or indirectly through military oppression.[96]

The violence of this encounter still traumatises Muslims' consciousness and haunts their imagination, and it explains the tensions that continue to characterise Muslims' relations with the west. Muslims experience a great sense of unease when the contrast between their historical glories and their present-day exclusion from the international arena stares them in the face. This translates into varied reactions to western 'intruders', ranging from confused emulation to outright rejection, or a flight from the bleak present into the glories of the past.

Despite the conciliatory and even incoherent nature of the reformist movement, it was nevertheless an invaluable aspect in Islam's renovation. It has helped to make Muslims more responsive to, and capable of dealing with, modern times. The Salafi movement, which found itself reeling from the 'shock of western modernity', sought to reactivate the principles of Islam and its internal concepts, giving them new significance while broadening Islam's intellectual outlook and extending its hermeneutics. For example, *ijtihad* has come to acquire a wider set of meanings in Salafi discourse than those it had before.

At this point we can derive the following conclusions. Islam was neither a maker of, nor indeed, a partner to modernity, the latter being a western phenomenon. Although the shock of modernity brought about by imperialist expansion left Muslim consciousness in turmoil, and caused enormous instabilities in many Islamic countries' historical development, it does contain elements that Muslims have learned and benefited from. As noted, the shocking encounter with western imperialism provoked the reformists to return to the past, with a view to 're-discovering the self' in the light of changed 'external' influences. This historical awareness, haunted by the spectre of decline in the present, sparked a yearning for resurgence and renovation.-

This also accounts for the modern Islamic reformists' return to aspects of Ibn Khaldun's *Muqaddimah*, which provides a review of Islamic history and problematises the rise and fall of dynasties. Ibn Khaldun was acutely aware of the dysfunctional condition of the socio-political institutions of Islamic *'umran* (civilisation) in his own times. In addition, he had an intuitive sense of the advancing military capabilities of the Europeans in the territories on the northern side of the Mediterranean that had been under the control of the Ottomans. It is interesting to distinguish between the historical consciousness portrayed in Ibn Khaldun's work and that shown by Hegel and Weber. Ibn Khaldun's approach to questions of political advance and decline used an Islamic moral and social yardstick, and he was acutely aware of the problem of historical fall and decline. By contrast, Hegel and Weber's primary concerns were with questions of rise and progress. Of course, Ibn Khaldun acquired his historical sensibility from witnessing the decline of the Islamic empire, while his European counterparts' perspectives evolved in the climate of the rise of modern Europe. Accordingly, words that echo frequently in Ibn Khaldun's work are extinction, decline and regress, while some of the words and phrases that permeate the Hegelian sphere are birth, emergence, new age, new world, emancipation and future.

Naturally, the philosophy of history largely, if not entirely, reflects historical conditions, and can never be isolated from feelings of torment or pride stirred by its labyrinthine trajectories. Thus, while the philosophers and intellectuals of Europe were joyously seeking to uncover the hidden secrets of their 'unprecedented progress', Muslim elites on the opposite shore of the Mediterranean were overwhelmed by the bleak task of identifying the reasons for their pitiful decline.

The principal object of Weber's historical concern can be summed up in the question: why is it that modern Europe alone was apt to engage in the historical process of rationalisation as embodied in capitalism and the modern state, leaving the rest of the world lagging behind, and staggering under the burdens of stagnation and the status quo? Since Kant posed the question that formed the title of his famous essay 'What is Enlightenment?', and Hegel's systematic elaboration of the Kantian view,[97] western philosophical consciousness has been consumed with the urge to account for the rise of modern Europe by transforming the Christian notion of eschatological salvation into the secular concept of teleological progress.

From Ibn Khaldun to contemporary Islamic reformism, Muslim consciousness has been engrossed in a quest to make sense of notions of decline and fall, and to find a way towards renovation and revivalism. Of course, this does not mean that modern reformism's historical awareness is identical to Ibn Khaldun's, or that it proceeds in a straight line from his work. For one, Ibn Khaldun never had to endure existence under the direct dominance of foreign powers; the ascendancies and declines he was concerned with were internal to Islamic politics. What is certain, however, is that when confronted with the historical shock of western victory over 'Islamdom' (to use Hodgson's term), the reformist elite returned to the work of Ibn Khaldun, and revived the questions he had posed centuries before.

Until then, the Khaldunian texts had largely been cast into the margins of intellectual tradition in the old universities of Egypt, Tunisia and Morocco, surviving only within the narrow circles of Ibn Khaldun's disciples and followers in North Africa and Andalusia.[98] It was after the dawn of the nineteenth century that the *Muqaddimah* again rose to prominence within the Islamic academic establishment. Ibn Khaldun's masterpiece became an essential reference for all Muslim reformists, and even state officials. Modern reformists revisited the questions raised by Ibn Khaldun about the rise and fall of states, and problematised the malaise affecting Islam, not only with reference to its internal dynamics but also by comparing it with those of modern Europe. In addition, they refuted Ibn Khaldun's deterministic view, which held that a state can never escape from weakness and decrepitude once plagued by them. The modern reformists insisted instead that the decline of Islamic civilisation was curable, and that a renaissance was possible if Muslims equip themselves with a clear historical consciousness and sufficient political will. For this reason, the Arab thinker Fahmi Jad'an claimed that for Arabs, modern times commenced with Ibn Khaldun in the fourteenth century, and not with Napoleon's invasion of Egypt as is generally thought to be the case.[99]

It can therefore be argued that the shock of western modernity did contribute to the renovation of the Islamic order of knowledge and the widening of its horizons. Countless attempts were made to revive the languages and symbols of Islam, and to clothe them in modern discourse. In this way, Islamic self-consciousness was able to rediscover itself and confidently stare at its reflection in the mirror of its own religious ideals and to compare them with those that are prevalent in present times. Thus the call to return to 'the fundamentals' – the Qur'an and the Sunnah – as advocated by the Salafi movement in the nineteenth and twentieth centuries that advanced alongside the revival of *ijtihad* and the condemnation of *taqlid*, was prompted by an attempt go beyond existing scholastic interpretations.

Reformist thought is emphatic that the crises experienced by Islam, as well as the manifest impotence of Muslims to deal with modern times and contemporary issues, are directly related to the power of blind tradition. Reformers argue that Muslims should bypass tradition and return directly to the Qur'an and the tradition of the Prophet without recourse to mediative interpretations. No doubt such calls are idealistic; no understanding or interpretation is possible without what Gadamer called the effectiveness of history, which allows conversations between an interpreter and a text or event to take place. There can be no escape from the gamut of prejudices that mark the hermeneutical situation of any readers of any text.[100] We can, however, distinguish between different modes of relating to 'the effectiveness of history'.

The reformist strategy reflected on history and tradition within the effectiveness of history, but was not unconsciously overwhelmed by history and tradition. It was capable of maintaining a certain distance from the past even when it sought to reconstruct and preserve continuity with it. The idea of distinguishing between the Qur'anic text and the tradition of the Prophet, on the one hand, and the traditional interpretations that had accumulated around these, on the other, was in itself innovative and revolutionary.

The reformist movement also deployed the idea of the first *salaf* (companions of the Prophet) as a means of emancipation from the past. To revert to the *salaf* implies a return to the first creative and *ijtihadi* spirit in relation to the texts, with no stringent or rigid commitments to any of the schools or interpretations that have arisen in between.

The spirit that runs through modern reformism is the reverse of that which stultifies madhhabism (sectarianism). The reformists dwelt in the vast horizon of the Islamic tradition, taking no notice of boundaries between schools of thought, ranging from the *mutakallimin* (theologians) and *fuqaha* to the philosophers and even the Sufis. The reformers looked to the encyclopaedic and intensely diverse spirit of Islamic culture. They were not concerned with safeguarding any particular 'sect' or granting it prominence, but with reconstructing and rejuvenating the entire Islamic intellectual sphere, in all its configurations. Their endeavour was to restore to Islam its status as a distinguished civilisation, and to show that it was powerful enough to ward off western imperialism.

The controversy over the work of al-Afghani aptly illustrates the diversity within the body of reformism. To many, al-Afghani was a mere spin doctor, a shrewd political player who artfully concealed his Shia leanings to secure his endorsement by mainstream Sunnis; a man who never tired of forging new political alliances and engaging in intellectual and political debates. This view is blind to the intellectualism of this great pioneer of reformism and to the priorities that steered his political agenda. What chiefly preoccupied al-Afghani was not Shia or Sunni Islam, but the all-encompassing value and utopia of the wide *ummah*, and the dream of pan-Islamism. This line of thought could only be conveyed through the medium of mainstream Sunni discourse. Nonetheless, his Shiism remained a prominent part of his intellectual grounding, not as a sectarian commitment, but as a collection of epistemological tools and a philosophical heritage. His anti-imperialism drove him to look at the entire Islamic map as a single phenomenon, and with no regard for narrow sectarianism or ethnic divisions.

The reformist movement created some space between religiosity as practised by the Muslim community in particular socio-historical contexts and 'religion' *per se* as embodied by the origins of its being. The proposition put forward by 'Abduh, for instance, is truly expressive of this view, albeit unsophisticated. He postulated that the Muslim *ummah* had regressed because it had deserted the path of true Islam, and begun to embrace Christian otherworldliness; meanwhile the Christian west was advancing because it was closer to reflecting the true spirit of Islam via its admiration for science, and its attempts to establish equality before the law.

It seems that the modern west 'Abduh was invoking, the west he found himself contending with, had retained some of its Christian characteristics, or at least appeared to be not only secular but Christian as well. As any reader of Abduh's dialogues with Renan knows, he spared no effort in his endeavours to undermine the postulates of European theologians and thinkers, pointing to the generally irrational character of Christian doctrine, while stressing Islam's rationality and superiority. But what 'Abduh found truly paradoxical about his time in France in the mid 1880s was that he was confronted with a 'Muslim society' practising Christian otherworldliness in its day-to-day existence and an opposing 'Christian society' living in ways that in some respects were more true to Islam.[101] When concluding his visit to France, 'Abduh commented that he had found Islam in France but no Muslims, and that he had come from a 'Muslim land' which had no Islam.

It is difficult to accept these views today given what we know of the modern west and historical Islam, but it is crucial that we take note of their underpinnings. In the late 1800s, 'Abduh faced a self-confident west, that was able to boast huge achievements, and was still unscarred by crises or defeat. In contrast, the Muslim world was injured and vulnerable, incapable of withstanding the power of its imperialist rivals. The paradox he observed while travelling in Europe enabled him to preserve some distance from the pitiful historical condition of Muslims while maintaining an unwavering esteem for and commitment to Islam.

'Abduh's reading of Islamic history in relation to the west is not uncontroversial. First, the idea of a historically decadent Islam is questionable, since we know from the works of Hodgson[102] and Lapidus[103] that Islam continued to flourish politically and militarily. Even when Islam was stripped of its political authority over Andalusia, the creativity of Muslim thinkers, jurists and philosophers did not suddenly cease. On the contrary, Islamic libraries still boasted huge, invaluable and truly unparalleled collections of works and treatises on science and literature, poetry, philosophy and theology, that embodied the spirit of the by then eclipsed Andalusia.[104] In addition, reaction to the schism plaguing the Muslim world, and the Christian advance that cost the Muslims Andalusia, sparked a vibrant intellectual movement of reassessment and renewal.

Second, 'Abduh looked at the west from a liberal point of view; that is, through the image that the modern west had created for itself. 'Abduh was unaware of the oppressive character of modernity. The modern west, to his mind, exemplified rationality, order, intellectual freedom and political justice. In this respect, his work can be seen as a step backwards from al-Afghani's, whose writings revealed an intense awareness of the west's dualistic and contradictory face as evident in its internally libertarian drives and its externally brutal imperialist force.

Notwithstanding their diverse and often conflicting strategies and agendas, the founders of modern Islamic reformism succeeded in bridging the gap between 'traditional Islam' and 'the modern world'. The reformists expanded discussions about Islam beyond the confines of 'traditional' teaching and learning establishments and into the 'modern' schools and universities. Thus, from being the exclusive terrain of traditional scholars, discussions about the nature of Islam spread out among Muslim intellectuals, professionals and political activists.

Even in the nineteenth and twentieth centuries, reformists spoke a simple, straightforward language that was accessible to Muslims in general. 'Abduh's text is that of a highly religious traditional scholar, but he wrote in a clear and simple style. This had a great impact on various fields of knowledge and learning within the different languages of Islam (Arabic, Persian and Turkish), appealing to new generations of Muslims and recruiting scores of students as followers. These intellectuals, in turn, spread the language of reformism to the fields of literature, education and the media.

The extension of discussions about Islam from the traditional circles of the *'ulama* into the broader spheres of the modern urbanised elite was, as Fazlur Rahman put it, 'a major basic revolution'.[105] It is widely known that when 'Abduh was appointed rector of al-Azhar University, he announced that he would not only introduce modern science and western knowledge to that institution, but would also seek to revive Islamic classics that had been driven to the margins of the Islamic educational establishment.[106] This included such works as Ibn Khaldun's *Muqaddimah*, and the theological works of the Mu'tazili School. This project lay at the heart of 'Abduh's reformist thinking, as he saw these works as the gates to uncovering 'modernity' within Islamic tradition.[107]

The Moroccan thinker Abdullah Laroui has argued that the reformist school failed to come up with anything new, and that all it did was translate what used to be said in the language of the old universities of al-Azhar or al-Zaytouna into the language of Oxford and the Sorbonne.[108] However, even if we were to accept that there is nothing novel in the discourse of Islamic reformism, the translation of a traditional scholarly language into a modern one is itself a creative contribution.

There is little doubt that the intellectual world of Islam suffered from intellectual impoverishment and instability in the nineteenth and twentieth centuries. Contemporary thinkers still find themselves powerless to fill the vacuum left by traditional scholars, or to generate an education system capable of replacing the old networks of traditional learning. In the Islamic world, many of the so-called modern universities still lag behind their western counterparts, and few can claim to have attained the elaborate levels of intellectual scholarship of the traditional universities. Nevertheless, the language of Islamic reformism has become the medium through which modern intellectual institutions express themselves, and even the traditional sectors have been infiltrated by this discourse. It seems therefore that, despite all the difficulties and obstacles, a bridge of communication between modern and traditional Muslims is being built.

Accordingly, the main questions that have engaged Islamic reformists since al-Afghani are:

- How can we reconstruct and restore Islam's internal energy so as to empower it to confront the imperialist challenge of the west?
- How should we incorporate western institutions and intellectual traditions into an Islamic renaissance?
- How do we maintain a balance between adapting western institutions and thought and safeguarding Islamic identity?

At the beginning of the twentieth century, Muslim consciousness found itself on unfamiliar ground, and having to cope with the disappearance of the Muslim state. In response to this, the reform movement sought to activate the mechanisms of self-regulation within the infrastructure of Islamic institutions, and to enable them to perform functions that had formerly been the responsibility of the state. Throughout Islamic history, tribal and village communities, family units, Sufi *tariqahs*, as well as artisan and merchant networks, had all maintained a certain degree of autonomy from the state. Reformism encouraged these groupings to withstand the changes brought about by the decline of the Islamic political establishment and the ascension of modern imperialism, in an effort to preserve the unity of Muslim society and preserve it from dissolution.[109] This served to shift political activity from the narrow confines of state apparatuses into the vast social realm, and activated all sectors of Muslim civil society.

In my view, this phenomenon is largely accountable for the emergence of the modern Islamic movements, or what is known as 'political Islam'. Reformist discourse consolidated the common identity of the Muslim *ummah* and strengthened social cohesion as individuals and Muslim organisations were called upon to shoulder some of the responsibilities of the state. Reformists then extended the concept of consensus from the confines of jurisprudence, and infused it with a fresh political dimension. For reformists, consensus is no longer limited to the agreement of scholars on a specific legal interpretation, but extends to the consensus of the whole *ummah*. In this way, the Muslim community has been able to preserve its identity and vital interests.

Furthermore, with the advance of secularisation, and the fading of Sufism along with other traditional religious alliances, Islam has become less ritualistic and even more intellectual and ethical. That is, the enormous energy within Islam, which had long been contained within the traditional sphere of the state and its allies among the political elites, has been transformed into a vast political movement that takes various forms, ranging from reactionary radicalism to peaceful reformism.

What appears to be common to most of these movements is that their leaders and their social bases are often linked to the modern universities. That is, the students are no longer trained only in seminaries and they tend to be more middle class. Thus the political language of modern Islam now reflects the discourse of urban middle- and upper-middle-class populations (students, professionals, new intelligentsia, technicians and bureaucrats), rather than the rural lineages and tribal communities.

It is interesting to note that this shift away from agrarian and rural roots and towards more socially mobile networks has not occasioned a shift away from Islam and towards secularism, but rather from traditional forms of Islam to a modern reformist one. For Gellner, this merely reflects a transformation from folk Islam to high scholarly Islam, or, as he likes to call it, a 'fundamentalist' Islam. The picture is in fact infinitely more complex. Contemporary reformists are not embracing a predetermined, ready-made, or 'correct' model of Islam; instead, they are participating in the reactivation of Islam's hermeneutical language, and finding ways of 'reconciling' this with the political discourse of modernity.

What is certain is that the reformist movement, in addition to its political role, helped to preserve Islam's cultural and intellectual integrity and unity. The reformist discourse opened the language of Islam to modernity and bridged the gap between its internal indigenous culture and the 'global' culture of modern times. To an outsider, this might seem like a tacit 'westernisation' of Islam that might in turn lead to the waning of tradition and ritual in favour of a secular modernity. However, Islamic reformism broadened the symbolic language of Islam, while keeping its internal integrity intact. Reformist discourse borrowed many concepts and terms from the modern west, but it did so as part of a selective and adaptive strategy aimed at Islamising western discourse. The reformist movement exposed Islamic consciousness and society to new possibilities beyond the confines of ritual and traditional religion, while avoiding the trap of western secular modernity. In my view, modern reformism laid the foundations of what may be called an Islamic modernity.

I think Gellner was correct in noting that reformist Islam has played a similar role in the Muslim world to that played by nationalism elsewhere.[110] The reformist movement established a widespread cultural and political identity in the name of pan-Islamism, which – despite the temporary dominance of nationalism or pan-Arabism, and the nationalist character of certain liberation movements – has remained a vivid source of legitimacy. Indeed, it has become difficult to envisage a 'national' identity without the presence of Islamic symbolic capital.

Arab nationalists (under the umbrellas of Nasserism in Egypt, Ba'thism in Iraq and Syria, and the various 'regional' nationalisms that emerged in the decolonisation of Tunisia, Algeria and other parts of the Islamic world) attempted to 'secularise' nationalism, but generally fell short of achieving this. To common consciousness, the term *ummah*, which can be translated as 'nation', remains a small part of the historical model and symbolic ideal of the broader *ummah*. Muslims remain unable to resolve the tension between 'utopian *ummah* and the 'real' *ummah*. Apart from the official ideologues of 'regional states' who continuously sing the praises of the 'modern nation state', most Arabic and Islamic intellectuals and political activists speak of a utopian *ummah*: an Arab and Muslim *ummah*. For Laroui, the only solution to this tension was to set aside the utopian dream and accept the fact of the Arab nation state as it is. Laroui contended that political utopia is still vividly present in the mind and the heart of the Arab and Muslim intellectuals only because they still read the political literature of the sultanate.

European imperialism generated massive upheaval within Islamic history and consciousness, but not so much as to cause their dissolution. Of course, this is not to deny the presence of calls for rupture with the past in the interests of fully embracing the western model outside from the likes of Salama Musa, Lotfi al-Sayyid, and other westernised liberal voices.[111] However, I think the continuity of transmitted symbols and social institutions is infinitely stronger and more solid than the wishes or ideological goals of such individuals or organisations.

The emergence of Islamic modernity

When the world of Islam faced the threat of western imperialism over two centuries ago, a kind of distinction, without complete separation, developed between traditional Islamic discourse and a new modern one. The former is still present, and has its own figures, spokespersons and social bases. However, the latter has exhibited greater activity and attained wider prominence, particularly among students, professionals and modern sectors of society. Indeed, one of the most striking features of contemporary Islamic revivalism is its appeal to the youth, through more modern forms of discourse. This is as evident in the intellectual background of the standard-bearers of modern Islamism as it is in that of its social base. Also noteworthy is the heterogeneous character that Islamic hermeneutics has assumed since its encounter with western modernity. Modern Islamism is far from being homogeneous or indigenous to any specific region or group of people. It is a highly heterogeneous sphere in which internal and external influences have become intimately entangled, and where the indigenous interacts with the foreign in a dual process of coexistence *and* confrontation. This was clearly highlighted by the Italian thinker Armando Salvatore, who wrote, 'Through the consolidation of trans-cultural dynamics between the "West" and "Islam", the originally endogenous process of reification of the latter became ineluctably heteronymous and no longer in pace with its subjectification.'[112] For Salvatore, modern Islamic reformism originated in 'new Sufism', Wahhabism and the *'ulama'*s reform movements of the nineteenth and twentieth centuries, and has provided the subjective conditions for the emergence of an intellectual modernity in the Islamic world.

> Differently from a *nahdha*, ground on a general level of civilisational rebirth, *islah* reflects a concern for the historical development of a responsible subject. Though it has some rooting in the Koran, the first conscious self-identification of some thinkers as committed to *islah* is contemporary and complimentary with the process of reification of Islam in public discourse that has taken place since the end of the nineteenth century.[113]

Although Islamic modernity looked less spectacular than the western model when it first emerged, its function, according to Salvatore, was largely similar. That is, Islamic modernity addresses the current social order through a new emphasis on the human subject as a social being, a denunciation of *taqlid* as a principal means of challenging the authority of the past, and the vindication of *ijtihad*. This general process, according to Salvatore, is essentially located in the Islamic region's major urban centres. As he put it, 'in spite of the fact that Muhammad's community functioned as a model, the novelty of *islah* is that it replaced an arbitrary sacralised consensus of the community (*ijma'*) with another kind of consensus based on the immanent rules of public communication'.[114]

Salvatore's general reading of *islahi* discourse might be valid, but his conclusions are contentious. Islamic reformism did not effect a shift from the 'transcendent' to the 'immanent', from 'transcendental consensus' to 'immanent public consensus'. This dualism derives from the political discourse of western modernity. In the philosophical discourse of Islamic reformism the 'transcendent' and the 'immanent' are already interconnected and inter-functional. As explained earlier in this chapter, the tenets of monotheism and *ijtihad* – the two pillars of Islamic rationalism – strip the validity from such dualism. In addition, when reformists extended the notion of consensus from the legal sphere to that of public politics, they did so through the hermeneutical framework of the *ummah*, whose will is realised as that of its members in their interaction with the religious text. As noted, the example of Madinah in the time of the Prophet was invoked, and *shari'ah*, as a representation of the discourse of society, juxtaposes transcendence with contractual immanence. Contrary to the Orientalist view that portrays *shari'ah* as expressing the transcendent and oppressive will of God in ways that leaves no room for mundane human presence, *shari'ah* has operated as a unifying discourse throughout Islamic history, providing a framework for social consensus.[115]

Contemporary radical Islamism tends to place the will of God in opposition to that of the people, and to depict *shari'ah* as the antithesis of human sovereignty. This created an image of stagnant and God-imposed law. Leaving its legalistic determination aside, *shari'ah* is best understood as a framework that regulates the social fabric. It has succeeded in performing this function through generating a vast network of consensual relations. In fact, the role *shari'ah* has played historically is in many respects comparable to that Habermas ascribed to communicative reason, which he saw as being workable only within a rational and secular life-world. In my view, Richard Khuri was right to argue that

> both the extended and short characterisations of reason given by Habermas…imply criteria that are easily met by the methods according to which the shari'ah has been drawn. If Habermas understands reason as consensus formation in a 'communication community', then the shari'ah is eminently rational, for it explicitly aims, through one of the three fundamental principles from which it is drawn, at the

consensus of a very large community indeed. For all the legal
competition it has run into, it persists as a popular token of
Muslim consensus.[116]

In Habermasian terms, the communicative function of *shari'ah* in Muslim society is based on a moralised life-world. Any Muslim follower of
a particular school of thought (*'alim*) is entitled to assert the Islamicity
and legitimacy of an *ijtihad* if it meets the requisite moral commitment
to the text and is able to defend itself argumentatively. These are the
criteria according to which acceptance of a given *ijtihad* is measured in
the wider community.

It is true that the transcultural dynamism that evolved between
'the world of Islam' and the 'world of the west' did not develop on
the basis of an equal footing in the balance of power; nor did it take
place in peaceful circumstances. Emerging within a climate of military control and imperial expansion, Islamic modernism has often
been both tentative and unstable in its analysis and concepts, alter-
nating between its own 'internal indigenous' authority and the 'external' western one. Nevertheless, transcultural interaction has helped
to enrich Islamic discourse in relation to its concepts, language and
guiding questions.

It is crucial to note, however, that Islamic reformism, from
al-Afghani onwards, has never been driven by a desire to reproduce or
copy western social or intellectual models. Its strategy has always been
to make the 'external' subservient to the 'internal' – a vessel for self-
reconstruction not self-abandonment. Indeed, since the development of
modern reformism, the intellectual world of Islam – as Iqbal made plain
– has found even more solid ground to stand on.[117]

The overwhelming majority of Orientalists and other western experts on the Middle East continue to expect the interaction between
western cultures and other cultures – including Islam – as necessarily
leading to the dominance of the western social model and the disappearance of any other. In their view, Islam will be lucky if it survives as
the folkloric expression of a faded culture that has been cast to the mar-

gins of modern life. Many might even see this as a sign of the victory of 'modernisation' over 'tradition', of the forces of rationality over those of rigidity. However, it seems to me that the reality in the 'world of Islam' is not what such 'experts' would have us believe. Islamic culture and society has never been a *tabula rasa* that was passively receptive to external influences. Islam possesses a vast cultural heritage accumulated over centuries. This culture is too rich, dynamic and vibrant to be easily dispensed with. Although Islam has faced enormous and unprecedented challenges in the past two centuries, the linguistic and cultural resilience of Muslim societies has made it possible for them to resist western hegemony on many fundamental levels, and to develop responses to it based on their own internal resources.

The Salafi movement of the nineteenth century is often seen as having merely reacted to the west by passively absorbing its external influences. Albert Hourani's analysis, for example, presents al-Afghani and 'Abduh as mere recipients of western ideas.[118] Hamilton Gibb's judgement in his book *Modern Trends in Islam* seems more balanced and profound. Gibb emphasised the complex nature of Islamic reformism, and saw that the influence of early Islamic thought, and particularly of al-Ghazali and Ibn Taymiyyah, was quite pervasive in modern reformism, arguing that

> It is commonly believed that since Islam was fast losing its vitality, the new factors were intrusions from without, impulses radiating out from Europe. This is in fact quite untrue. The new tensions arose within Islam itself by the operation of its own forces.[119]

Of special significance in Gibb's analysis was his awareness of three crucial factors, as advanced throughout this chapter, namely:
- the long history of Islamic reformism, which made it possible for al-Afghani and 'Abduh to draw on the work of much earlier thinkers such as al-Ghazali and Ibn Taymiyyah;
- the great potential for revivalism and internal resurgence within Islam, which has translated into successive movements of reform;

- the fact that when the reformist movement introduced western ideas into the Islamic intellectual order, it did so within an Islamic frame of reference.

In later years, Hourani accepted Gibb's view, and even critiqued his own early work, noting that he had overlooked the force of authentic continuity of the reformist discourse and over-emphasised the role of external influences.[120]

As Hamid Enayat insisted, ideas have an existence of their own and are possessed of great powers that enable them to survive and prosper. Modern Islamic reformism was never bereft of new concepts or terms, and its discourse and analyses did not emerge from a vacuum. Instead, old ideas and terms were resurrected and enriched by western ideas or by their contrast with western ideas. For Enayat, the primary response of modern reformism vis-à-vis the modern west roughly paralleled the strategy adopted by the Mu'tazilah in relation to Greek thought. The Mu'tazilah saw no harm in absorbing Greek philosophy and logic with the aim of strengthening their own capabilities in relation to polemical debates with Christianity and other creeds. Enayat noted that 'the modernists overtly or covertly apply categories of thought derived from Western philosophy, political theory and science to enrich their own reformist or revolutionary propositions'.[121]

The main priority for the modern reformists was to eliminate the theological and canonical elements that they saw as sources of stagnation and redundancy. To achieve this, they invited all the 'progressive' tenets of Islam to prove their internal rationality as a religion of freedom, justice and prosperity. At the same time, they rejected all thought, conduct and values operating in Muslim society that they saw as contradicting the rational bases of 'true Islam'. In the process, they ended up rejecting much in Islamic history, and took the era of the Rightly Guided Caliphs (632–661) as the basis for their understanding of the Qur'an and the Prophet.[122]

The elements of continuity in the history of Islam have their origins not only in the deeply rooted Islamic social structure, and in Muslims' strong attachment to tradition, but also in the fact that Islam – as a religious and moral authority – is still alive and active in the consciousness of the vast Muslim masses. This remains true, even though many social institutions and much of the 'infrastructure' that Islam rested upon in the past has been dissolved and weakened by the impact of western colonialism and the destructive 'modernisation' policies of many post-colonial states.

While external events have radically confronted Islam's moral and symbolic authority, its values and culture remained ever-present and deeply embedded in the social fabric and social structures of Muslim societies. Islam has never been banished from private or public life, and, in the decades since the 1979 Iranian revolution, Islam has returned to the political sphere and its political language has been revived. Today, the Muslim world responds to western colonialism with calls for *jihad*, and even the most secular national elites use Islamic slogans in pursuit of their goals.

7

The new Islamic reformists

As this book draws to a close, I explore the contours of Islamic discourse over the last century, and attempt to explain why I believe that a new phase of Islamic reformism has begun. I offer some criteria that allow for the distinction between 'old 'and 'new', and discuss the work of some of the intellectuals who have and still are pioneering this discourse. I also outline some of the great questions around which this new phase revolves.

First, let me acknowledge that all acts of classification and categorisation are arbitrary to some degree; classification attempts to impose some order on that which is fragmented and dispersed, and this is one of the principal difficulties facing any endeavour to group the various trends in Islamic thought. What some might designate new might be labelled old by others, while what some see as reformist can appear to others to be liberal, or even conservative. I must also admit to a certain emotional relationship with this topic, and I take comfort that the claims to objectivity, much emphasised by classical epistemology, are illusory: our relationship with any text is, I submit, always interactive. Thus readers may observe that my reading of the precepts of Islam overlaps significantly with what I outline as new reformist discourse.

Having made these admissions, let me define the new Islamic discourse as I see it: it is a mode of discourse that derives its authority from Islam's referential framework, and problematises the issues of modern times using Islamic terms and frames of reference, with the aim of reviving Islam and contributing to its adaptation to the present conditions of the world.

As Nietzsche noted, to name something is to attempt to master and exert power over it. Since no knowledge is possible without order and methodology (that is, selection and intervention), this epistemological dilemma is part of any act of classification. However, the typology I have used is not intended to be rigid or finite; it deals with a multitude of discourses pregnant with unfinished and unexpected interpretations. What I refer to as 'new Islamic reformism' is an ideal type in the Weberian sense of the term – a flexible model that may be subject to revision, or renaming. It is heterogeneous, with a great variety of embedded texts, figures and possible interpretations. Thus the new discourse of reformism lives within an overlapping and cumulative lineage, in which the 'classical' coincides with the 'modern', the 'old' with the 'new', the 'revivalist' with the 'reformist', and the 'secular' with the 'religious'. Like a newborn in need of naming to acquire some kind of existential legitimacy, it is my view that this phenomenon needs to be named in order to acquire ontological legitimacy.

Many creative phenomena have died in their infancy in the land of Islam, their existence unknown to the wider world, simply because they remained nameless, or have been given pseudo-names by the hegemonic discourses of the west.[1]

The two crucial questions that I attempt to answer in this chapter are: how does Islamic reformism appear today, over two centuries after the emergence of the modern reformist movement; and have contemporary scholars made any significant contributions to this discourse?

Generally speaking, most of the issues raised by the modern reformists and outlined in Chapter 6 remain acutely relevant, although some of the answers have evolved and acquired more sophistication. Their questions about the rise and fall of civilisations, their diagnoses of the great maladies within Muslim societies and consciousness, and their suggestions for dealing with the challenges of modern times, have dominated Islamic discourse for two hundred years, and are still in a process of formation and growth.

My object here is not to depict the cumulative vanguard of modern Islamic thought, but to shed some light on the labyrinthine and complex development of modern Islamic discourse since it came face to face with the western challenge that marked the start of the contemporary age. No doubt, much of what was produced by earlier generations of reformists was deeper, or more erudite, than some of what is written today, but the general picture reveals a degree of evolution and maturation.

My classification of old and new is not intended to be chronological. My focus is more on the quality and nature of the questions raised than on when they emerged. For example, no serious reader of Islamic thought can overlook the writings of the Indian philosopher Muhammad Iqbal (1877–1938), who is renowned for the depth of his critical insights. Iqbal can be classified as a leading force in the new Islamic discourse, even though he wrote in the early part of the twentieth century. Similarly, the work of Algerian writer Malek Bennabi (1905–1973) is profound and sophisticated even though his writings date back to the middle of the twentieth century. The same can be said of the founder of modern reformism, Jamal ad-Din al-Afghani, who showed an acute awareness of the frightening bleakness of western modernity. Conversely, many of those who write today can only be categorised as following the classical or 'old' discourse of Islam. For me, what distinguishes new reformism from modern reformism is its attitude towards western modernity, and the distinct levels of comprehensiveness that each discourse developed.[2]

Western readings of contemporary Islam

What seems to keep western academics, politicians and intellectuals from perceiving the intellectual dynamism of modern Islam is their obsession with the radical but marginal voices within Islam, who are engaged in a ruthless crusade against women, modernity, democracy, and all that is deemed to be of value to the modern west. Three main factors have conspired to produce this outrageously stereotypical and prejudiced image of Islam: ignorance, fear and the instability of vast areas of the Muslim world (which is partially related to foreign powers' involvement in the geo-politics of the region). As a result, the far-flung, diverse and complex world of Islam is often reduced to the militant face of the Taliban or other reactionary factions in Egypt or Algeria, for example. These marginal elements reduce the wide world of Islam to a generic picture of a 'world deprived of reason'.

One example of this perspective was presented by Samuel P Huntington, who consigned the vast geography of the Muslim world to what he calls Islam's 'bloody borders', blaming the religion's inability to co-exist with other creeds.[3] Accordingly, Huntington warned western policymakers and strategists of the dangers presented by the turbulence of the Muslim world, and went on to encourage their engagement in 'a conflict of civilisations'. Particularly alarming for him was the possibility of an alliance between the Chinese and Islamic civilisations. Francis Fukuyama, as if he were a prophet, proclaimed that with western neoliberalism, and particularly the American era, history has come to its end. This, too, implies a biased and simplistic reading of Islam, and that the fundamentalist reactionary currents that are allegedly peculiar to Islam will not remain impervious to western liberalism. Fukuyama, with his historical determinism, or poor attempt at Hegelianism, has insisted – implicitly and explicitly – that Islam is a reactionary anti-modern force consumed by fundamentalism, and will have to choose between conforming to American liberalism and being consigned even further into the margins of the world.[4]

The unanimously dismissive position assumed by many western academics and institutions in relation to Islam is striking. To the western imagination, Islam is still flawed, violent and fanatical; at worst, a deluded sect. The effect of global power games in shaping such discourses is obvious. What may be less clear is how the 'demonisation' of the other serves as a catalyst for the construction of views of the self. The modern secular west presents itself as civilised, superior, developed and progressive. However, all these qualities can only be fully appreciated with reference to the negation of everything that the west imagines or desires itself to be.[5] In this case, a great religion and a deeply rooted civilisation have been forced to stand as objects of preconceived prejudice.

Hans-Georg Gadamer's reading of prejudice as a crucial and active factor in the generation of knowledge is apposite here.[6] The set of prejudices through which Islam is seen, and in terms of which it is devalued, are crucial for the preservation of the west's self-image. Nietzsche's conception of illusion as an existential condition of life also seems appropriate.[7] Indeed, if illusion is often the ontological condition of a historical community and culture, as well as of its internal self-confidence, then it may be argued that without such illusions, the modern west might be considered little more than a historical accident.

It is no accident, however, that Islamic thought is widely excluded from departments of theology, philosophy, history, etc. in western universities. Underlying this is the west's perception of Islam as an impoverished culture with no real contributions to make to the field of thought. And some religious studies departments even exclude Islam from the study of the monotheistic traditions, arguing that Islam is a special case, and that the monotheistic tradition is primarily Judeo-Christian.[8] Nevertheless, the emergence of the new Islamic discourse is intimately associated with the birth of the new Muslim intellectual. Interestingly, such intellectuals are not encountered only in the traditional centres of Islam, but also in western Europe and North America, which have growing Muslim minorities. The decline of traditional Islamic institutions of learning, and the waning role of scholars of Islam, has brought the new Muslim intelligentsia to the fore. The part that modern reformism has played in shifting the discourse of Islam and its symbolic heritage away from the traditional learning institutions and into modern schools and universities has been truly significant. Indeed, contrary to the prevalent view that modern schools and universities are the vanguard of secularisation, these establishments have acted as the principal generator of the new Muslim intellectual elite.[9]

A circle of strong intellectuals, academics and other figures who combine an intellectual background with political activism have come to represent the new Islamic discourse. What is common to all these individuals is their concern with the great questions confronting the world of Islam and modernity. American researcher Charles Kurzman tried to subsume a great variety of Muslim intellectuals and scholars under the umbrella of liberal Islam. He identified three traditions within Islam. The first, which he called *customary Islam*, is marked by the combination of regional practices (such as reverence for saints, ritual displays of spirituality and power that express regional cultural traditions) with those that are common to the entire Islamic world. The second, which he called *revivalist Islam*, he designated as fundamentalism or Wahhabism, and, he argued, is governed by a desire to renew the Arabic language, destroy illegitimate local political institutions, and assert the authority of revivalists as sole legitimate interpreters of Islam.[10] The third tradition, designated by Kurzman as *liberal Islam*, subsumes a wide array of intellectual figures and conflicting views under one label. Kurzman argued that like revivalist Islam, liberal Islam 'defines itself in contrast to customary tradition and calls upon the precedent of the early period of Islam in order to legitimate present-day practices'.[11] He argued that what distinguishes the two is that the first recalled the past in the name of modernity, while the second appeals to modernity in the name of the past.

Kurzman had no qualms about identifying revivalist Islam with Wahhabism and liberal Islam with 'the enlightened elite' whom he saw as receptive to western liberalism. He offered liberal Islam as proof of 'modern' Islam's ability to accept and take to western liberalism. Thus, for Kurzman, if modern Islam showed signs of dynamism and openness, it was only because it had come under the influence of western liberalism. It follows that for him the most westernised voices of modern Islam are both the most 'liberal' and the most creative on the Islamic intellectual map. For such thinkers, the intellectual *telos* of modern Islam seems to begin with to the intellectual 'revivalism' of Waliullah al-Dahlawi in eighteenth-century India, and stretches forward to the voices of contemporary westernised liberals.

Unlike Kurzman, I see reformist Islam as the clearest and most expressive face of Islam's *internal* intellectual dynamism. Some of the figures he cited do indeed belong in this group. Others, however, are better classified as westernised liberals. Islamic reformism is a wide field that speaks in different tones and languages, and some Islamic reformists do have some liberal inclinations, but it would be a travesty to overlook the 'Islamicity' that forms the core of their identity. This does not mean that new Islamic reformism is merely an endogenous phenomenon since, as shown in the previous chapter, it has been subject to influences from the west since its emergence. However, the language best suited to characterise this phenomenon is not 'indigenous versus exogenous', since elements from both are engaged in an ongoing process of interaction and entanglement, and are being continuously reinterpreted and reinvented.

The typology of Islamic discourse drawn by Esposito and Voll seems more useful, although their chronological evolutionary approach might also be flawed. For Esposito and Voll, Muslim activist intellectuals – as they refer to the new reformists – represent a bridge to the tradition of radical *tajdid*, and can be divided into three groups: the early activists of the mid twentieth century; the 'second generation' that formed the core of the Islamic resurgence in the 1970s and 1980s; and the 'third generation' that has participated in an increasingly sophisticated and complex discourse since the early 1990s.[12]

For me, what distinguishes the new form of Islamic discourse is its dual concern with Islam and modernity, and its use of complex language that is both Islamic and modern. In addition, a clear chain of continuity exists between early, modern and contemporary Islamic reformism. Perhaps the expression that most aptly characterises this phenomenon is 'the new phase of modern reformism'. This highlights the peculiarity of this new stage, and emphasises the fact that a clear chain of continuity stretches back to early reformism, late reformism, modern reformism (as outlined in Chapter 6), and continues on through this important contemporary trend in Islamic thought.

Enabling Islam to articulate and express its thought in a modern language was one of the great achievements of Islamic reformism. Contemporary reformists are all descendants of al-Afghani and 'Abduh, and remain in intimate affinity with them, even as they seek to critique or go beyond them. Al-Afghani's legacy of reinterpreting Islam using a modern language, combined with his intense consciousness of the demands of the age and his resentment of imperialism, remains influential in reformist discourse. The history of ideas, it seems, is destined always to be governed by continuity with the past, even when it manifests signs of departure and rupture from earlier traditions.[13] This is not to say that the history of thought is merely a cumulative chain, but simply to highlight the power of continuity within moments of shift.

The pioneers of reformism since al-Afghani have continued to define their enterprise as a return to the *salaf* and to pristine Islam, but their effect has been much wider than instilling the idea of a simple return to a golden age. Far from being merely a call to revert to the past, modern Islamic reformism has reshaped the entire Islamic intellectual map.

In my view, Esposito summarised the intellectual map of the Muslim world accurately when he said:

> The old elitist visions of the secularists, which have few roots in the Islamic traditions and which were important to the newly educated and urban masses, and the social and political institutions that had been created by Western-style modernisers, had proven to be woefully inadequate. Among the modern educated classes, a new style of Muslim intellectual emerged who was committed to effective transformation of society but within the framework of ideologies and programs that could be identified as authentically Islamic.[14]

As noted, the massive defeat of Islam at the hands of western imperialism forced Muslim reformists to direct their energy towards reconciling western modernity with Islam. Thus, their aim was to instil 'western modernity' within Islam's worldview; that is, to adopt western modernity while preserving the cultural and moral identity of Islam.

In general, these reformists saw science as a neutral tool, adaptable to different contexts and universally applicable. They were rationalists in the sense that they were convinced that reason was incapable of dealing with metaphysical subjects, but that what is within the reach of reason is entirely transparent and may be absolutely grasped. In addition, these modern reformists endorsed the notion of progress, but sought to purge it of its positivist connotations and recycle it within a religious framework.[15]

The philosophical discourse of new reformism

What distinguishes the bearers of new Islamic reformism from their predecessors is their greater familiarity with western modernity, including its pitfalls. They are more aware of the complexity of modernity, its emancipatory character as well as its shackles and its shadows. Many of the new reformists were trained in western universities or in the modern universities of the Muslim world, and only later came to rediscover their Islamic roots. Thus many contemporary Muslim intellectuals endeavour to advance an Islamic approach to modernity that combines both western and Islamic references.[16] This sets them apart from the modern reformists from traditional Islamic backgrounds who went on to discover western modernity and attempted to readapt it into an Islamic framework.

To the new wave of reformists, the modern west is no longer an enchanting secret, or an attractive model. Admittedly, the modern west is also utterly different from what it was in the nineteenth or early twentieth centuries. Modernity's underbelly could no longer remain hidden after the First and Second World Wars, or during the Cold War, and has continued to make itself felt ever since, in the massive environmental destruction and social disintegration that it has generated.

Critiques of modernity flowed from among the ranks of the new Islamic elite. Two interconnected factors are relevant here. The *first* is that from the dawn of the twentieth century, western modernity stopped boasting about itself. Nietzsche's hammer shattered the foundations of its great narrative about global emancipation, and the world wars, with their horrifying atrocities, violently shook the pillars of western modernity. A wide gap opened up between what Paul Ricœur called the 'space of experience' and that of expectation.[17] The *second* factor is that these crises helped to restore the confidence of the Muslim elites and fostered a critical view of the west that traversed the camp of the conservatives, who were utterly averse to the west, and that of the liberals, who had earlier been enchanted by it. As a result, the new Islamic discourse created what I call counter-narratives to those of western modernity, the principal features of which can be summed up as a vivid awareness that:

- The nature of western modernity is complex and intricate; while it can harness great power in favour of emancipation, it also possesses a massive force of destruction and annihilation.
- There is no such thing as a single unique and uniform modernity even if most Muslims are familiar with the aggressive violent face of western imperialism and the various forms of political and economic restrictions it has since imposed.
- External expansion is not a digression from historical process but a substantial and intrinsic aspect of western modernity; the will to master the universe and achieve hegemony over its vast population has always been integral to it.[18] Internally, this takes the form of ever-expanding institutions of control and discipline – as Max Weber, the Frankfurt School and Michel Foucault have made plain. Externally, it is in various forms of imperialism that this will has been manifest.

From the very beginning, the discourse of modernity was haunted by contradictory perspectives and goals. The Kantian spirit of utopian universal liberation that ran through it aspired to create a rational free subject. However, this spirit was overwhelmed with a raging sense of national glory and a Hobbesian Leviathan expansionism. Modernist discourse was thus always torn between articulating a humanist utopia and national self-interest. Readers of western philosophical literature of the eighteenth and nineteenth centuries are all too familiar with this conflict, and with attempts to reconcile the two, such as can be found in the writings of Alexis de Tocqueville. Tocqueville's work is discussed in more detail in an earlier chapter of this book, but it is interesting to note that he spent some time in Algeria, which offered him a chance to become acquainted with the Qur'an and to 'contemplate' a Muslim society with the keen eyes of a French colonialist. Tocqueville was interested in studying the moral influence of religion on society. In his view, the Christian spirit of American society made democracy possible there, while Muslim morality crushed its followers with its materialism and fatalism. As he wrote to Gobineau:

> I studied the Koran a great deal, mainly because of our position vis-à-vis the Muslim populations of Algeria and throughout the Near East. I must tell you that I came away from that study with the conviction that by and large, there have been few religions in the world as deadly to men as that of Muhammad. As far as I can see, it is the principal cause of the decadence so visible today in the Muslim world, and though it is less absurd than the polytheism of old, its social and political tendencies are, in my opinion, infinitely more to be feared, and I therefore regard it as a form of decadence rather than a form of progress in relation to paganism.[19]

Of course, western discourse on Islam and so-called Oriental society is inseparable from the mechanisms of constraint and control that the modern west attempted to impose on the planet. As discussed in Chapter Two, western political hegemony was accompanied and consolidated by the establishment of the dualisms of 'west' versus 'east', and 'Occident' versus 'Orient'. In this enterprise, the west armed itself with a solid paradigm of a 'scientific and methodological' approach to 'Oriental' societies. New reformist discourse has devoted much intellectual energy to deconstructing western modernity, undermining its internal homogeneity, and delegitimising its 'great narratives'. In fact, this, too, sets the new reformists apart from their predecessors, who were more interested in absorbing modernity and incorporating it within their own religious paradigms.

The new reformists are intensely aware of the enormous gap between what modernity preaches and the way it actually functions in the world. Egyptian thinker Abdelwahab Elmessiri (1938–2008), for instance, read western modernity through the faces of fascism, Nazism and imperialism.[20] Palestinian writer Munir Shafiq distinguished between modernity as a discourse and a utopia, and modernity as a socio-historical movement. He insisted that it is misleading to read western modernity through its philosophical doctrines or its intellectual formulations, and argued that the dark side of western modernity is evident in the international structures of hegemony and monopoly established by the modern west.[21]

The United Nations offers just one example of the west's inconsistent amalgamation of universal liberation and conflicting national interests. On the one hand, this institution draws its roots from the Enlightenment utopia of a unified and peaceful human community, and claims to represent the universal and common will of humanity. On the other hand, its permanent members monopolise the right of veto, thereby embodying the will and interests of the great nations that have seized the reins of global economics and politics.

Part of a wider discourse

Many features of the new reformism coincide with those of post-modernism. Both traditions share a clear awareness of the limits of the philosophical foundations of western modernity. Where they part company, however, is in their response to these limitations. The postmodernists are committed to playing the game of internal deconstruction. The new reformists' tendency is to attempt to offer 'constructive' answers to the issues confronting the modern human condition – fragmented and dispersed though their answers may be.

Thus, as Shafiq noted, the new Islamic discourse is only part of a wider global trend.[22] One can say that, while modern reformism tried to legitimise modernity within an Islamic frame of reference, the new reformism assimilates critiques of western modernity within an Islamic frame of reference. Its proponents go beyond the nihilism and scepticism of post-modernism, drawing on Islamic values and highlighting Islamic alternatives in their critiques. Deconstruction is seen as a procedural step in a constructive process aiming at a 'new model' of modernity.

Habermas, for one, expressed fear and dismay at the possibility of an alliance between anti-modernists and post-modernists. Many Arab thinkers, including Muhammad Arkoun, Hashim Salih and others, frequently warned that 'Islamism' may use such criticism to destroy modernity altogether. These concerns appear to emanate largely from a fear that the type of modernity to which this class of intellectuals subscribes might be abolished. Their fears conceal the fact that the new Islamic discourse has found solid grounds for discrediting the western model, highlighting its limits, *as well as* formulating different solutions from an Islamic perspective.

In other words, the new Islamic discourse is not confined to rethinking Islam, but seeks to introduce a new approach to the problem of modernity. The Moroccan philosopher Taha Abdurrahman, for example, has called for a new *ijtihad* of modernity. To him, the so-called Arab modernist discourse lacks novelty and rigour, and is but a blind reproduction of western discourse. Abdurrahman appealed for vibrant investment in the energy of the Arabic language and Islamic hermeneutics. A philosopher of language and logic with a wonderful mastery of several European languages, Abdurrahman conducted an archaeological study of the texts of the great European philosophers, unveiling the etymological mechanisms in terms of which they produced their terminology and discourse. Abdurrahman then showed how the lexicons of such philosophers reflected their national languages and informed their worldviews in ways that relate directly to the Greek and Christian traditions. Such traditions, he contended, remain active even in the discourse of the most radical of western atheists.[23]

Abdurrahman not only called for fresh *ijtihad*, he himself embarked on the project, drawing on various spheres of Islamic knowledge, ranging from theology to Sufism, from jurisprudence to philosophy. He is acutely aware of the limits of Islamic rationalism, as championed by Ibn Rushd, and has pointed this out in his work.[24] Similarly, the remarkable Muslim philosopher Abu Ya'rub al-Marzuqi rejected Rushdism as a possible foundation for what he referred to as an 'Islamic renaissance'. For al-Marzuqi, an Islamic renaissance will only be possible if Islamic consciousness rises to the level of the universal and provides answers to the deep concerns of our age. He has argued that this can only happen when Islam's spiritual revolution incorporates the tools or means of modernity in a synthetic and critical manner.[25] In al-Marzuqi's eyes, al-Ghazali's thinking offers a firmer basis for 'Islamic rationalism'.

Immanence

The new reformists stand strongly against what they call the metaphysics of immanence, as Parvez Manzoor pointed out:

> Against this, theology should guard the radical transcendence of God, whose voice comes into being from without, is fully consonant within Islamic sentiment that stems from its non-negotiable commitment to transcendence. For without transcendence, there is neither ethics nor politics. The immanentist philosophical foundation of secularism cannot withstand any normative edifice that houses a morally binding theory of politics.[26]

For Manzoor, peace in the city and bliss in the soul are different aspects of human longing. He summed up his attitude to western modernity as follows:

> The ultimate conflict between Islam and modernity, it ought to be clear by now, is neither over governance nor over technology, not even over society and social engineering, but over transcendence and the nature of ultimate reality. As against the immanent claim of modernity, Islam holds that the ultimate reality is transcendent. Consequently, human reality, in as much as it is part of the ultimate reality, stretches beyond the authority of the state and the coercive world-order that sustains it.[27]

In a nutshell, the object of new reformists' efforts may be summarised as: to generate a vibrant heart within the heartless world of modernity, and to invite the spirit that illuminated the works of al-Ghazali and Ibn Taymiyyah to remedy the ills of modern times.

For Taha Abdurrahman, the root of western modernity's failures can be traced to an absence of teleological and moral objectives. Western modernity is a culture of power and means, moving within its own self-enclosed framework, and interested in nothing but effectiveness and pragmatism, regardless of ends or goals.

Secularism

The problem of secularism is another central theme in the discourse of new Islamism. Its adherents take issue with Muslims who paint secularism as a uniform and unified phenomenon that should be wholeheartedly endorsed or completely rejected.

The new reformists firmly oppose the philosophical and moral foundations of secularism, which they identify as reflecting the philosophy of immanentism, and rejecting any reference to transcendence. Instead, they position transcendence at the heart of worldly affairs, insisting that, 'without transcendence, neither ethics nor politics exist'. As Manzoor observed, 'the immanentist philosophical foundation of secularism cannot withstand any normative edifice that houses a morally binding theory of politics'.[28]

For new reformists, politics and civility are inseparable from a solid commitment to transcendence that bestows meaning on the world and saves human consciousness from the darkness of nihilism. They argue that the elimination of transcendence from the province of human thought not only causes westerners much agony, but its consequences have been deadly for all fields of modern endeavour. They also point out that the utopian idea that historicism has the power to heal the past without appealing to transcendental morality is little more than wishful thinking.

Nevertheless, the new Islamists' philosophical and moral rejection of secularism has not prevented them from analysing secularisation's labyrinthine historical processes or its great variety of expressions. Secularism, as Manzoor noted, does not represent a systematic doctrine. This allows for aspects of modernity to be adapted and incorporated within Islam's moral framework. Manzoor summed this up as follows:

We must also avoid looking to the ideational landscape of our times as a battlefield between Islamic theocracy and Western secularism. The contest is not between Islam and modernity; neither is it between Islamic faith and secular rationality; indeed not even between Muslim will-to-power and the secular world order (whose rhetoric solicits a cultural and political pluralism but whose institutions dictate monism), but between faith in a Transcendent Being and the totalitarian project for an immanent social Utopia conceived as the End (*al-akhirah*). So long as the western man, has taken upon himself to act as the advocate of secularism, so long as modern man, whatever his descent and persuasion, is adamant upon renouncing transcendence, *homo Islamicus* has no other option but to stand firm in his faith in an ultimately trans-secular order of reality.[29]

Alongside the deconstruction of secularism as a theory of truth, new Islamists have attempted to expose the various forms that secularism takes in the Muslim world. For example, Rachid Ghannouchi has shown that what is often seen as a necessary relationship between secularism and democracy is an illusion.[30] As shown in Chapter Three, secularism in the Muslim world, and the Arab region in particular, has in fact long been associated with political despotism.

The new reformists are, however, keen to functionalise the political and social features of *democracy*, including political representation, freedom of expression and tolerance of difference. They insist that these values are embedded in Islamic texts and traditions, or could easily be incorporated based on the values of Islam. They point out that secularism is not necessarily an ally of civil liberty or political tolerance, even in the west. The most brutal instances of modern totalitarianism, from Nazism to Fascism and Stalinism, were all secular in essence. This is also not to condemn secularism *per se*, since many of western modernity's political achievements are indebted to the secularisation of the political sphere. Although it expressed itself in the Jacobin terror in the aftermath of the French Revolution and in various other dark species of political totalitarianism, secularism has also fostered a culture of tolerance and political representation as a remedy to religious and sectarian schisms. Secularism, the new reformists point out, is, like all political concepts, a historical phenomenon and can assume a variety of expressions and formulations that shape its general character – closed or open, intolerant or tolerant, despotic or democratic.

Democracy

What all the pioneers of new Islamic reformism share is a pragmatic attitude to democracy. To the new reformists, democracy is a political system based on instrumental mechanisms – political accountability, the rule of law, the separation of powers etc. – with the potential to cure the political malady of despotism. In addition, in countries where Muslims are in a clear majority, many new reformists have remained loyal to the view that democracy and freedom of thought and expression would empower the Muslim *ummah* to defend its interests in the face of the incessantly aggressive west. More importantly, democracy does not stand in opposition to Islamic values or principles, which remain of supreme significance. In countries where Muslims are not in a clear majority, or where they exist as small minorities, democracy is conceived as a tool that could serve to protect the interests and freedoms of different groups in multi-religious and multi-ethnic societies.[31]

American historian Bernard Lewis has argued that democracy remains an unwelcome guest in the Muslim world because of the dominant political tradition of command and obedience, and the absence of liberal concepts. Lewis cited the absence of the notion of citizenship from Islamic political culture to substantiate his case.[32] Despite the views propagated by Lewis and many other western academics, the new reformists have devoted much energy to the project of enriching democracy, both theoretically and practically. They are seeking to adapt and reactivate elements of Islamic political culture that they deem compatible and reconcilable with democratic values. These include the norms of equality before the law, consultation (*shura*), the accountability of the ruler, freedom of expression and belief, etc.

For example, modern reformism has extended the concept of *shura* beyond its traditional meanings. While traditional jurists spoke of governance as a contract between the ruler and the ruled, they ended up defining *shura* as an optional consultation between the ruler and a few carefully selected individuals. In opposition to this, modern reformists have stressed that *shura* is an obligation and they have elaborated on the notion of the political contract that is embedded in classical Islamic political thought, defining its distinct and crucial characteristics.

In this process they have come to understand the nature of the relationships between democracy, secularity and modernity more deeply. Rachid Ghannouchi, for example, has argued that the vaunted reciprocity between democracy and secularism is illusory because democracy is a collection of pragmatic tools, not a dogmatic belief system that stands opposed to religious conviction. He pointed out that to make use of the tools of democracy, one does not have to decide between being a believer or a democrat; commitment to one does not require belief in the other.[33]

Generally speaking, liberal democracy has worked reasonably well in the context of secularised but nominally Christian countries, but for Ghannouchi, and others such as Muhammad Salim al-'Awa, Fahmi Huwaidi and Tariq al-Bishri, liberal democracy is merely one historical possibility, and does not exhaust other historical possibilities or the 'great narrative' of democracy (if such a narrative does exist).

Democracy, as understood by the new reformists, offers a pragmatic system of rules and regulations that can help to 'rationalise' the political sphere and exclude physical violence. Their priority is to apply the tools of liberal democracy within the moral and religious framework of Islam, or to dissolve liberal democracy into *shura*. Although Ghannouchi refused to engage in what he called linguistic games that contrast *shura* with democracy, what primarily concerned him were the institutional tools of democracy that allow for the dismantling of despotism and the limiting of state power. In this respect, Ghannouchi displayed a pragmatism characteristic of the politician. He was vividly aware of the limits of Islamic *shura*, which, he insisted, remains a mere apologetic morality in Islamic political culture and history, that was implemented for only a brief time during the Prophet's lifetime and the Rightly Guided Caliphate. With its mechanisms that enable the peaceful transfer of power and power-sharing, modern democracy holds the promise of being able to reactivate, renew and historicise *shura*. This also seems to be what Iranian president Mohammad Khatami hopes to achieve by incorporating the notion of democracy into his discourse, and applying it in state policies.[34]

Although the new reformists often refer back to the earlier generation of reformists who aspired to reconcile Islamic thought and democracy, the two groups differ on this issue in several ways. It is worth noting that democracy preoccupied Muslim thinkers as far back as the nineteenth century. Rifaʻa al-Tahtawi (1801–1873) was the first to advocate borrowing from the modern west that which does not conflict with the established values and principles of Islamic *shura*.[35] After living in Paris for some time, al-Tahtawi published his first book, *Takhlis al Ibriz fi Talkhis Bariz*, on his return home to Cairo in 1834. Here he recorded his thoughts on the French way of life, and wrote several passages on democracy, having witnessed its defence and reassertion during the 1830 revolution against King Charles X.[36] Al-Tahtawi endeavoured to convince his readers that it is possible to reconcile Islamic *shariʻah* with liberal democracy, arguing that democracy is compatible with Islam, which values justice *(ʻadl)* very highly. Like al-Tahtawi, many Muslim reformists have equated the concepts of political freedom and justice, despite the fact that justice is the term used in classical Islam. The concept of political freedom is a new one, and is associated with the penetration of western political thought into the Islamic order of knowledge. Nevertheless, the renowned reformist Khayr al-Din attributed the west's victories over the Islamic world to the vast scope it accorded to freedom and justice. Being a pragmatic statesman, Khayr al-Din saw democracy not as having value in itself but as an efficient tool with a potential to 'revive' the Muslim *ummah*. His strategy of reform revolved around three key points. The first was to borrow from Europe the institutions and instruments that stood behind its rise to power. The second was to remove absolutism and despotism and limit the power of rulers using the *shari'ah*. The third was to rebuild the Islamic *'umran* through a modern system founded on the principle of freedom.[37]

Thus, even if the new Islamic discourse is significantly more synthetic and elaborate than the classical discourse of *islah*, it remains heavily indebted to it, particularly in relation to the notion of democracy, and certain apologetic dimensions inherited from modern reformism are present in the discourse of new reformists, since the latter are forced to navigate through conflicting arguments. On the one hand, new reformists devote much of their energy to defending democracy by appealing to the principle of *maslahah* (public interest). On the other hand, they often have to defend themselves from most of the Arab regimes, as well as from Arab and Muslim secularists, who accuse them of using democracy as a means to attain power, while planning to renounce democracy as soon as they achieve this goal.[38] In straddling this line, the new reformists have developed a vivid awareness of the limits and pitfalls of liberal democracy, and are fully aware of the mechanisms of discipline and control embedded in it, as exposed by its early alliance with imperialism. In other words, they are acutely aware that the oppressive forces of imperialist expansion have always propped up the libertarian side of democracy that westerners experience inside their own national borders.[39] In addition, most new reformists are more interested in the functional aspects of democracy than in its theoretical foundations, and warn against wasting too much time and energy on attempting to reconcile the political culture of Islam with democracy. With a deeper awareness of the limitations of both, they show great flexibility and practicality in their attitudes.

Universality

This relates to another characteristic of new Islamic reformism, namely, its endeavour to historicise or relativise the modern west by divesting it of all claims to universal validity. In new reformist discourse, the modern west is shown to be nothing more than a historical contingency that is seeking to lay claim to universalism. The fact that modern western culture has spread widely throughout the globe via military expansion and capitalist globalisation[40] does not free it of its historicity, and should not mislead us into thinking that the west is unique. All great civilisations, be they Greek, Persian, Babylonian, Chinese or Islamic, have contained elements of universalism. It is by virtue of what is known in French as *technologisation*, combined with its monopoly on world resources, that western civilisation has expanded in such unprecedented ways.

Martin Heidegger maintained that the universalisation of the west is less a historical phenomenon than an ontological destiny, and observed that the possibility of dialogue with non-western cultures is precluded by 'the complete Europeanization of the earth'.[41] For Heidegger, technology, which has so profoundly and extensively transformed the face of the planet, is the historical realisation of western metaphysics, and has transformed nature into *techne* in the Greek sense (that is, into a world of objectified power that consumes the 'human subject' and strips it of all meaning and depth).[42]

For all its rigour and complexity, Heidegger's reading lacks what Nietzsche calls 'historical sense'.[43] Heidegger's views are so immersed in ontology that they leave very little scope for history. What is missing from his analysis is attention to the complexity of the historical circumstances surrounding the spread of modern technology. It can be argued that the engulfing of the planet by modern technology is more than an expression of westernisation, and can as easily be associated with bids to de-westernise and de-Europeanise, to technologise without stripping the world of value and meaning. I mention Heidegger's thesis to stress the point that the new Islamic discourse is not Heideggerian in its approach, meaning or values. Far from bestowing the west with an ontological determination, it seeks to historicise it and deconstruct its universal claims.

For all of Heidegger's prophecies, nihilism has not turned into the 'voice of existence'. The conception of the planet as a mere mechanical object laid bare for mastery by an intentional subject armed with modern equipment and devoid of all feelings of responsibility to the environment has, indeed, been as catastrophic for westerners as it has for the Earth and all its inhabitants. As Hannah Arendt has shown, the inescapable eclipse of transcendence in modern times did not lay the world bare before modern eyes. Instead, it drove humanity to alienation from the world and into the secluded prison of the self. The great problem for humanity today, Arendt contended, does not lie in self-alienation, as Marx assumed, but in alienation from the world.[44]

The new Islamic discourse emphasises the historicity of the west, and all of the cultures of the world, but questions whether specificity is an inescapable trap or whether it is possible for the 'particular' to lay claim to universal validity. Essentially, new Islamic discourse perceives universalism as a historical activity, not a given metaphysical fact. It is a quest for transcendence over the individual and collective self towards universalism through what is referred to in the Qur'an as *ta'aruf* or knowledge of others.

> We created you from a single male and female, and made you into nations and tribes, that you may know each other. Verily the most honoured of you in the sight of Allah is the most righteous of you...And Allah has full knowledge and is well acquainted with all things.[45]

Thus, for new Islamic reformism, the modern west is neither a universal omnipotent power holding the reins of the universe, nor indeed – in spite of its many evil facets – is it seen as demonic. It is seen as a historical phenomenon that deserves to be evaluated, and whose power games and limits need to be deconstructed. 'By virtue of their open-ended, critical, interactive approach to Western modernity, the bearers of the new Islamic discourse are able to benefit in a creative way from this modernity without being engulfed by it.'[46]

Although the new phase of Islamic reformism manifests a more rigorous understanding of the question of democracy, its position on the neutrality and 'universality' of the liberal mechanisms of western democracy seems to suffer from some intellectual superficiality. No doubt, certain forms of life, to use Wittgenstein's terminology, do hold greater potential for universalisation than others, in the sense that they have an ability to overcome their national and cultural limits. But to seek to extricate these mechanisms from the 'will to power' inherent in them is little more than wishful thinking, as these mechanisms sometimes possess energy and power that do not submit to the dictates of their users.

The postulate upon which the entire political theory of the new reformists is founded may be summarised as the possibility of separating the content of liberal democracy from its means. The new generation of reformists is adamant that although liberal democracy has operated within the secular cultural context of the west, it is possible to dismantle the system and borrow the means without their content. But is it really possible to purge these instruments of the marks of their cultural and historical content? Are the political mechanisms of democracy neutral tools that can be separated from their historical and hermeneutical contexts?

In my view, the bid to incorporate western liberal democracy within the framework of Islamic *shura* may not necessarily work as well as most new reformists seem to hope. This is not because I see liberal democracy as a solid package to be fully accepted or completely rejected. It is because I question the neutrality of the mechanisms of western democracy, and wonder whether it is possible to purge these of their historical and cultural heritage.

If we accept that democracy is an instrument that serves to monitor and maintain a balance of power and rationalise political affairs, is it really possible to divest these institutions of the 'forms of life' – to use Wittgenstein's vocabulary – and specific history they emerged from, and within which they have operated for so long? Is it possible to accord them a claim to universal validity?[47]

These questions remind me of al-Ghazali's view that Aristotelian syllogism was a neutral tool that could be used in pursuit of Islamic knowledge, and especially in *fiqh*. A jurist's inability to master logic must cast serious doubt over his knowledge and even his faith, al-Ghazali conjectured. However, what he saw as a transparent and neutral instrument came to transform the whole structure of the Islamic episteme. As Iqbal observed, the post-Ghazalite Islamic mind shifted towards the abstract and the immutable due to the influence of Greek rationalism, thereby losing its vibrant pragmatism and realism.[48]

It is not easy to predict whether an Islamic political system will have the ability to successfully incorporate the mechanisms of liberal democracy, but Mohammad Khatami's time in office in the Islamic Republic of Iran does provide a concrete example upon which we can base some predictions and conclusions.

The state and civil society

Modern political Islam has always been haunted by the idea of the state as the saviour of the political *ummah* and the redeemer of its integrity. The demolition of the Islamic caliphate in Istanbul by the Young Turks in 1924 has long tormented Islamic consciousness. For the first time in modern history, Muslims felt that they were deprived of the political body of an Islamic state. It is no accident that modern political Islam was born in 1924 – the year in which the caliphate was demolished. The Muslim Brotherhood led by Hassan al-Banna in Egypt was the first modern Islamic movement to emerge and to assume responsibility for re-establishing the lost Islamic state. Rashid Rida strongly influenced al-Banna's political vision and agenda. Rida saw a great need for the Islamic caliphate, and stood firmly against assertions that the Prophet was a purely spiritual leader whose mission was not political. In response, the modern reformists have tended to exaggerate the role of the state, seeing its restoration as the moral and religious obligation of every Muslim. For this reason, slogans calling for the establishment of an Islamic state have come to the forefront of modern Islam's political agenda.

In this regard, modern Islam was deeply influenced by étatisme, discussed in earlier chapters. The political and economic conditions of the Muslim world in the mid to late 1900s encouraged the idea that the state should be the main player in modernising yet preserving the political unity of a disintegrated society. Kemalism in Turkey,[49] Ba'thism in Iraq and Syria,[50] Nasserism in Egypt,[51] socialism in Algeria, and Bourguibism in Tunisia, all provide telling examples of the role accorded to the state in catalysing modernisation and generating a sense of political identity.

Although Islamic movements reacted to secularist ideologies at this time, they also came to accept many aspects of modernism in the name of the Islamic state. The most flagrant example of the inclination towards étatisme was Hizb ut-Tahrir, an international pan-Islamic political organisation working for the re-establishment of the caliphate. Its leader and founder, Taqiuddin al-Nabhani, championed the notion of a top-down, state-led Islamisation programme. Not only did al-Nabhani argue for a vanguard Islamic state, he advocated military coups as the principal means of revolutionary change and as a vital instrument in the return of the caliphate. The head of state, as envisaged by Hizb ut-Tahrir, would be an unlimited sovereign reminiscent of Hobbes's *Leviathan*.[52]

Modern Islamic political discourse championed what the contemporary scholar Basheer Nafi has described as 'Islamisation by injection', meaning an attempt to Islamise post-colonial Muslim states by injecting them with *shari'ah*.[53] At the heart of this project lies the supremacy of a state's ideological identity over its political identity. The Islamic Republic of Iran provides a contemporary example of this position. The founder of the Islamic Republic and its first supreme leader, Ayatollah Khomeini, was opposed to the Akhbari School in traditionalist Shiism, which holds that a condition for the establishment of a state is the presence of the *mahdi*, a messiah-like figure. Khomeini therefore aligned himself with Shia reformism, and the theory of *imamah* which stipulates that in the absence of the imam, the *velayat-e-faqih* should provide political leadership. Khomeini's political thought was highly complex, and emphasised the value of the *ummah* as well as the autonomy of society to some extent – including the prestigious religious institutions of Qumm. However, the notion that the state could be embodied in the person of the *velayat-e-faqih* was perhaps the view he advanced most strongly. The idea of a central state dissolved in the charismatic body of the imam remains a central reference point in political Shiism. It has been incorporated into the Iranian constitution, and lies behind the ambiguous nature of the present Iranian state, which exhibits a strange mixture of theocracy and democracy.

At the forefront of the Iranian president's agenda was the construction of a well-organised civil society, the members of which are allied to one another on the basis of ideas and beliefs rather than blood ties, and are united in attempting to follow the example of the city of the Prophet. President Khatami of Iran tried to engage in a dual mission. On the one hand, he sought to reconcile Islamic political thought – within the Shia tradition – with modern democracy. This task required fresh interpretations of both traditional Islamic political thought and modern democracy. On the other hand, Khatami attempted to democratise the Islamic Republic, and in doing so had to maintain a highly delicate balance between the conservative and progressive forces in his country. Khatami wavered between the masses' aspirations for reform and the demands of conservatives who were reluctant to relax the grip they had on Iran's religious and political establishment. The most significant aspect of Khatami's project was its attempt to build a form of Islamic democracy. His government was not merely seeking to achieve a theoretical reconciliation between Islamic *shura* and liberal democracy in the fashion of nineteenth-century Islamic reformism, but to concretely test the attainability of a modern Islamic democracy.

Perhaps the main factor that distinguishes the new Islamic reformists from their forebears is that they no longer see the modern state as a magic wand in the process of Islamisation. New Islamic reformism is intensely conscious of the political dangers immanent in the modern state. The state is not perceived as a neutral tool to which the destiny of society may be entrusted. Fully cognisant that state institutions are capable of violence and of tormenting citizens, the new Islamic reformists do not consider the state to be the bearer of an ethical project in the Hegelian sense, or a means of reshaping people's political and cultural identity. No armed territorial state is necessarily a protector of peace or guarantor of stability and welfare, and its co-existence with its citizens can never be taken for granted.[54]

Rachid Ghannouchi has championed the idea of the minimum state, calling for a vast array of state functions to be shifted on to civil society (this is mostly referred to as *ahli* in his writings). For Ghannouchi, while the Kharijite view has an anarchist tendency, its elevation of the value of the *ummah* and the ideals of justice remain valid. Ghannouchi dismissed the idealistic tendencies of Kharajite thought but highlighted the principle that the *ummah* should prevail over the state. Recalling Ibn Khaldun's conjecture that *mulk* (political authority) tends by its nature to monopolise power, Ghannouchi argued that the state should be limited to the arena of civil governance, and be restricted by institutions that ensure checks and balances on its powers. Ghannouchi also extended Ibn Khaldun's view that tribal ties were the only means of curtailing state hegemony,[55] noting that the kinds of civic ties that are fostered by well-organised Muslim societies have the power to restrict state violence and weaken the intrinsic inclination to dominance and despotism.[56]

In a similar vein, Munir Shafiq has observed that with modern technology's ability to ensure centralisation, surveillance and control, nation states have the potential for great violence and intense interference in individuals' private lives. He also argued that states are irreligious by nature, and impose their own inner imperatives on citizens, whether they are religious or not. In his view, this means that the Islamic project's main priority should be to transfer as much as possible of the state's jurisdiction to civil society, so as to ensure the latter's integrity and welfare.[57]

Notes

Introduction

1   Fukuyama (2001).
2   Foucault (1969).
3   Mitchell (1991).
4   See Heidegger (1999: 296–305).
5   Said (1995). Orientalism as treated by Said is not a specific intellectual school but a general style of thought based on an ontological and epistemological distinction made between the 'Orient' and the 'Occident'.
6   See Hentsch (1988).
7   Djait (1985: 18).
8   Mitchell (1991: 166).
9   Mitchell (1991: 166).
10   Salvatore (1997: 169).
11   Gellner (1992: 38).
12   Ibn Rushd (1998).
13   See, for example, Lewis (1961).
14   Said (1995).
15   See Manzoor (2000).
16   Foucault (1972).
17   Rorty (1999: 169).
18   The word 'genealogist' is used here in the Nietzschean sense, to denote a search for remote historical roots, which, although only faintly perceptible, remain vividly active and highly influential.

19   Touraine (1992: 42–43).
20   This view is confirmed by German *Aufklarung* and the British Enlightenment's intimate entanglement with religion (Touraine 1992: 48).
21   Vattimo (1988: 100).
22   Vattimo (1992: 95).
23   Vattimo (1992: 97).
24   Vattimo (1988: 103).
25   Rorty (1999: 169).
26   Rorty (1999: 169).
27   Rorty (1998: 196).
28   Rorty (1998: 170).
29   Rorty (1998: 197).
30   The case of the United States casts some doubt on the proposition that 'the west' equals secularity or secularism. Secularisation is an undeniable reality in the modern 'west', but to claim that the west has undertaken a complete transition from the 'religious' to the 'secular', or from the sacred to the profane, seems to be too rushed a proposition to make.

Chapter 1

1   Foucault (1972).
2   See the Introduction by HH Gerth and C Wright Mills in Weber (1946/1991: 51).
3   Tenbruck (1989: 50).
4   See Kontos (1994).
5   Weber (1946/1991: 293).
6   Weber (1905/1998: 26).
7   See Morrison (1997: 217–220).
8   See Morrison (1997: 217–221).
9   See the Introduction by HH Gerth and C Wright Mills to Weber (1946/1991: 56–57).
10   Aron (1967b: 180–181). Adopting a roughly similar view, Habermas contended that the various forms of practical rationalisation

do not exhaust the concept of rationalisation itself, since Weber still maintains a certain gap between the idea of rationality itself and rationality as action. Weber thus appears to follow the Kantian distinction between value judgements and facts, as well as between theoretical and practical reason.

11   Löwith (1960/1993).
12   Weber (1922/1989: 13).
13   Weber (1922/1989: 17).
14   Weber (1922/1989: 13).
15   Poole (1994).
16   See Chapter 14 of Giddens (1993).
17   Foucault (1972).
18   Weber (1922/1989: 22–23).
19   Schluchter (1981: 22).
20   Weber (1922/1989: 24).
21   Mitzman (1969: 190).
22   Weber (1922/1989: 23).
23   Weber (1922/1989: 18).
24   Mitzman (1969: 205–220).
25   Schluchter (1981: 44–45). Throughout his reading of Weber's texts, Schluchter distinguished between three forms of ethics: normative ethics (or law), which are based on a religious worldview; principle ethics, which are founded on a rationalisation of religious interpretation; and the ethics of responsibility, which are grounded in a subjective choice with no reference to sources of behaviour that stand outside or beyond the active subject.
26   See Hekman (1994).
27   Warren (1994).
28   Weber (1927/1978, Vol. 1: 402).
29   Weber (1927/1978, Vol. 1: 402).
30   Weber (1927/1978, Vol. 1: 403). The Weberian reading of the history of religion bears much similarity to Durkheim's, as illustrated in *The Elementary Forms of Religious Life* (1912/1965). For Weber as well as for Durkheim, the sacred progressively tends to

be transformed into social norms and shifts its energy from transcendence to the immanent 'social order'.

31   Habermas (1984).

32   Tenbruck (1989: 72).

33   By 'brotherly religion', Weber meant an advanced stage in the long process of religious rationalisation, associated with the breakdown of blood ties in favour of spiritual bonds founded on the norm of religious community. This necessarily leads to tension with the uncommunal world, based on conflicts of interests and polarisation between the two value spheres. Here, we see a clear similarity between the Weberian view and the Hobbesian world.

34   Weber (1946/1991: 350–351).

35   Habermas (1984: 342).

36   Weber asserted that the world, as human beings experience it, is separated into different and often opposing 'life orders' or 'value spheres', which function in terms of their own internally constructed, autonomous principles. These principles define the kinds of actions, choices and roles and norms available to human beings as participants in different contexts. Indeed, the rationalisation of a worldview becomes effective only when it is transformed into a practical rationality; that is, when it is transposed to rationalise actions and orientations, and 'life orders'.

37   Habermas (1987:166–188).

38   Weber (1964: 226).

39   Weber (1946/1991: 323).

40   Weber (1946/1991: 324).

41   Weber (1946/1991: 330).

42   Weber (1946/1991: 325).

43   Weber (1946/1991: 326).

44   Habermas (1987: 186–215).

45   Weber (1946/1991: 328).

46   Weber (1946/1991: 278).

47   Weber (1946/1991: 330).

48 Weber (1946/1991: 281).

49 Weber (1927/1978, Vol. 1: 578–579).

50 See Mitzman (1969: 176–177).

51 This typology was used by Habermas in his constructive reading of the sociological discourse of modernity as expressed in Weber's writings. I applied this treatment of modernity to my own analysis of secularity.

52 Schluchter (1981: 26).

53 Aron (1967b: 216).

54 Weber (1905/1988: 80).

55 Habermas (2002: 214–215). In most of his contributions, Weber stressed the peculiarity of Greek philosophy, referring to the emergence of the concepts in Greek philosophy and the ethical norms of Christianity, which were later reactivated in Protestantism.

56 Weber (1905/1998: 105).

57 Aron (1967b: 214).

58 Weber (1946/1991: 332).

59 Weber (1905/1998: 55).

60 Weber (1927/1978: 95).

61 Warren (1994: 87).

62 Keane (1984: 33).

63 Keane (1984: 44).

64 Warren (1984: 84–85).

65 Weber (1905/1998: 70).

66 Weber (1946/1991: 331).

67 Weber (1946/1991: 333–334).

68 Weber (1946/1991: 79).

69 Brubaker (1984: 71).

70 Weber (1946/1991: 335).

71 Weber (1946/1991: 335).

72 Any alert reader of Weber's texts will sense Nietzsche's overwhelming presence, whether in Weber's advocacy of an existential form of nihilism, or his perspectivist understanding of morality.

73 Turner (1994: 154). Allow me also to point briefly to the argument that binds Weber to Durkheim. The latter insists that modern society will forsake the authority of the traditional sacred in favour of the immanent. Traditional relationships will thereby dissipate, making way for an array of organic relations founded on the norm of the individual. The culmination of the process will lead to the disappearance of the old gods, in Durkheim's own words, 'the old gods are growing older or already dead and others are not yet born': Durkheim (1912/1965: 475).

74 See Jaspers (1966).

75 Nietzsche (1882/1974: S125).

76 Nietzsche (1885/1990: 140).

77 Kaufman (1974: 100).

78 See Heidegger (1977).

79 Nietzsche (1879/1996: 29).

80 Nietzsche (1882/1974: S343).

81 Heidegger (1977: 61).

82 Nietzsche (1888/1990: S6).

83 Nietzsche (1888/1990: 47).

84 See Jaspers (1966: 186).

85 Vattimo (1988).

86 Vattimo (1988).

87 Heidegger (1982: 4).

88 Nietzsche (1888/1990: 77).

89 Kaufman (1974: 110).

90 Heidegger (1977: 61–62).

91 Schute (1984).

92 Ansell-Pearson (1994: 138).

93 Vattimo (1988: 165).

94 Nietzsche (1956: S27).

95 Hotton and Turner (1989: 83).

96 It seems astonishing that the term secularity, with all its offshoots and ambiguities, has not previously been the subject of scholarly interrogation. However, it is fair to say that, in the present

era, the term seems to be overwhelmed by a rhetorical discourse that takes for granted that secularisation is irreversible. Thus, the modern world, as secularists conceive of it, with its drive towards rationalisation, is indifferent if not hostile to religious commitment, and secularisation is now 'less a scientific concept than a tool of counter-religious theology' (Martin 1964: 9).

97   Cox (1966: 19).
98   Keane (2000).
99   Addis and Arnold (1957).
100   Keane (2000: 6). To secularise someone is to convert them from an ecclesiastical to a secular life. To secularise a public affair or organisation is to transfer it from the possession of the church into the hands of the state, or some other representative of the public interest.
101   Bauberot (1996).
102   Blumenberg (1983).
103   Blumenberg (1983: 23).
104   Blumenberg (1983); see also Löwith (1997).
105   Blumenberg (1983: 16).
106   Manzoor (2000: 89).
107   Gadamer (1977: 46).
108   Arendt (1963/1990: p. 186).

Chapter 2

1   Gibb (1947/1972).
2   See al-ʿAzma (1992); Laroui (2001); Tibi (1988).
3   Ruedy (1994).
4   Davison (1998: 3).
5   Barbier (2000) (my translation); see especially Chapter 7, pp. 212–224.
6   Maurice Barbier is just one of a vast stream of writers who have no real knowledge of Islamic intellectual traditions or the complex conditions of Muslim societies, but who, nonetheless, have no qualms about declaring themselves experts on Islam.

7　It is interesting that the majority of writers who insist on Islam's resistance to secularisation tend to emphasise – rather joyously –the unique ways in which Christianity determined the development of western history. Islam is invoked as the antithesis of Christianity and the Islamic world's history is perceived as all that Europe's is not. In this, even the most radical champions of secularisation turn into Christian theologians.

8　See Weber (1946/1991).

9　Bin Ashur (1998: 177–183).

10　Izetbegovic (1994: 196).

11　Izetbegovic (1994: 224).

12　Eliade (1958).

13　Iqbal (1988).

14　See Kersten (2011).

15　See Gardet (1978: 29).

16　Qur'an, 51:56, my translation.

17　Historically speaking, Islam successfully maintained a balance between the three main institutions around which Muslim life revolved (the mosque, the school and the *suq*). The traditional Muslim city was quite dynamic and, in some respects, cosmopolitan. Whether Muslim societies are capable of recovering the balance between these three fundamental elements remains to be seen.

18　Asad (2003: 206–207).

19　See Lewis (1988: 117).

20　Davison (1998: 90–133).

21　Al-Afghani (1999).

22　Berkes (1999).

23　See Kenny (1973).

24　'Abed al-Jabri (1982).

25　'Abed al-Jabri (1982).

26　Spinoza (1673/2002).

27　Ibn Khaldun (1377/1991: 152–153).

28　Southern (1962).

29　Nietzsche (1885/1990: 162).

30 Iqbal (1988: 9).

31 Iqbal (1988: 155). Iqbal also said: 'Islam, recognising the contact of the ideal with the real, says "yes" to the world of matter and points the way to master it, with a view to discovering a basis for a realistic regulation of life' (10).

32 At the time of writing, Iran appeared to be moving towards the first option by beginning to establish an Islamic democracy within an Islamic framework.

33 A small minority of Christian liberation theologians and feminist theologians follow a tradition that militates against Augustinian dualism, and argue that participation in liberatory forms of politics is grounded in early Christian theology.

34 Laroui (2001: 11–41).

35 In some ways these efforts were similar to those undertaken in relation to Shia Islam by Ayatollah Ruhollah Khomeini, who re-interpreted the concept of *al-mahdi* (the expected saviour). Prior to the Khomeini era, Shia political thought was founded on a kind of historical redundancy, resulting from the illusion of waiting for the saviour. Khomeini put forward the concept of 'waiting' within a 'mundane' context, proposing that the mullah would represent the saviour in his absence. For more on this, see Enayat (1982) and Keddie (1983).

36 See Badie (1986).

37 Von Grunebaum (1981: 127–137).

38 Ibn Khaldun was a statesman, jurist, historian and scholar who was born in Tunis in May 1332. He was from an aristocratic family that, for several centuries, was prominent in the political leadership of Moorish Spain, and crossed over to North Africa a few years before Seville fell into the hands of the Christians in 1248. The love of learning and intellectual pursuits for which his father and grandfather were noted, coupled with the political aspirations that had inspired a long line of his Moorish forebears, produced the rare combination of philosopher and statesman that we find in Ibn Khaldun. He died in 1406.

39 Skinner (1979).

40 Ibn Khaldun (1377/1987).

41 This point has been well illustrated by Iqbal (1988).

42 Laroui (2001).

43 Lapidus (1988).

44 Laroui (2001: 19).

45 Lapidus (1988: 260).

46 Martin (1964).

47 Gauchet (1998).

48 For example, Abu Nasr al-Farabi (AD 872–950) opted for this strategy when he set about reconciling the views of the Aristotle and Plato. And Ibn Rushd (Averroes), despite being a strong advocate of Aristotle (referring to him as the First Teacher), also steered away from the materialism of Aristotelian philosophy, and subjected Aristotle's work to a fresh interpretation based on a theory of creation.

49 Al-Afghani (1999).

50 Milbank (1998: 89).

51 Althusser (1970/2009).

52 Durkheim (1912/1965: 62).

53 Manzoor (2000: 84).

54 Cox (1966: 4).

55 Berger (1973); see also Berger (1967).

56 Kolakowski (1990).

57 Sandel (1998).

58 Manzoor (2000: 3).

59 Kolakowski (1990: 66).

60 Yemen, where the Islamic movement has been able to strike an alliance with the tribal forces under the auspices of the Yemeni Assembly for Reform, is the sole exception. However, this alliance is the product of a society with a tribal structure that cannot be overlooked by either the ruling groups or the opposition, and, at the time of writing, it seemed liable to dissolve at any moment. The Communists who ruled South Yemen from 1967 to

1990 were obliged not only to deal with tribalism, but also to find a social base therein.

61   Gellner (1992: 5).

Chapter 3

1   Sparks (1999).
2   Aristotle *Politics* 2.1255a (trans. Barker).
3   Koebner (1951: 275).
4   Richter (1977: 45).
5   Aristotle *Politics* 5.1311a (trans. Barker)
6   Grosrichard (1979: 11).
7   Aristotle noted: 'Another type of kingship is the sort which is to be found among some uncivilized [that is, non-Hellenic] peoples. All kingships of this sort possess an authority similar to that of tyrannies, but are nonetheless constitutional and descend from father to son. The reason is that these uncivilised peoples are more servile in character than Greeks (as the people of Asia are in turn more servile than those of Europe) and will, therefore, tolerate despotic rule without complaint. Kingships among uncivilized people are, thus, of the nature of tyrannies, but being constitutional and hereditary at the same time' (*Politics* 3.1285a, trans. Barker).
8   Grosrichard (1979: 23).
9   Aristotle *Politics* 1.1252b (trans. Barker).
10   Nicolas d'Oresme translated Aristotle's *Politics* into French in 1489, and Jean Bodin translated the *Republic* in 1576.
11   Anderson (1993).
12   Machiavelli (1513/1979: 26–27).
13   Richter (1977: 46).
14   This seems to have been a reworking of the Greek classification of governments into monarchies, aristocracies and democracies.
15   Plamentaz (1992: 17).
16   Palmentaz (1992: 19).
17   Palmentaz (1992: 19).

18 'Les Grecs et ensuite les Romains entendaient par le mot Grec *despotès* un père de famille, un maître de maison…il me semble qu'aucun Romain ne se servit du mot *despote*, ou d'un dérivé de *despotès* pour signifier un roi. *Despoticus* ne fut jamais un mot latin…Aujourd'hui les empereurs de Turquie, du Maroc, de L'Indoustan, de la Chine, sont appelés par nous despotes, et nous attachons à ce titre l'idée d'un fou féroce qui n'écoute que son caprice, d'un barbare qui fait ranger devant lui ses courtisans prosternés, et qui pour se divertir, ordonne à ses satellites d'étrangler à droite et d'empaler à gauche' [The Greeks and then the Romans understood the Greek word *despotes* to mean the father of a family, the head of the household…It is my view that no Greek or Roman ever used the word *despote*, or any derivation of *despotes*, to signify a king. *Despoticus* was never a Latin word…Now, the emperors of Turkey, Morocco, Hindustan and China were called despots by us; and we attach to this title the idea of a ferocious madman who heeds only his own whims; of a barbarian who has his courtesans lined up to prostrate themselves before him, and who, for entertainment, orders his satellites upon a riot of strangulation and impalement] (Montesquieu 1748/1994: 409).

19 Koebner (1951).

20 Montesquieu (1748/1994: 77).

21 'Comme tous les hommes naissent égaux, il faut que l'esclavage est contre la nature, quoique dans certains pays il soit fondé sur une raison naturelle, et il faut bien distinguer ces pays d'avec ceux où les raisons naturelles mêmes le rejettent comme les pays d'Europe où il est heureusement aboli' [As all men are born equal, slavery must necessarily be against nature, although in some countries it is founded on natural reason, and it is necessary to distinguish these countries from those in which the very same natural reason rejects it as in the European countries where it has happily been abolished (Montesquieu 1748/1994: Ch. VII, my translation).

22 Grosrichard (1979: 52–53).

23 Je cherche en vain moi-même une expression qui reproduise exactement l'idée que je m'en forme et la renferme; les anciens mots de despotisme et de tyrannie ne conviennent point. La chose est nouvelle, il faut donc tâcher de définir puisque je ne peux la nommer (Tocqueville 1840/1991: 415, my translation).

24 Keane (1988: 55).

25 'Il dégradait les hommes sans les tourmenter' (Tocqueville 1840/1991: 414). Tocqueville goes on: 'il ne brise pas les volontés, mais il les amollit, les plie et les dirige, il force rarement d'agir; mais il s'oppose sans cesse à ce qu'on agisse; il ne détruit point, il empêche de naître, il ne tyrannise point, il gêne, il comprime; il énerve, il éteint, il hébète' [it does not break wills, but softens, bends, and guides. It rarely bothers to act, but constantly opposes what acts; it destroys nothing, but it prevents existence; it does not tyrannise, it hinders, it compresses, enervates, extinguishes, bewilders'] (416, my translation).

26 Keane (1988: 58.)

27 Lefort (1988: 26).

28 Keane (1988: 57).

29 'On le met aisément à part, et on le foule impunément aux pieds' (Tocqueville 1840/1991: 424).

30 In French : 'Le monde politique change, il faut désormais chercher de nouveaux remèdes à des mots nouveaux' (Tocqueville 1840/1991: 249). Note the pun on *mots* – the original saying is 'chercher de nouveaux remèdes à des maux nouveaux'– with *maux* meaning ills, injuries or diseases.

31 Arendt (1967: 125).

32 Arendt (1967: 125).

33 Arendt (1967: 137). Interestingly, Arendt contrasted power with violence. In her view, power corresponds to the human ability to act correctly and communally; power is never the property of an individual, it belongs to a group and remains in existence only so long as a group coheres.

34 Arendt (1967) referred to Joseph-Arthur de Gobineau's *Essai sur l'inégalité des races humaines* (1853) and to Edmund Burke's *Reflections on the Revolution in France* (1790) as two examples of race-thinking in Europe. De Gobineau proposed the notion of 'race aristocrats' as opposed to a 'nation' of citizens, while Burke elaborated on the rights of the English versus the rights of others.

35 See Canovan (1974: 39).

36 Arendt (1967: 186).

37 Canovan (1974: 33).

38 Arendt (1967: 137).

39 Arendt (1967: 186).

40 Arendt (1970: 52–53). Arendt insisted that any political order that isolates its citizens from one another, and in which elites separate themselves from the political community, will degenerate into domination based on violence because this separation destroys the communicative structures that might allow citizens' power to emerge.

41 That Arendt preserved the traditional classification of the Orient as despotic can be seen in the following quote: 'The very integrity of the British administration made despotic government more inhuman and inaccessible to its subjects than Asiatic rulers or reckless conquerors had ever been' (1967: 211–212).

42 Galtung (1980).

43 Galtung (1971:83)

44 Badie (1992: 22).

45 Badie (1992: 37).

46 Salvatore (1997).

47 Berques (1979).

48 Hourani (1991b: 129).

49 Gellner (1997).

50 See Gibb (1947/1972: 109).

51 Cromer (1908: 538–539).

52 Mitchell (1991: 154–159).

53 Tachan (1975).

54 Hourani (1981: 18).

55 Hourani (1981).

56 Hale (1994: 81).

57 Hale (1994).

58 Hale (1994: 80).

59 Latouche (1996).

60 **See** Manço (1996: 341).

61 See Cantori (1989).

62 Arendt (1967).

63 Ricœur (2001: 155).

64 Gueniffey (2000).

65 Arendt (1963/1990: 215).

66 Arendt (1963/1990: 222).

67 Tamimi (2001).

68 Tamimi (2001).

69 Quoted in Lewis (1961: 404).

70 Tamimi (2001: 113).

71 Former Tunisian president Habib Bourguiba, who saw himself as the founding father of the nation and of the project of 'modernisation', once announced in a public speech, 'The era of the independence of national organisation is over. There is no more room for the party to stand as an independent unit, or for the general labourers' union to stand as an independent unit, or for the national union of farmers to stand as an independent unit, or for the union of industry and commerce to stand as an independent unit, or for the general union of students to stand as an independent unit. Tunisians, whether they are in the general labourers' union, the national union of farmers, the union of industry and commerce, or in the general union of the students, are before anything else members of the national constitutional party' (from a speech by Bourguiba on 2 April 1963).

72 Hermassi (1994: 92).

73 Nationalism in this context is a 'race-thinking ideology', where a certain homogenous 'race' deems itself superior to another.

74 Ghalioun (1997: 166), emphasis added.
75 Ghalioun (1997: 174).
76 Ghalioun (1997: 188).
77 Djait (1991: 222).
78 Djait (1991: 236).
79 'Abed al-Jabri (1982).
80 Keane (2000).
81 See Esposito and Voll (1996).
82 Rawls (1996).

Chapter 4

1 Weber (1905/1998: 26).
2 Parsons (1993).
3 Aron (1967a: 532).
4 Weber (1905/1998).
5 Weber (1927/1978, Vol. 2: 439).
6 Peters (1967).
7 Weber (1920/1966: 262).
8 Weber (1927/1978: 472).
9 Becker was an Orientalist, served as Prussian secretary of higher education and was Weber's colleague at Heidelberg University. His views on Islam greatly influenced Weber.
10 See Goldziher (1971).
11 Hourani (1981: 60).
12 Weber (1920/1966: 263).
13 Weber (1920/1966: 263).
14 Weber quoted by Turner (1992: 42).
15 Turner (1994: 14–15).
16 Weber (1920/1966: 263).
17 Weber (1947/1966: 347).
18 Turner (1994: 75).
19 Weber (1958/2000).
20 Marx (1867/2007: 393).
21 Marx and Engels (1979: 217).

22 Hegel (1899/2004: 18).
23 Turner (1981: 272–273).
24 Weber (1921/1958: 88).
25 Turner (1992).
26 Hourani and Stern (1970).
27 Al-Attas (1995: 42–44).
28 Messick (1993).
29 Hodgson (1974).
30 Messick (1993: 154). *Shari'ah,* as noted by the jurist Ibn al-Qa-yyim al-Jawziyyah, can be summed up in the norm of *'adl* (justice). That is, *shari'ah* is not restricted to the Qur'an and the Sunnah, but is also immanent in human language and practice. As al-Jawziyyah argued, any norm that is compatible with the ideal of *'adl* and which promises to improve the existential status of humanity – whether within the Muslim community or not – can be deemed part of the *shari'ah* even if this is not explicitly stated in the texts.
31 Weber (1927/1978).
32 Parsons (1941).
33 Weber (1927/1978: 426).
34 Weber (1927/1978: 426.
35 Weber (1927/1978: 343).
36 Aron (1967a: 537).
37 Weber (1905/1998: 13).
38 Weber (1922/1989).
39 Weber (1905/1998: 16).
40 Keane (1984: 31).
41 Weber (1927/1978: 512).
42 Weber (1927/1978: 625).
43 Weber (1927/1978: 626).
44 Turner (1981: 146).
45 Turner (1981: 147).
46 This is different from the Weberian determination of *jihad.*
47 Albrow (1990: 15).

48 Albrow (1990: 21, 22).
49 Albrow (1990: 33).
50 See Lewis (1993: 3–14).
51 Weber (1927/1978: 400).
52 Hourani (1967/1980: 71–72).
53 Mastinak (1994: 3).
54 Hodgson (1974: 184–185).
55 Hodgson (1974: 177).
56 Kant (1784/1996: 59).
57 See Weber (1922/1989: 17).
58 Quoted in Keane (1984: 31).
59 Weber (1947/1966: 182).
60 Gellner (1964: 3).
61 Vattimo (1992).
62 See Armstrong (1991).
63 Hourani (1967/1980: 24).
64 Hourani (1967/1980: 25).
65 See Rodinson (1980).
66 Djait (1985: 15).
67 Rodinson (1980: 15).
68 Djait (1985: 13).
69 Hourani (1967/1980: 71).
70 Iqbal (1988: 102).

Chapter 5

1 To use Habermas's words, this involved a 'pre-understanding an-
   chored in modern orientations' (1984: 44).
2 Habermas (1996a: 45).
3 Habermas (1979: 104–105).
4 Habermas (1979: 157–158).
5 Habermas (1984: 68).
6 Schmid (1982: 165).
7 Habermas (1984: 48).
8 Quoted in White (1988: 95).

9   Quoted in White (1988: 59).
10   Habermas seems to have taken this from Gellner who, in turn, drew
     on the work of Karl Popper (1972). See also Sheamur (1996).
11   Alexander (1991: 52).
12   Shills (1981: 5).
13   McCarthy (1982).
14   McCarthy (1993: 140).
15   Benhabib (1986: 239).
16   Benhabib (1986: 255).
17   See McCarthy (1998).
18   Habermas (1998: 84).
19   Habermas (1998: 7).
20   Habermas (1996a: 45–46).
21   Couzens Hoy (1996: 126).
22   In this, Habermas stood against Horkheimer and Adorno, who
     attempted to relate the prevalence of instrumental rationality in
     modern society to the inner structure of the dialectic of Enlighten-
     ment. For Habermas, the distortions of reason and the reifications
     in modern societies were simply negative counter-images of true
     reason (see Wellmer 1991: 46–47).
23   Habermas (1996a: 52).
24   Habermas (1996a: 51).
25   Dallmayr (1996: 82–83).
26   Dallmayr (1996: 86).
27   Dallmayr (1996: 90).
28   Habermas (1996b: 414).
29   McCarthy (1993: 134, original emphasis).
30   Habermas (1996b: 416).
31   Weber (1905/1998: 10).
32   Benhabib (1986: 255–256).
33   Touraine (1992: 23–24).
34   This is taken from the *Marriam-Webster Online Dictionary*,
     http://www.merriam-webster.com/dictionary/secularize?show=
     0&t=1419804140.

35   See Touraine (1992: 21).

36   Gray (1997).

37   MacIntyre (1981).

38   Habermas (1998: 94).

39   See al-Ghazali (2000).

40   Al-Farabi (c.943/1982).

41   See Ibn Sina (1965).

42   See Ibn Rushd (1998).

43   See Imara (1988).

44   Ricœur (1996).

45   Lapidus (1988: 880).

46   Arendt (1963/1990: 197).

Chapter 6

1   Voll (1983: 32).

2   This applies particularly to Sunni Muslims who revere the four Rightly Guided Caliphs as representing the ideals of Islamic justice. The Rightly Guided Caliphs is a term that Sunni Muslims use to refer to the first four leaders of the Muslim community after the death of Muhammad: Abu Bakr, 'Umar, 'Uthman and 'Ali. Shia Muslims, on the other hand, have a deep reverence for 'Ali and see the imams among his descendants as infallible.

3   See Ibn Khaldun (1377/1991: 199–209).

4   It seems to me that what really distinguishes Islam from other great religions, including other monotheistic religions, is its grounding in a book that was written and memorised from the beginning of the prophetic message. The Qur'an also forms the basis of the interconnectedness of all Muslim schools and sects regardless of their differences.

5   See al-Ghazali's *Ihya' 'ulum al-din,* Volumes 1–5 (1981).

6   See Rahman (2000).

7   Dekmejian (1995: 18).

8   Brown (1996: 110).

9   Brown (1996: 110).

10   Smith (1944).
11   Al-Ghazali (2004).
12   Al-Ghazali (1960).
13   Watt (1979: 117).
14   Gardet (1977).
15   Watt (1979).
16   Ibn Tufayl (1999); see also Dammen McAuliffe (1999).
17   Al-Ghazali (1985).
18   Ibn Rushd (1964).
19   Ibn Taymiyyah (1971); see also Ibn Taymiyyah (1993).
20   Ibn Khaldun (1377/1987: 352). In addition, Ibn Khaldun notes
     that al-Ghazali's work epitomises the difference between what he
     described as the methods of the ancient and the modern theologi-
     ans: pre-Ghazalite theologians held the view that the refutation of
     an argument implies the falsity of the subject, but for al-Ghazali,
     the falsity of an argument had no bearing on the truth-value of the
     subject (1377/1991: 294).
21   See Gimaret (1990) and Ibn Furaq (1987).
22   See Ibn al-Balkhi (1974).
23   See al-Ghazali (1925).
24   Al-Ghazali (1912).
25   See Salah ad-Din (1976).
26   Nafi (2000: 16).
27   See Ibn Taymiyyah (1987: 145–154).
28   See Rahman (2000: 134).
29   Nafi (2000).
30   Muhyiddin Ibn 'Arabi, known by his disciples and admirers as
     'Sheikh al-Akbar' (Great Master), was born in Spain. At the age
     of thirty, he left Spain, travelling first to Tunis, and then to Cairo
     and Jerusalem. He died in Syria in 1240.
31   See al-Hallaj (1974). Available at http://godlas.myweb.uga.edu/
     Sufism/tawasin.html
32   Through radical critiques of Muslim philosophers and theologi-
     ans, and motivated by his mystical inclinations, al-Hallaj largely

contributed to the endorsement of Sufism by Sunni Islam. After al-Ghazali's work became known, popular Sufism began to move rapidly into the circles of the *'ulama* and high Islam. Al-Ghazali syntheticised Ash'arite Sunni theology with mysticism. It may not have been altogether coincidental that the first Sufi order or *tariqah*, known as the Qadiriyyah, was founded within a generation of al-Ghazali's death in 1111. Al-Ghazali himself established a Sufi spiritual centre in Tus late in his life.

33   See Ibn Taymiyyah (1961).

34   Ibn Taymiyyah (1951).

35   See Ibn Taymiyyah (1982).

36   Nafi (2000: 17).

37   See Ibn 'Abd al-Wahhab (1987).

38   Rahman (2000: 132).

39   Nafi (2000: 21).

40   Hourani (1981).

41   See al-Jabarti (n.d.).

42   Lewis (1993: 136–137).

43   Gibb (1986: 119).

44   Hodgson (1974: 180); see also Lewis (1994).

45   Hodgson (1974: 176, 182).

46   See Hourani's introduction in Hourani et al. (1993: 4).

47   See Muñoz (1999: 6).

48   Nafi (2000: 48).

49   *Maqasid* is the plural of *maqsad*, which means the aims and goals underlying a given religious proposition. *Maqasid ash-shari'ah*, as understood by the Andalusian jurist al-Shatibi (d. 1388), was the framework upon which the system of *shari'ah* is based. According to al-Shatibi, the whole of the *shari'ah* can be summed up as the protection of the self, religion, reason, property and honour.

50   Gibb (1947/1972).

51   Hourani (1981).

52   See Hourani (1981: 29–54).

53   Lapidus (1988: 599–601).

54   Lewis (1973: 272).
55   Hodgson (1974: 253–256).
56   See Hourani (1991a: 52).
57   Al-Tunsi (1972: 82–83).
58   al-Kawakibi (1993).
59   See Nafi (2000).
60   See Delumeau (1978).
61   See Delumeau (1978).
62   Al-Afghani (1999).
63   In a polemic against French philosopher Ernest Renan, al-Afghani firmly opposed Renan's positivist materialism. Renan believed in the great utopia of a humanity liberated from all traditional religions and transcendental beliefs in favour of a new pseudo-scientific religion.
64   See Mehdi (1990: 5–6).
65   Al-Afghani (1999: 110).
66   See Pakdman (1969).
67   See Pakdman (1969: 246).
68   Ramadan (1998).
69   See Ibn Khaldun (1377/1987: 131).
70   'Abduh discussed the concept of *tawhid* in depth in his work *Risalat al-Tawhid* (1980); see also 'Imara (1973).
71   See 'Abduh (1928).
72   'Abduh (1980: 132).
73   'Abduh (1980: 142).
74   See al-Iji (1958).
75   Nafi (2000: 46).
76   See Iqbal (1988: 95).
77   Iqbal (1988: 102).
78   Iqbal (1988: 102).
79   Iqbal (1988: 80–83).
80   Enayat (1982: 9).
81   This also explains why children and the mentally ill are exempted from religious obligations.

82 Gibb (1947/1972: 110).
83 See 'Imara (1973: 214).
84 'Abduh (1966/1980: 127).
85 'Abduh (1980); see also Ramadan (1998: 78).
86 See Esposito (1998: Chapter 4).
87 Ibn Rushd (1997).
88 See Ibn Taymiyyah (1971).
89 Crow (1999: 51).
90 'Abduh (1966/1980: 127).
91 Nafi (2000: 47).
92 See Rida (1931).
93 See al-Shatibi (1998).
94 See Rida (n.d.).
95 See H Laoust's translation of Rida's *al-Khilifah* (Rida 1938); see also Rida (1980).
96 See Hourani (1981).
97 Hegel (1899/2004).
98 See Ibn al-Azraq (1977).
99 Jad'an (1988).
100 Gadamer (1977).
101 'Abduh (1928: 65–66).
102 See Hodgson (1974).
103 See Lapidus (1988).
104 See Eche (1967); Southern (1962: 10–13).
105 Rahman (1984: 70).
106 Within this project, 'Abduh revived a number of valuable classics including *Maqamat abil-Fadl Badi' al-Zaman al-Hamadhani* and 'Ali Ibn Abi Talib's *Nahj al-Balaghah*. He also revived the theology of the Mu'tazilah, and the philosophical works of Ibn Rushd and Ibn Taymiyyah in his own well-known work, *Bayn al-Falsafah wa al-Kalamiyyin* (1958).
107 'Abduh (1928: 67).
108 Laroui (2001: 7).
109 Lapidus (1988: 883).

110 See Gellner (1992: 15–16).

111 See Musa (1960; 1963); As-Sayyid (1959) and Hourani (1991a).

112 Salvatore (1997: 76).

113 Salvatore (1997: 83).

114 Salvatore (1997: 84).

115 Hodgson's account of the inner mechanisms of Muslim society is particularly useful in reversing the dominant conception of *shari'ah* as a transcendental God-made system superimposed on a passive society: see Hodgson (1974).

116 Khuri (1998: 164).

117 Iqbal (1988: 92).

118 Hourani (1991a).

119 Gibb (1947/1972: 25).

120 Hourani et al. (1993).

121 Enayat (1982: 8).

122 Enayat (1982: 14–15).

Chapter 7

1 For example, the term 'Islamic fundamentalism' totally fails to reflect, or do justice to, the dynamic and contingent character of Islamic discourse, yet a myriad of discourses that display Islamic features or reference points tend to be stereotyped and dismissed as fundamentalist.

2 Elmessiri (1997).

3 Huntington (1996a).

4 Fukuyama (1992).

5 Venn (2000: 3).

6 Gadamer (1977).

7 Nietzsche (1873/1968).

8 Arkoun (1987).

9 As Gibb noted, since the nineteenth century, modern Islamic reformism has played a crucial role in reshaping the intellectual framework of Islam and shifting its energy from a traditional environment to the modern world: see Gibb (1986).

10 Kurzman (1998).

11 Kurzman (1998: 6).

12 Esposito and Voll (2001: 21).

13 Michel Foucault's reading of thought as a successive shift from one order of knowledge to another appears questionable, since what appears to be a radical form of transformation is often little more than deceptive appearance.

14 Esposito and Voll (2001: 20).

15 See Jad'an (1988: 191–255); see also Keddouri (1997: 43–65).

16 Esposito and Voll (2001: 17).

17 Ricœur (1988).

18 See Domenach (1995). Although the violent faces of modernity have received much attention, far less effort has been directed at gauging the cruelties perpetrated in the name of 'civilisation'.

19 Quoted in Jardin (1990: 318).

20 Elmessiri (1997).

21 Shafiq (1999).

22 Shafiq (1999: 52).

23 Abdurrahman (1995).

24 Abdurrahman (2000).

25 Al-Marzuqi (1999).

26 Manzoor (1999: 56).

27 Manzoor (1999: 59)

28 Manzoor (1999: 56).

29 Manzoor (2000: 96).

30 Ghannouchi (2000a).

31 This view is widely held by various Muslim thinkers in the Middle East, of the likes of Muhammad Salim al-'Awa, Tariq al-Bishri, Fahmi Huwaidi in Egypt, Mohammad Khatami in Iran, Rachid Ghannouchi in Tunisia, Anwar Ibrahim in Malaysia, Muhammad Fathi Osman in the USA and various others.

32 The word is a derivative of the Latin *civis* and relates to the Greek *polites*, meaning one who participates in the affairs of the *polis*; see Lewis (1996).

33   See Ghannouchi (1993).

34   Khatami (1998).

35   Al-Tahtawi was a graduate of al-Azhar University in Egypt. He was appointed as an imam to an Egyptian regiment that was dispatched to France. Once there, he applied himself to European thought with great enthusiasm. He acquired a precise knowledge of French, and read ancient history, Greek philosophy and mythology, geography, mathematics and logic. He also translated some French texts into Arabic. Returning home five years later, he recognised the malaise of the Muslim *ummah* under the reign of political despotism and advocated a multi-party system as the remedy. He stood strongly against those who refused to learn from Europeans, saying: 'Such people are deluded, for civilisations are turns and phases. These sciences were once Islamic when we were at the apex of our civilisation. Europe took them from us and developed them further. It is now our duty to learn from them as they learnt from our ancestors' (quoted in Hourani 1991a: 69); see also al-Husry (1980) and al-Tahtawi (1973).

36   Tamimi (1997).

37   Al-Tunsi (1868); see also Karru (1973) and Van Kriekden (1976).

38   This kind of discourse is popular among a great many left-inclined journalists, politicians and intellectuals in several Middle Eastern countries such as Turkey, Algeria, Egypt and Tunisia who dread the advance of Islamisation.

39   It is no accident that most of the theoreticians of liberal democracy were satisfied with the marriage between democracy and military imperialism. Tocqueville's approval of the French occupation of Algeria is by no means unique amongst western intellectuals, as it encapsulates the complexity of modernity, libertarian in some aspects, oppressive and expansionist in others.

40   McNeill (1964).

41   Heidegger (1971: 15).

42   Heidegger (1977).

43   Nietzsche (1888/1990).

44   Arendt (1981: 321–322).
45   Qur'an, 49: 13.
46   Elmessiri (1997: 55).
47   For analyses of the relationship between tradition and democratic politics, see Mouffe (1988).
48   Iqbal (1988).
49   See CCCCNA (1981).
50   See al-Husari (1985); Abu Jaber (1966); Sallam (1982).
51   See Choueiri (1989); Beattie (1994); al-Tikriti (2000).
52   See Taji-Farouki (1996).
53   Nafi (2000); see also el-Affendi (2001).
54   Keane (1998).
55   Ibn Khaldun (1377/1987).
56   Ghannouchi (1993; 2000a; 2000b).
57   Shafiq (1990).

Bibliography

'Abad al-Jabri, Mohammed (1982). *al-Khitab al-'Arabi al-Mu'asir.* Beirut.

'Abd as-Salim, Ahmad (1987). *Mawaqif Islahiyyah fi Tunis Qabla al-Himayah.* Tunis.

'Abduh, Muhammad (1889). *Maqamat Abi al-Fadl Badi' al-Zaman al-Hamadhani.* Beirut.

'Abduh, Muhammad (1928). *al-Islam wa al-Raddu 'ala Muntaqidih.* Cairo.

'Abduh, Muhammad (1958). *Bayn al-Falsafah wa al-Kalamiyyin.* Cairo.

Abduh, Muhammad (1966/1980). *The Theology of Unity* (translated by Ishaq Musa'ad and Kenneth Cragg). London.

'Abduh, Muhammad (1980). *Risala al-Tawhid.* Beirut.

'Abduh, Muhammad (1999). *al-Tha'ir al-Islam Jamal ad-Din al-Afghani.* Beirut.

Abdurrahman, Taha (1995). *Fiqh al-Falsafah: al-Falsafah wa at-Tarjamah,* Vol. 1. Beirut.

Abdurrahman, Taha (2000). *Su'al al-Akhlaq.* Casablanca and Beirut.

Abu Jaber, Kamal (1966). *The Arab Ba'th Socialist Party: History, Ideology, and Organization.* New York.

Addis, William E and Thomas Arnold (1957). *A Catholic Dictionary.* London.

el-Affendi, Abdelwahab (ed.) (2001). *Rethinking Islam and Modernity: Essays in Honour of Fathi Osman.* Leicester.

al-Afghani, Jamal ad-Din (1999). *Risalat ar-Radd 'Ala ad-Dihriyyin.* Beirut.

Ahmed, Akbar S (1988). *Discovering Islam: Making Sense of Muslim History and Society.* London, New York.

Albrow, Martin (1990). *Max Weber's Construction of Social Theory.* London.

Alexander, Jeffrey (1991). 'Habermas and critical theory: beyond the Marxian dilemma?' in Axel Honneth and Hans Joas (eds.), *Communicative Action.* New York.

Althusser, Louis (1970/2009). *Reading Capital.* New York.

'Amara, Muhammad (1984). *'Abd ar-Rahman al-Kawakibi: Shahid al-Hurriyah wa Mujaddid al-Islam.* Cairo.

Anderson, Perry (1993). *Lineage of the Absolutist State.* London, New York.

Ansell-Pearson, Keith (1994). *An Introduction to Nietzsche as a Political Thinker: The Perfect Nihilist.* Cambridge.

Arendt, Hannah (1963/1990). *On Revolution.* London.

Arendt, Hannah (1967). *The Origins of Totalitarianism.* London.

Arendt, Hannah (1970). *On Violence.* London.

Arendt, Hannah (1981). *Condition de l'homme moderne.* Paris.

Arendt (1990)

Aristotle. *Politics* (translated by Ernest Barker). London.

Aristotle. *Politics* (translated by John Warrington). London.

Arkoun, Mohammed (1987). *Rethinking Islam.* Washington.

Armstrong, Karen (1991). *Muhammad: A Western Attempt to Understand Islam.* London.

Aron, Raymond (1967a). *Les etapes de la pensée sociologique.* Paris.

Aron, Raymond (1967b). *Main Currents in Sociological Thought,* Vol. 2 (translated by H Weaver). London.

Asad, Talal (2003). *Formations of the Secular: Christianity, Islam, Modernity.* Stanford, MA.

al-Attas, Sayed Muhammed Naquib (1995). *Prolegomena to the Metaphysics of Islam.* Kuala Lumpur.

al-'Azma, 'Aziz (1992). *al-'Ilmaniyyah fi Maniur Mukhtalif.* Beirut.

Badie, Bertrand (1986). *Les deux états, pouvoir et societé en occident et en terre d'Islam.* Paris.

Badie, Bertrand (1992). *L'état importé: essai sur l'occidentalisation de l'ordre politique.* Paris.

Barbier, Maurice (2000). *La modernité politique.* Paris.

Bauberot, Jean (1996). 'Genèse du concept de la laïcité en occident', in Michel Bozdémir (ed.), *Islam et laïcité: approches globales et régionales.* Paris.

Beattie, James Kirk (1994). *Egypt during the Nasser Years: Ideology, Politics and Civil Society.* Boulder, CO.

Benhabib, Seyla (1986). *Critique, Norm and Utopia.* New York.

Berger, Peter (1967). *The Sacred Canopy: Elements of a Sociological Theory of Religion.* New York.

Berger, Peter (1973). *The Social Reality of Religion.* Harmondsworth.

Berkes (1998)

Berkes, Niyazi (1999). *The Development of Secularism in Turkey.* London, New York.

Bernstein, Richard J (1991). *Habermas and Modernity.* Oxford.

Berques, Jacques (1979). *L'Égypte: impérialisme et révolution.* Paris.

Bin Ashur, Muhammad al-Tahir (1998). *Maqasid ash-Shari'ah al-Islamiyyah.* Beirut.

Blumenberg, Hans (1983). *The Legitimacy of the Modern Age* (translated by Robert Martin Wallace). Frankfurt.

Brown, Alan (1986). *Modern Political Philosophy: Theories of the Just Society.* London.

Brown, Daniel William (1996). *Rethinking Tradition in Modern Islamic Thought.* Cambridge.

Brubaker, Rogers (1984). *The Limits of Rationality: An Essay on the Social and Moral Thought of Max Weber.* London.

Canovan, Margaret (1974). *The Political Thought of Hannah Arendt.* London.

Cantori, Louis (1989). *Comparative Politics in the Post-Behavioral Era.* Boulder, CO.

CCCCNA (Conseil de Coordination pour la Célébration du Centenaire de la Naissance d'Atatürk) (1981). *Atatürk: pensées et témoignages, hommage de la Commission Nationale Turque pour l'Unesco à l'occasion du centenaire de sa naissance (1881–1981)*. Ankara.

Choueiri, Youssef M (1989). *Arab History and the Nation-State: A Study in Modern Arab Historiography, 1820–1980*. London.

de Condorcet, Nicolas (1795). *Outlines of an Historical View of the Progress of the Human Mind*. http://oll.libertyfund.org/titles/1669.

Coole, Diane (1996). 'Habermas and the question of alterity', in Maurizio Passerin d'Enreve and Seyla Benhabib (eds.), *Habermas and the Unfinished Project of Modernity*. Cambridge.

Couzens Hoy, David (1996). 'Splitting the difference: Habermas's critique of Derrida', in Maurizio Passerin d'Enreve and Seyla Benhabib (eds.), *Habermas and the Unfinished Project of Modernity*. Cambridge.

Cox, Harvey (1966). *The Secular City*. New York.

Cromer, Evelyn Baring (1908). *Modern Egypt*, Vol. 2. New York.

Crow, Karim Douglas (1999). 'Between wisdom and reason: aspects of *'aql* in early Islam', *Islamica* 3 (1): 51.

Dallmayr, Fred (1996). 'The discourse of modernity: Hegel, Nietzsche, Heidegger and Habermas', in Maurizio Passerin d'Enreve and Seyla Benhabib (eds.), *Habermas and the Unfinished Project of Modernity*. Cambridge.

Dammen McAuliffe, Jane (ed.) (1999). *Encyclopedia of Islam* (CD-ROM edition, Volume X). Leiden.

Davison, Andrew (1998). *Secularism and Revivalism in Turkey: A Hermeneutic Reconsideration*. New Haven, London.

Dekmejian, Hrair Richard (1995). *Islam in Revolution: Fundamentalism in the Arab World*. Syracuse, New York.

Delumeau, Jean (1978). *La peur en occident (XIVeme–XVIIIeme siècles)*. Paris.

Djait, Hichem (1985). *Europe and Islam: Cultures and Modernity* (translated by Peter Heinegg). London.

Djait, Hichem (1991). *al-Ijtihad* 10/11: 222–236.

Domenach, Jean Marie (1995). *Approches de la modernité*. Paris.

Durkheim, Émile (1912/1965). *The Elementary Forms of Religious Life* (translated by Joseph Ward Swain). New York.

Eche, Yusef (1967). *Les bibliothèques arabes publiques et semi-publiques en Mésopotamie, en Syrie et en Égypte au moyen âge*. Damascus.

Eliade, Mircea (1958). *Patterns in Comparative Religion* (translated by R Sheed). New York.

Elmessiri, Abdelwahab M (1997). 'Features of the new Islamic discourse', *Encounters* 3 (1): 45–63.

Enayat, Hamid (1982). *Modern Islamic Political Thought*. London.

Esposito, John L (ed.) (1983). *Voices of Resurgent Islam*. New York, Oxford.

Esposito, John L (1998). *Islam: the Straight Path* (third edition). New York, Oxford.

Esposito John L and John Voll (1996). *Islam and Democracy*. New York, Oxford.

Esposito, John L and John Voll (eds.) (2001). *Makers of Contemporary Islam*. Oxford.

al-Farabi, Abu Nasr Muhammad Ibn Muhammad (c.943/1982). *Ara' ahl al-Madinah al-fadilah* [The Virtuous City] (revised by A Nasri Nadir, fourth edition). Beirut.

Foucault, Michel (1969). *L'archéologie du savoir*. Paris.

Foucault, Michel (1972). *The Archaeology of Knowledge* (translated by Alan Mark Sheridan-Smith). New York.

Freund, Julien (1970). *The Sociology of Max Weber* (translated by Mary Illford). London.

Friedman, Richard Elliot (1997). *The Disappearance of God*. New York.

Fukuyama, Francis (1992). *The End of History and the Last Man*. London.

Fukuyama, Francis (2001). 'The west has won: radical Islam can't beat democracy and capitalism', *The Guardian*, 11 October.

Gadamer, Hans-Georg (1977). *Philosophical Hermeneutics* (translated and edited by David E Linge). Berkeley, CA.

Galtung, John (1971). 'A structural theory of imperialism', *Journal of Peace Research* 8 (2): 83.

Galtung, John (1980). *The North/South Debate: Technology, Basic Human Needs and the New International Economic Order*. New York.

Gardet, Louis (1977). *Les hommes de l'Islam: approche des mentalités*. Paris.

Gardet, Louis (1978). *Islam: religion et communauté*. Paris.

Gauchet, Marcel (1998). *La religion dans la démocratie, parcours de la laïcité*. Paris.

Gellner, Ernest (1964). *Thought and Change*. London.

Gellner, Ernest (1992). *Post-Modernism, Reason and Religion*. London.

Gellner, Ernest (1994). *Conditions of Liberty: Civil Society and its Rivals*. London.

Gellner (1997)

Ghalioun, Burhan (1997). *Islam et politique: la modernité trahie*. Paris: La Découverte.

Ghannouchi, Rashid (1993). *al-Hurriyyat al-'Ammah fi al-Dawlah al-Islamiyyah*. Beirut.

Ghannouchi, Rashid (2000a). 'Secularism in the Arab Maghreb', in John L Esposito and Azzam Tamimi (eds.), *Islam and Secularism in the Middle East*. London.

Ghannouchi, Rashid (2000b). *Muqarabat fi al-'ilmaniyyah wa al-Mujtama' al-Madani*. Beirut.

Ghannouchi (2001)

al-Ghazali, Abu Hamid Muhammad Ibn Muhammad (1912). *Maqasid al-Falsafah*. Cairo.

al-Ghazali, Abu Hamid Muhammad Ibn Muhammad (1925). *Mihakk al-Nadar fi al-Mantiq* (revised and edited by M Badr ad-Din Ibn Faras an-Na'sani al-Halabi and Mustapha Ibn Muhammad al-Qabbani). Cairo.

al-Ghazali, Abu Hamid Muhammad Ibn Muhammad (1960). *al-Munqidh min al-Dalal* (revised by J Saliba). Damascus.

al-Ghazali, Abu Hamid Muhammad Ibn Muhammad (1981). *Ihya' 'Ulum al-Din*, Vols. 1–5. Beirut.

al-Ghazali, Abu Hamid Muhammad Ibn Muhammad (1985). *Iljam al-'Awam 'an 'Ilm al-Kalam*, edited by Muhammad al-Mu'tasim billah al-Baghdadi. Beirut.

al-Ghazali, Abu Hamid Muhammad Ibn Muhammad (2000). *The Incoherence of the Philosophers/Tahafut al-Falasifah: A Parallel English/Arabic Text* (translated and annotated by ME Marmura, second edition). Provo, UT.

al-Ghazali, Abu Hamid Muhammad (2004). *Deliverance from Error: Five Key Texts Including his Spiritual Autobiography, al-Munqidh min al-Dalal.* Louisville, KY.

Gibb, Hamilton Alexander Rosskeen (1947/1972). *Modern Trends in Islam.* Chicago.

Gibb (1954)

Gibb, Hamilton Alexander Rosskeen (1986). *Islam.* Oxford, New York.

Giddens, Anthony (1993). *Sociology.* Oxford.

Gimaret, Daniel (1990). *La doctrine d'al-Ash'ari.* Paris.

Goldziher, Ignaz (1971). *Muslim Studies: Muhammedanische Studien* (edited by Samuel Miklos Stern and translated from the German by CR Barber and Samuel Miklos Stern). London.

Gray, John (1997). *Enlightenment's Wake: Politics and Culture at the Close of the Modern Age.* London, New York.

Grosrichard, Alain (1979). *Structure du sérail: la fiction du despotisme asiatique dans l'occident classique.* Paris.

Gueniffey, Patrice (2000). *La politique de la terreur: essai sur la violence révolutionnaire 1789–1794.* Paris.

Habermas, Jürgen (1979). *Communication and the Evolution of Society* (translated by T McCarthy). Boston.

Habermas, Jürgen (1996a). 'Modernity: an unfinished project', in Maurizio Passerin d'Enreve and Seyla Benhabib (eds.), *Habermas and the Unfinished Project of Modernity.* Cambridge.

Habermas, Jürgen (1996b). 'The unity of reason in the diversity of its voices', in J Schmidt (ed.), *What Is Enlightenment? Eighteenth Century Answers and Twentieth Century Questions.* Berkeley, CA.

Habermas, Jürgen (1984). *The Theory of Communicative Action, Volume 1: Reason and the Rationalization of Society* (translated by Thomas A McCarthy). Boston.

Habermas, Jürgen (1987). *The Theory of Communicative Action, Volume 2: Lifeworld and System, A Critique of Functionalist Reason* (translated by Thomas A McCarthy). Boston.

Habermas (1997)

Habermas, Jürgen (1998). *The Philosophical Discourse of Modernity* (translated by Frederick G Lawrence). Oxford.

Habermas, Jürgen (2002). *Religion and Rationality: Essays on Reason, God and Modernity*. Cambridge: MIT Press.

Hale, William (1994). *Turkish Politics and the Military*. London, New York.

al-Hallaj, Mansur (1974). *The Tawasin of Mansur al-Hallaj* (translated by Aisha 'Abd ar-Rahman at-Tarjumana). London.

Hegel, Georg Wilhelm Friedrich (1899/2004). *The Philosophy of History*. London.

Heidegger, Martin (1971). *On the Way to Language*. New York.

Heidegger, Martin (1977). *The Question Concerning Technology and Other Essays* (translated by William Lovitt). London.

Heidegger, Martin (1982). *Nietzsche*, Vol. 4: *Nihilism*. New York.

Heidegger (1997)

Heidegger, Martin (1999). *Basic Writings* (edited by David Farrell Krell). London.

Hekman (1994)

Hentsch, Thierry (1988). *L'Orient imaginaire: la vision politique occidentale de l'Est méditerranéen*. Paris

Hermassi, Abdelbaki (1994). 'The political and the religious in the modern history of the Maghrib', in John Ruedy (ed.), *Islamism and Secularism in North Africa*. Basingstoke, New York.

Hodgson, Marshall Goodwin Simms (1974). *The Venture of Islam*, Vol. 3. Chicago.

Hotton, Robert James and Bryan Stanley Turner (1989). *Max Weber on Economy and Society*. New York.

Hourani, Albert (1967/1980). *Europe and the Middle East.* London.

Hourani, Albert (1981). *The Emergence of the Modern Middle East.* London.

Hourani, Albert (1991a). *Arabic Thought in the Liberal Age, 1798–1939.* Cambridge.

Hourani, Albert (1991b). 'How should we write the history of the Middle East?' *International Journal of Middle East Studies* 23 (2): 125–136.

Hourani, Albert, Philip Shukry Khoury and Mary Christina Wilson (eds.) (1993). *The Modern Middle East.* London, New York.

Hourani, Albert and Samuel Stern (eds.) (1970). *The Islamic City.* Oxford.

Huntington, Samuel P (1996a). *The Clash of Civilizations and the Remaking of World Order.* New York.

Huntington, Samuel P (1996b). 'Democracy for the long haul', *Journal of Democracy* 7 (2): 3–13.

al-Husari, Sati' (1985). *Ara'wa dirasat fi al-Fikr al-Qawmi.* Kuwait.

al-Husry, Khaldun Sati (1980). *Origins of Modern Arab Political Thought.* New York.

Ibn 'Abd al-Wahhab, Muhammad (1987). *Majmu'at al-Fatawa wa al-Rasa'il wa al-Ajwibah: Khamsuna Risalah fi al-Tawhid* (edited by 'Abd Allah as-Sayyid Ahmad Hajjaj, second edition). Beirut.

Ibn Abi Talib, 'Ali (1963). *Nahj al-Balaghah* (revised by Muhammad 'Abduh). Beirut.

Ibn 'Arabi, Muhyiddin (1883). *Fusus al-Hikam* (with commentary by Dawud Ibn Mahmud al-Qaysari). Bombay.

Ibn 'Arabi, Muhyiddin (1972). *al-Futuhat al-Makkiyyah* (revised by Ibrahim Madkur with a commentary and preface by 'Uthman Yahya). Cairo.

Ibn al-Azraq, Muhammad Ibn 'Ali (1977). *Badai' as-Silk fi Tabai' al-Milk* (edited by Muhammad Ibn 'Abd al-Karim). Tunis.

Ibn al-Balkhi, Ahmad (1974). *Fadl al-I'tizal wa Tabaqat al-Mu'tazilah.* Beirut.

Ibn Furaq, Muhammad Ibn al-Hassan (1987). *Mujarrad Maqalat al-Shaykh Abi al-Hassan al-Ash'ari.* Beirut.

Ibn Khaldun, 'Abd ar-Rahman (1377/1987). *The Muqaddimah* (translated by F Rosenthal, edited by NJ Dawood). London.

Ibn Khaldun, 'Abd ar-Rahman (1377/1991). *al-Muqaddimah.* Beirut.

Ibn al-Khatib, Muhammad 'Abd al-Latif (1948). *al-Furqan.* Cairo.

Ibn al-Khatib, Muhammad 'Abd al-Latif (1964). *'Awdat al-Tafasir.* Cairo.

Ibn Rushd, Muhammad al-Walid (1964). *Tahafut at-Tahafut* (edited by S Dunya). Cairo.

Ibn Rushd, Muhammad al-Walid (1997). *Fasl al-Maqal fi Taqrir ma Bayn al-Shari'ah wa al-Hikmah min al-Ittisal aw-Wujub al-Nadar al-'Aqli wa Hudud at-Ta'wi* (edited by MA al-Jabiri). Beirut.

Ibn Rushd, *Muhammad al-Walid (1998). al-Kashf 'an Manahij al-Adillah fi 'Aqa'id al-Millah (edited by M 'Abd al-Jabiri). Beirut.*

Ibn Sina, Ahmad (1965). *al-Shifa'* (edited by GC 'Anawati and S Zayed). Cairo.

Ibn Taymiyyah, Ahmad Ibn 'Abd al-Halim (1951). *Naqd al-Mantiq* (revised by Muhammad Ibn 'Abd ar-Razzaq Hamzah, Sulayman Ibn 'Abd ar-Rahman at-Thani' and Muhammad Hamid al-Faqi). Cairo.

Ibn Taymiyyah, Ahmad Ibn 'Abd al-Halim (1961). *al-Iman.* Damascus.

Ibn Taymiyyah, Ahmad Ibn 'Abd al-Halim (1971). *Dar Ta'arud al-'Aql wa al-Naql* (edited by MR Salim). Cairo.

Ibn Taymiyyah, Ahmad Ibn 'Abd al-Halim (1982). *al-Siyasah al-Shar'iyyah fi Islah al-Ra'i wa-r-Ra'iyah.* Beirut.

Ibn Taymiyyah, Ahmad Ibn 'Abd al-Halim (1987). *al-Furqan Bayn al-Haqq wa al-Batil.* Beirut.

Ibn Taymiyyah, Ahmad Ibn 'Abd al-Halim (1993). *Jahd al-Qariha fi Tajrid al-Nasiha* (translated into English by W Hallaq in *Ibn Taymiyya against the Greek Logicians*). Oxford.

Ibn Tufayl, Muhammad Ibn 'Abd al-Malik (1999). *Two Andalusian Philosophers* (translated by Jim Colville). London.

al-Iji, 'Abd ar-Rahman Ibn Ahmad (1958). *al-Sheikh Muhammad 'Abdu Bayn al-Falasifah wa al-Kalamiyyin* (edited by S Dunya). Cairo.

'Imara, Muhammad (1973). *al-A'mal al-Kamilah li al-Imam Muhammad 'Abdu.* Beirut.

'Imara, Muhammad (ed.) (1988). *Rasa'il al-'Adi wa at-Tawhid: al-Hassan al-Basri, Qadi 'Abd al-Jabbar, al-Qasim al-Rassi, al-Sharif al-Murtada wa Imam Yahya Ibn al-Husayn*, Vols. 1 and 2. Cairo.

Iqbal, Allama Muhammad (1988). *The Reconstruction of Religious Thought in Islam*. Lahore.

Izetbegovic, Alija (1994). *Islam between East and West*. Plainfield, IN.

al-Jabarti, 'Abd ar-Rahman (n.d.). *'Aja'ib al-Athar fi al-Tarajim wa al-Akhbar*, Vol. 4. Cairo.

Jad'an, Fahmi (1988). *Usus al-Taqaddum 'inda Mufakkir al-Islam*. Amman.

Jamros, Daniel (1994). *The Human Shape of God: Religion in Hegel's Phenomenology of Spirit*. New York.

Jardin, Andre (1990). *Tocqueville: A Biography* (translated by Lydia Davis and Robert Hemenway). Toronto.

Jaspers, Karl (1966). *Nietzsche: An Introduction to the Understanding of his Philosophical Activity* (translated by CF Wallraff). New York.

Karru, Abu-l-Qasim Muhammad (1973). *Khayr al-Din al-Tunsi: Hayatuhu*. Tunis.

al-Kawakibi, 'Abd ar-Rahman (1970). *Umm al-Qura, al-A'mal al-Kamilah li al-Kawakibi* (edited by Muhammad 'Amara). Cairo.

al-Kawakibi, 'Abd ar-Rahman (1993). *Taba'i al-Istibdad wa Masari' al-Isti'bad* [The Nature of Despotism]. Beirut.

Khalaf, Allah Muhammad Ahmad (1956). *al-Kawakibi: Hayatuhu wa Ara'uhu*. Cairo.

Khatami, Muhammad (1998). *Mutal'at fi al-Din, al-Islam wa al-'Asr* [A Study of Religion, Islam and Time]. Beirut.

Kant, Immanuel (1784/1996). 'An answer to the question: what is enlightenment?' in James Schmidt (ed.), *What Is Enlightenment? Eighteenth Century Answers and Twentieth Century Questions*. Berkeley, Los Angeles, London.

Kaufman, Walter (1974). *Nietzsche: Philosopher, Psychologist, Antichrist*. New York.

Keane, John (1984). *Public Life and Late Capitalism: Toward a Socialist Theory of Democracy*. London.

Keane, John (ed.) (1988). *Civil Society and the State.* London.

Keane, John (1998). *Civil Society: Old Images, New Perspective.* Cambridge, Oxford.

Keane John (2000). 'The limits of secularism', in John Esposito and Azzam Tamimi (eds.), *Islam and Secularism in the Middle East.* London.

Keddie, Nikki (ed.) (1983). *Religion and Politics in Iran: Shi'ism from Quietism to Revolution.* New Haven.

Keddouri, Elie (1997). *Afghani and 'Abduh: An Essay on Religious Unbelief and Political Activism in Modern Islam.* London.

Kenny, Anthony (1973). *Wittgenstein.* London.

Kersten, Carool (2011). 'Mohammed Aziz Lahbabi and the "anthropological turn" in Muslim thinking', Blogpost, 28 May. http://caroolkersten.blogspot.co.za/2011/05/mohammed-aziz-lahbabi-and.html

Khumayni et al. (1998)

Khuri, Richard K (1998). *Freedom, Modernity and Islam: Towards a Creative Synthesis.* London.

Koebner, Richard (1951). 'Despot and despotism: vicissitudes of a political term', *Journal of Warburg and Courtauld Institutes 14* (3/4): 275–302.

Kolakowski, Leszek (1990). *Modernity on Endless Trial.* Chicago.

Kontos, Alkis (1994). 'The world disenchanted, and the return of gods and demons', in Asher Horowitz and Terry Maley (eds.), *The Barbarism of Reason: Max Weber and Twilight of Enlightenment.* Toronto.

Kurzman, Charles (ed.) (1998). *Liberal Islam: A Sourcebook.* New York, Oxford.

Lapidus, Ira M (1988). *A History of Islamic Societies.* Cambridge.

Laroui, Abdullah (2001). *Islam et modernité.* Casablanca.

Latouche, Serge (1996). *The Modernization of the World: The Significance, Scope and Limits of the Drive towards Global Uniformity* (translated by R Morris). Cambridge.

Lefort, Claude (1988). *Democracy and Political Theory* (translated by David Mary). London.

Lewis, Bernard (1961). *The Emergence of Modern Turkey*. London, Oxford.

Lewis, Bernard (1973). *Islam in History: Ideas, Men and Events in the Middle East*. London.

Lewis, Bernard (1988). *The Political Language of Islam*. Chicago.

Lewis, Bernard (1993). *Islam and the West*. Oxford.

Lewis, Bernard (1994). *The Muslim Discovery of Europe*. London.

Lewis, Bernard (1996). 'Islam and liberal democracy: a historical overview', *Journal of Democracy* 7 (2): 64–75.

Löwith (1982)

Löwith, Karl (1993). *Max Weber and Karl Marx* (edited by Tom Bottomore and William Outhwaite). New York: Routledge.

Löwith, Karl (1997). *Nietzsche's Philosophy of the Eternal Recurrence of the Same* (translated by J Harvey Lomax, foreword by B Magnus). Berkeley.

MacIntyre, Alasdair (1981). *After Virtue: A Study in Moral Theory* (third edition). Notre Dame, IN.

Machiavelli, Niccolò (1513/1979). *The Prince*. London.

Manço, Ural (1996). 'Les conféries Soufies et l'avenir de la laïcité en Turquie: hypothèse sur la polarisation de la société turque', in Michel Bozdémir (ed.), *Islam et laïcité: approches globales et régionales*. Paris.

Manzoor, Parvez (1999). 'Modernity, transcendence and political theory', *Encounters* 5 (1): 56–63.

Manzoor, Parvez (2000). 'Desacralising secularism', in John L Esposito and Azzam Tamimi (eds.), *Islam and Secularism in the Middle East*. London.

Martin, David (1964). *The Religious and the Secular*. London.

Marx, Karl (1867/2007). *Capital: A Critique of Political Economy*, Vol.1. New York.

Marx, Karl (1970). 'Contribution to a critique of Hegel's philosophy of right', in *Critique of Hegel's 'Philosophy of Right'* (translated and edited by Joseph O'Malley). Cambridge.

Marx, Karl and Friedrich Engels (1979). *Collected Works*, Vol. 12. New York.

al-Marzuqi, Abu Ya'rub (1999). *Afaq an-Nahdah al-'Arabiyyah wa Mustaqbal al-Insan fi Mahabb al-'Awlamah*. Beirut.

Mastinak, Tomaz (1994). *Islam and the Creation of European Identity*. London.

McCarthy, Thomas (1982). 'Rationality and relativism: Habermas's "overcoming" of hermeneutics', in John B Thompson and David Held (eds.), *Habermas: Critical Debates*. London.

McCarthy, Thomas (1993). *Ideals and Illusions: On Reconstruction and Deconstruction in Contemporary Critical Theory*. Cambridge, MA.

McCarthy, Thomas (1998). 'Introduction', in Jürgen Habermas, *The Philosophical Discourse of Modernity* (translated by Frederick G Lawrence). Oxford.

McDonald, Duncan B (ed.) (1903). *Development of Muslim Theology, Jurisprudence and Constitutional Theory*. London.

McNeill, William Hardy (1964). *The Rise of the West: A History of the Human Community*. Chicago, London.

Mehdi, Muhsin (1990). 'La philosophie islamique dans la pensée islamique contemporaine', in *Études Orientales*, Vol. 6. Paris.

Messick, Brinkley (1993). *The Calligraphic State*. Oxford.

Milbank, John (1998). *Theology and Secular Theory: Beyond Secular Reason*. Oxford.

Mitchell, Timothy (1991). *Colonizing Egypt*. Los Angeles.

Mitzman, Arthur (1969). *The Iron Cage: A Historical Interpretation of Max Weber*. Oxford.

Montesquieu (1721/1993). *Lettres persanes*. Paris.

Montesquieu (1748/1994). *De l'esprit des lois, Vols. 1–3*. Tunis.

Morrison, Kenneth (1997). *Marx, Durkheim and Weber*. London.

Mouffe, Chantal (1988). 'Radical democracy: modern or post-modern', in Andrew Ross (ed.), *Universal Abandon?* Minneapolis.

Muir, William (1924). *The Caliphate: Its Rise, Decline, and Fall* (revised edition by TH Weir). Edinburgh.

Muñoz, Gema Martin (ed.) (1999). *Islam, Modernism and the West.* London, New York.

Musa, Salama (1960). *Kitab al-Thawrah.* Cairo.

Musa, Salama (1963). *Maqalat Mamnu'ah.* Cairo.

Nafi, Basheer M (2000). *The Rise and Decline of the Arab-Islamic Reform Movement.* London.

Nietzsche, Friedrich (1873/1968). 'On truth and lies in a nonmoral sense' (translated by Walter Kaufmann), in *The Portable Nietzsche.* New York.

Nietzsche, Friedrich (1876/1983). *Untimely Meditations* (translated by RJ Hollingdale). Cambridge.

Nietzsche, Friedrich (1878/1996). *Human, All Too Human: A Book for Free Spirits.* New York.

Nietzsche, Friedrich (1879/1996). *Hammer of the Gods* (compiled, edited and translated by S Metcalf). London.

Nietzsche, Friedrich (1882/1974). *The Gay Science, With a Prelude of Rhymes and an Appendix of Songs* (translated by Walter Kaufman). New York.

Nietzsche, Friedrich (1883–1885/1968). *Thus Spake Zarathustra* (translated by Walter Kaufmann, in *The Portable Nietzsche*). New York.

Nietzsche, Friedrich (1885/1990). *The Anti-Christ* (translated by RJ Hollingdale). London.

Nietzsche, Friedrich (1885/1997). *Beyond Good and Evil: Prelude to a Philosophy of the Future* (translated by Helen Zimmern). London.

Nietzsche, Friedrich (1887/1956). *On the Genealogy of Morality* (translated by F Golffing). New York.

Nietzsche, Friedrich (1888/1990). *Twilight of the Idols* (translated by R J Hollingdale). London.

Nietzsche, Friedrich (1895/1992). *Ecce homo: Nietzsche contre Wagner* (translated by Eric Blondel). Paris.

Nietzsche (1957)

Pakdman, Homa (tr.) (1969). *Djamal-ed-din Assad Abadi dit Afghani.* Paris.

Parsons, Talcott (1941). *The Structure of Social Action*. Chicago.

Parsons, Talcott (1993). 'Introduction', in Max Weber, *The Sociology of Religion*. Boston.

Passerin d'Enreve, Maurizio and Seyla Benhabib (eds.) (1996). *Habermas and the Unfinished Project of Modernity*. Cambridge.

Peters, Richard Stanley (1967). 'Authority', in Anthony Quinton (ed.), *Political Philosophy*. Oxford.

Plamentaz, John (1992). *Man and Society: Political and Social Theories: From Machiavelli to Marx*, Vol. 2. London.

Poole, Ross (1994). *Morality and Modernity*. London.

Popper, Karl Raimund (1972). *Conjectures and Refutations: The Growth of Scientific Knowledge* (fourth edition). London.

Rahman, Fazlur (1984). *Islam and Modernity*. Chicago, London.

Rahman, Fazlur (2000). *Revival and Reform in Islam: A Study of Islamic Fundamentalism* (edited by Ebrahim Moosa). Oxford.

Ramadan, Tariq (1998). *Aux sources du renouveau Musulman: d'al-Afghani à Hassan al-Banna, un siècle de réformisme islamique.* Paris.

Rawls, John (1996). 'The domain of the political and overlapping consensus', in Robert M Stewart (ed.), *Readings in Social and Political Philosophy*. New York, Oxford.

Richter, Melvin (1977). *The Political Theory of Montesquieu.* Cambridge.

Ricœur, Paul (1988). *Time and Narrative*, Vol. 3 (translated by K Blanny and D Pellaner). Chicago.

Ricœur, Paul (1996). *The Hermeneutics of Action* (edited by Rob Kearney). London.

Ricœur, Paul (2001). *La critique et la conviction: entretien avec François Azouvi et Marc Launay.* Paris.

Rida, Muhammad Rashid (n.d.). *Muhawarat al-Muslim wa al-Muqallid.* n.p.

Rida, Muhammad Rashid (1931). *Tarikh al-Sheikh Muhammad 'Abdu.* Cairo.

Rida, Muhammad Rashid (1938). *Le califat dans la doctrine de Rasid Rida* (translated by H Laoust). Paris.

Rida, Muhammad Rashid (1980). *Mukhtarat Siyasiyyah min Majallat 'al-Manar'* (edited by W. Kawtharani). Beirut.

Rodinson, Maxime (1980). *Europe and the Mystique of Islam* (translated by R Venus). London.

Rorty, Richard (1998). *Truth and Progress.* Cambridge.

Rorty, Richard (1999). *Philosophy and Social Hope.* London.

Ruedy, John (ed.) (1994). *Islamism and Secularism in North Africa.* Basingstoke, New York.

Ruthven, Malise (2000). *Islam in the World.* London.

Said, Edward (1995). *Orientalism: Western Conceptions of the Orient.* London.

Salah ad-Din, M (1976). *Shaykh al-Islam Ibn Taymiyyah: Siratuhu wa Akhbaruhu 'ind al-Mu'arrikhin.* Beirut.

Sallam, Kassim (1982). *Le Ba'th et la patrie arabe.* Paris.

Salvatore, Armando (1997). *Islam and the Political Discourse of Modernity.* Reading.

Sandel, Michael J (1998). 'Religious liberty: freedom of choice or freedom of conscience', in Rajeev Bhargava (ed.), *Secularism and its Critics.* Delhi, Oxford.

as-Sayyid, L (1959). *Mushkilat al-Hurriyyah fi al-'Alam al-'Arabi* Cairo.

Schluchter, Wolfgang (1981). *The Rise of Western Rationalism.* Berkeley, Los Angeles, London.

Schmid, Michael (1982). 'Habermas's theory of social evolution', in John B Thompson and David Held (eds.), *Habermas: Critical Debates.* London.

Schmidt, James (ed.) (1996). *What Is Enlightenment? Eighteenth-Century Answers and Twentieth Century Questions.* London.

Schute, Ofelia (1984). *Beyond Nihilism, Nietzsche without Masks.* London.

Shafiq, Munir (1990) *al-Islam fi Muwajahat ad-Dawlah al-Hadithah.* Beirut.

Shafiq, Munir (1999). *Fi al-Hadathah wa al-Khitab al-Hadathi.* Beirut and Rabat.

al-Shatibi, Abu Ishaq (1998). *al-Muwafaqat fi Usul al-Shari'ah*, Vols. 1–4 (revised by A Darraz and MA Darraz). Beirut.

Sheamur, Jeremy (1996). *The Political Thought of Karl Popper.* London.

Shills, Edward (1981). *Tradition.* London.

Skinner, Quentin (1979). *The Foundations of Modern Political Thought*, Vol. 1: *The Renaissance.* London.

Smith, Margaret (1944). *al-Ghazali the Mystic: A Study of the Life and Personality of Abu Hamid Muhammad at-Tusi al-Ghazali, Together with an Account of his Mystical Teaching and an Estimate of his Place in the History of Islamic Mysticism.* London.

Southern, Richard William (1962). *Western Views of Islam in the Middle Ages.* Cambridge.

Sparks, Christopher S (1999). *Montesquieu's Vision of Uncertainty and Modernity in Political Philosophy.* New York.

Spinoza, Baruch (1673/2002). 'Theological-political treatise', in *Spinoza: Complete Works* (translated by Samuel Shirley). Indianapolis.

Tachan, Frank (1975). *Political Elites and Political Development in the Middle East.* London.

al-Tahtawi, Rifa'a (1973). *al-A'mal al-Kamilah li Rif'ah Rafi' al-Tahtawi*, Vols. 1–3. Cairo.

Taji-Farouki, Suha (1996). *A Fundamental Quest: Hizb at-Tahrir and the Search for the Islamic Caliphate.* London.

Tamimi, Azzam (1997). 'Democracy in Islamic political thought', *Encounters* 3 (1): 3–20.

Tamimi, Azzam (2001). *Rachid Ghannouchi: A Democrat within Islamism.* Oxford.

Tenbruck, Friedrich H (1989). 'The problem of thematic unity in the works of Max Weber', in Keith Tribe (ed.), *Reading Weber.* London.

Tibi, Bassam (1988). *The Crisis of Modern Islam: A Pre-industrial Culture in the Scientific-Technological Age.* Salt Lake City.

al-Tikriti, Buthaynah 'Abd ar-Rahman (2000). *Jamal 'Abd an-Nasir: Nash'at wa Tatawwur al-Fikr al-Nasiri.* Beirut.

de Tocqueville, Alexis (1840/1991). *De la démocratie en Amérique*, Vol. 2. Algiers.

Touraine, Alain (1992). *Critique de la modernité*. Paris.

al-Tunsi, Khayr al-Din (1868). *La plus sûre direction pour connaître l'état des nations*. Paris.

al-Tunsi, Khayr al-Din (1972). *Aqwam al-Masalik*. Tunis.

Turner, Bryan Stanley (1981). *For Weber: Essays on the Sociology of Fate*. London.

Turner, Bryan Stanley (1992). *Max Weber: From History to Modernity*. London.

Turner, Bryan Stanley (1994). *Weber and Islam*. London.

Van Kriekden, GS (1976). *Khayr ad-Din et la Tunisie: 1850–1881*. Leiden.

Vattimo, Gianni (1988). *The End of Modernity* (translated by JR Synder). London.

Vattimo, Gianni (1992). *The Transparent Society* (translated by D Webb). Cambridge.

Venn, Couze (2000). *Occidentalism, Modernity and Subjectivity*. London, New Delhi.

Voll, John O (1983). 'Renewal and reform in Islamic history: *tajdid* and *islah*', in John L Esposito (ed.), *Voices of Resurgent Islam*. New York, Oxford.

Von Grunebaum, Gustav E (1981). *Essays in the Nature and Growth of a Cultural Tradition*. Westport, CT.

Warren, Mark E (1994). 'Nietzsche and Weber: when does reason become power?' in Asher Horowitz and Terry Maley (eds.), *The Barbarism of Reason: Max Weber and Twilight of Enlightenment*. Toronto.

Watt, Montgomery William (1979). *Islamic Philosophy and Theology*. Edinburgh.

Weber, Max (1905/1998). *The Protestant Ethic and the Spirit of Capitalism* (translated by Talcott Parsons). London.

Weber, Max (1920/1966). *The Sociology of Religion*. London.

Weber, Max (1921/1958). *The City* (translated by Don Martindale and Gertrude Neuwirth). Glencoe.

Weber, Max (1922/1989). *Science as a Vocation.* London.

Weber, Max (1927/1978). *Economy and Society: An Outline of Interpretive Sociology,* Vols. 1 and 2 (edited by Guenther Roth and Claus Wittich and translated by Ephraim Fischoff). Berkeley, London.

Weber, Max (1929/1982). 'The social psychology of the world religions', in *From Max Weber: Essays in Sociology.* London.

Weber, Max (1946/1991). 'Religious rejections of the world and their directions', in *From Max Weber: Essays in Sociology* (translated by Hans Heinrich Gerth and C Wright Mills). London.

Weber, Max (1947/1966). *The Theory of Social and Economic Organization.* New York.

Weber (1948)

Weber, Max (1958/2000). *The Religion of India* (translated by Hans Heinrich Gerth and Don Martindale). New Delhi.

Weber, Max (1964). *The Religion of China: Confucianism and Taoism.* New York.

Wellmer, Albrecht (1991). 'Reason, utopia and the dialectic of enlightenment', in RJ Bernstein (ed.), *Habermas and Modernity.* Oxford.

White, Stephen K (1988). *The Recent Work of Jürgen Habermas: Reason, Justice and Modernity.* Cambridge.

Glossary

ahli – society/the people; indigenous
'aql – reason
'aqli – rational
dahriyyah – secularism
din – religion; the contract between God and humanity
falasifah – philosophers
fatwa – decree; legal opinion
fiqh – jurisprudence
fitnah – civil disorder; strife
fuqaha – jurists
hadith – tradition; the sayings of the Prophet and his companions
hikmah – philosophy
ijma' – consensus
ijtihad – lit. 'exertion': the exercise of independent judgement
'ilm – knowledge, science
'ilmaniyyah – secularity
islah – reform
madhhab – pl. *madhahib*: classical school of jurisprudence
maqsad – pl. *maqasid*: the aims and goals underlying a given religious proposition
maslahah – pl. *maslahat*: public interest
mutakallimun – theologians
mutasarrif – administrative elite
salaf – companions of the Prophet

shahadah – the declaration of faith bearing witness to the unity of God and the prophethood of Muhammad

shar'i – religious

shari'ah – Islamic law; constitution

shura – consultation; democracy

tajdid – renovation, renewal

taqlid – imitation; stagnation; following the rulings of one particular jurisprudent on religious laws and commandments uncritically, and without requesting or offering any explanations

tariqah – pl. *turuq*; Sufi order; way or path

tawhid – the oneness of God

ta'wil – interpretation

'ulama – (sing. *'alim*: religious scholars; followers of a particular school of thought

ummah – the global Muslim community; nation

'umran – civilisation

velayat-e-faqih – Iran: rule by the jurist

Index

220; and equality 230; in
educational institutions 29,
244, 247, 265; and immanence
270–1; 'Islamic renaissance'
269–70; and *ijtihad* 203,
204, 205, 212, 214, 215,
220, 226, 234–6, 269; and
imperialism 237–9, 242; late
213–15; and liberalism 237,
249, 262–3; modern 215–36;
and modernity 27, 100, 199,
201–84; and monotheism
225–7; and nationalism 248;
new 257–83; and nihilism 271;
philosophical basis of 225–36,
265–83; and politics 212, 247;
and postmodernism 268–70;
and rationality 230–2, 234;
and secularism 271–3; and
secularity 199; and *shari'ah*
234–5, 281; Shiite 281–2;
and social conservatism 220;
spread of 244–6; the state
and civil society 280–3; and
Sufism 220, 225, 228, 250; and
transcendence 271; and *'ulama*
225, 250; and universality
276–80; and Wahhabism 250;
western culture and 216–20,
224–5, 236–8, 253–4, 265–6,
267–8, 270, 276–7; see also
Islah; revivalism, Islamic;
tajdid
religion 77–9, 95–7, 159–60,
164–5: bureaucratisation of
128–35; and culture 226;

development of 232; French
Revolution and 124; Freudian
view of 96; as irrational 19,
32, 95; Marxist view of 95–6,
97; nationalisation of 128,
129, 130; and philosophy 233;
and politics 57, 68, 73, 76, 82,
84–95; rationalisation and 141,
151–3, 190; and reason 226–7,
233–4; routinisation of 141–2;
and science 233; the state and
134; and tolerance 188; as
worldly 211; see also *din*
Renaissance: view of Islam during
168
Renan, Ernest 243, 307n63
revelation 227: and consensus
94; as foundation of Islam 16;
'natural religion' and 16, 76;
and reason 209–10, 230; as
supreme 230; as will of God
210
revivalism, Islamic 15, 16, 28, 99,
216, 253: and democratisation
136–7; al-Ghazali and 203–4;
in modernised societies 99,
118, 123; Sufis and 91, 204;
and Wahhabism 262; and
youth 249; see also reformism,
Islamic
Ricœur, Paul 125, 197, 265
Rida, Rashid 221, 224, 235, 237,
280
Rightly Guided Caliphs/Caliphate
85, 202, 203, 254, 275, 304n2
Rijal al-Tanzimat 216, 221

About the author

Rafik Abdessalem is the founder and director of the Centre for Strategic and Diplomatic Studies, a think tank that focuses on Tunisia's political, security and economic concerns, and has a regional focus on the broader Middle East and North Africa region.

Abdessalem played a prominent role in founding the Tunisian Students General Union in the late 1980s. After a heavy government crackdown on dissent in general and on the student movement in particular, he was forced into exile in England, where he lived for twenty-one years. There, he founded the Maghreb Centre for Research and Translation, and chaired the London Forum for Dialogue, which offered a platform to various Arab political figures in the United Kingdom. He later worked at the Al Jazeera Centre for Studies in Doha as director of research. From 2011 to 2013, Abdessalem served as Tunisia's foreign minister in the country's first democratically elected government after the fall of Zine El-Abidine Ben Ali in 2011.

Abdessalem has a BA in philosophy from Mohammed V University in Rabat, Morocco, and obtained his PhD in politics and international relations from the University of Westminster in England in 2003. He is the author of two other books – *On Religion, Secularity and Democracy*, and *The United States of America: Between Hard Power and Soft Power*, as well as numerous journal and newspaper articles.

www.ingramcontent.com/pod-product-compliance
Lightning Source LLC
Chambersburg PA
CBHW060023030426
42334CB00019B/2158